Media Ecologies of Literature

Media Ecologies of Literature

Edited by
Susanne Bayerlipp, Ralf Haekel and Johannes Schlegel

BLOOMSBURY
NEW DELHI • LONDON • OXFORD • NEW YORK • SYDNEY

BLOOMSBURY INDIA
Bloomsbury Publishing India Pvt. Ltd
Second Floor, LSC Building No. 4, DDA Complex, Pocket C–6&7,
Vasant Kunj, New Delhi 110070

BLOOMSBURY, BLOOMSBURY ACADEMIC INDIA and the Diana logo are trademarks of Bloomsbury Publishing Plc

First published in India 2025
First published in the United States of America 2024

Cover design: Eleanor Rose
Cover image © The Trustees of the British Museum

This edition published with permission from Bloomsbury Publishing Plc, 50 Bedford Square, London, WC1B3DP, UK

A catalogue record for this book is available from the British Library.
A catalog record for this book is available from the Library of Congress.

ISBN: 978-93-61312-49-6

Typeset by Deanta Global Publishing Services, Chennai, India
Printed and bound in India by Replika Press Pvt. Ltd.

To find out more about our authors and books visit www.bloomsbury.com and sign up for our newsletters

CONTENTS

FIGURES

CONTRIBUTORS

Susanne Bayerlipp: Institut für England- und Amerikastudien, Goethe-Universität Frankfurt, Germany.

Sebastian Domsch: Institut für Anglistik/Amerikanistik, Universität Greifswald, Germany.

Zita Farkas: School of Humanities, Education and Social Sciences, Örebro University, Sweden.

Ralf Haekel: Institut für Anglistik, Universität Leipzig, Germany.

Rieke Jordan: Rieke Jordan holds a PhD in North American Studies and studies Psychology in Berlin.

Balázs Keresztes: General Literary and Cultural Studies, Eötvös Loránd University, Budapest, Hungary.

Birgitte Stougaard Pedersen: School of Communication and Culture, Aarhus University, Denmark.

Ralph Pordzik: Institut für Anglistik/Amerikanistik, Julius-Maximilians-Universität Würzburg, Germany.

Christoph Reinfandt: Englisches Seminar, Eberhard Karls Universität Tübingen, Germany.

Johannes Schlegel: Institut für Anglistik/Amerikanistik, Julius-Maximilians-Universität Würzburg, Germany.

Alexander Starre: John F. Kennedy Institute for North American Studies, Department of Culture, Freie Universität Berlin, Germany.

Mirna Zeman: Institut für Neuere deutsche Literatur- und Medienwissenschaft, FernUniversität Hagen, Germany.

Sabine Zubarik: Evangelische Akademie Thüringen, Germany.

ACKNOWLEDGEMENTS

The editors would like to thank the contributors of this edited collection for their diligence, patience and smooth collaboration. Without their combined efforts, this volume would not have materialized. We are also immensely grateful for all the hard work our student assistants put into this project. Adam Badstübner, Max Oehmichen, Ella Scholz, Selina Stranz and Janina Goetzmann have proven invaluable for meticulously formatting the manuscript as well as for their careful and prudent proofreading. We would also like to thank Katja Brunsch for reading and correcting the manuscript. Not least, we wish to extend our gratitude to Haaris Naqvi of Bloomsbury for supporting the project throughout the process of publication and to the anonymous peer reviewer, whose insights and suggestions improved the project.

Introduction

The media ecologies of literature

Susanne Bayerlipp, Ralf Haekel and Johannes Schlegel

Introduction

This book explores the media ecologies of literature – the ways in which a literary text is interwoven in its material, technical, performative, praxeological, affective and discursive network and which determine how it is experienced and interpreted. The aim is to develop a comprehensive yet flexible media theory of literature. The following chapters discuss the various possibilities for regarding literature from a media-theoretical angle and thus they respond to the current and ongoing crisis of literary theory. In the past twenty years, give or take, the term 'medium' and its derivatives have become buzzwords within cultural and literary studies, opening up a new research area with hardly any limits or boundaries. Numerous theoretical and methodological approaches – such as intermediality, transmediality and remediation – are by now firmly established in literary studies. The *media concept*, however, is far from being a fixed and defined theoretical or practical entity. For a long time now, its scope has comprised considerably more than simply the means of communication – particularly the technology of mass communication such as radio, television and newspapers. Numerous theoretical approaches have been deployed in order to refer to phenomena that are categorically different from the technical-mechanical 'extensions of man' famously described by Marshall McLuhan in his classic study *Understanding Media* (1964), which include, for instance, the typewriter, the wheel and the bicycle. Indeed, advanced media theory has observed and described an astonishing breadth of phenomena including, as Stefan Münker and Alexander Roesler have shown, the classroom and the waiting room (Flusser); the general strike, the electoral system and the street (Baudrillard); the horse, the dromedary and the elephant (Virilio); money, power and influence (Parsons); and art, faith and love (Luhmann) (see Münker and Roesler 2008, 11). Next to this puzzling spectrum of media phenomena, there is a discernible movement away from a conception of technological instruments towards cultural techniques and practices of mediation (see Bayerlipp, Haekel and Schlegel 2018).

The word 'medium', then, appears to stand for a concept which functions as an umbrella term across literary, cultural and social studies (see O'Malley 2002; Golding 2019) – and it is hard to decide whether this is despite, or, rather, because of its semantic ambiguities. In her introduction to the *Blackwell Companion to Media Studies* – in itself a key marker of the concept's institutionalization – Angharad N. Valdivia describes media studies as a necessarily 'amorphous and porous field' that is 'diverse, contested, and growing' (2003, 1). It thus seems apt to classify *medium* as one of the so-called 'essentially contested concepts', which, according to Walter Bryce Gallie, involves the following: 'Recognition of a given concept as essentially contested implies recognition of rival uses of it (such as oneself repudiates) as not only logically possible and humanly "likely", but as of permanent potential critical value to one's own use or interpretation of the concept in question' (1956, 193).

Because of the wide range of media concepts, it makes little sense to insist on a single – supposedly correct, normative and prescriptive – definition. Instead, we propose *media ecology* as an appropriate approach to the entire field, because it provides the opportunity to investigate literature using the full scope of media theories while retaining a conceptual focus. We argue that the most recent developments in media ecology provide a theoretical frame to encompass this wide range of approaches, most notably the dichotomy between so-called techno-deterministic and materialist approaches, on the one hand, and approaches that are performative, dynamic and self-reflexive by nature, on the other hand. This collection explores and navigates the productive possibilities of this conceptual openness. By doing so, we address prevalent problems that inevitably arise when literature is observed as a medium in its own right. We argue, in other words, that the outlined diversity can be turned into a methodological strength: the fact that a media approach to literature may encompass everything from book history and manuscript research via discourse history and systems theory to metamedial reflexions within literary works underlines the variety and versatility of the field. Before we delineate the concept of a media ecology of literature, we thus need to address media-theoretical approaches to literature in a more general vein.

Literature – media – theory

In the wake of the digital revolution and the omnipresence of the Internet, fundamental changes in society at large have had an enormous impact on traditional forms of mediation – including art and literature. There is a sense that we are still in the midst of a general transformation of established cultural manifestations, institutions and practices (see Schlegel 2017). This has had an effect on literature and its institutions as well. What is sometimes described as the crisis of literature (see Iser 1993; Reinfandt 2009; for an assessment of the specific quality of literature as a print medium, see Wutz 2009) should, rather, be discussed as a re-negotiation of literature in the wake of the digitization of all forms of mediation (see Hansen 2006; Hayles 2002 and 2008; Tabbi and Wutz 1997; Starre 2015). This development goes hand in hand with the so-called crisis of theory: since the early 2000s, a surge of publications proclaiming the end of theory and the erosion of the post-structuralist paradigm (e.g. Cunningham 2002; Eagleton 2003; Birns 2010; Middeke and Reinfandt 2016) have created a situation where 'there seems to be no single orthodoxy' (Selden, Widdowson and Brooker 2005, 268) within literary studies anymore. Currently, the humanities are still engaged in a pervasive reconceptualization of their future role in response to this change. Digital humanities, medical humanities and cognitive poetics are just some examples of a long list of recent disciplinary expansions of, or 'turns' within, the study of literature (see Bachmann-Medick 2016) – the medial turn (see e.g. Purdon 2018) featuring prominently among them.[1]

As far as literature and literary studies are concerned, however, a seemingly paradoxical situation can be observed. While decisive impulses for the instigation and development of media studies originated in and radiated from literary studies – both McLuhan and Kittler were literary scholars, after all – literature was soon abandoned and left behind. Neither Valdivia's companion cited earlier, nor Oullette and Gray's *Keywords for Media Studies* (2017) nor Mitchell and Hansen's *Critical Terms for Media Studies* (2010), to name just a few instances, feature articles on literature. What has been investigated extensively, however, are various representations of other media in literature (see e.g. Griem 1998; Nünning and Rupp 2011; Glaubitz 2014; Paulson and Malvik 2016), the transposition of a literary text into another medium (including classics such as Stam 2005; McFarlane 1996; Aragay 2005 and many others) or the technologies that underlie the invention, production and dissemination of literature such as writing, typing and printing (Gieseke 1991; Gumbrecht 1998; Assmann 2012, 55–84). While these are substantial research contributions in their own right, they do not consider literature's own medial status – or they reduce this medial status to the material dimension of a given text. Both approaches, however, are ultimately reductive, as they contradict the constitutive ambiguities of a contested concept. In fact, as Oliver Jahraus has repeatedly argued, these myopic perspectives fail to take something fundamental into account: what media actually *do* is hardly recognizable when only their technological dimension is taken into view (see Jahraus 2017). A media concept that aims solely at its technological status, in other words, runs the risk of reducing its complexities to a mere carrier of a given message – such as the book.

One theorist who has repeatedly – and unjustly – been accused of this form of techno-determinism is Friedrich Kittler. Friedrich Kittler's impressive media theory is one of the most interesting and controversial positions in this field. Methodologically, this concept is based primarily on Michel Foucault's discourse analysis, which describes the inherent rules of the organization of discursive systems. Kittler extends the concept of discourse by a media-technical dimension to the concept of the *Discourse Networks*: 'The term discourse network,' he states, 'can [. . .] designate the network of technologies and institutions that allow a given culture to select, store, and process relevant data' (Kittler 1990, 369). Kittler's position does indeed rely on a technological notion of media – in fact, he even claims that media technology determines literature and culture, which is sometimes referred to as his hardware-determinism. But Kittler does not stop here. Rather, he proposes a radical revaluation of the term by not using it in the sense of a technology, but as an *a priori* explanatory figure. For this very reason, Kittler's basic idea consists precisely in the fact that he does not introduce technology itself technically, as a surface phenomenon, but systemically, that is, as a statement of justification. Geoffrey Winthrop-Young (2011) and Sybille Krämer (2004) have furthermore stressed the performative dimension and the dynamic dimension of Kittler's groundbreaking theory. A case in point is the first half of his study *Discourse Networks, 1800 – 1900,* in which he describes the changes in the practice of reading at the turn of the nineteenth century. At the heart of the paradigm shift described by him are not new technologies but the development and transformation of key cultural techniques: the growth of literacy and the practice of silent reading.

The revaluation of the relation between technology and literature has led to severe criticism, but also, more importantly, to profound reconsiderations of literature as a medium. Alexander Starre (2015), for instance, has investigated the medial self-reflexivity of contemporary literature, using a traditional and yet flexible concept of the literary medium as a technical storage and communication device. What is more, Kittler's insights have been productively extended by systems theories and cybernetic theories such as Niklas Luhmann's distinction of medium and form (see e.g. Luhmann 2000, 102–31). Oliver Jahraus (2003), in his study of literature as a medium, even rejects the theorization of the material dimension of the storage medium of the book altogether.[2] Instead, he argues that literature is able to mediate between communication and cognition by its ability to create meaning. Christoph Reinfandt likewise pleads for the necessity to differentiate between a material and a conceptual understanding of literature as a medium (2009, 163), arguing for a historical conception of literature as a mediating instance between the social condition of modernity and the emergence of subjectivity as the key cultural component of modern literature (see Reinfandt 2009, 168). What these approaches have in common is that they conceive of literature and its technological and systemic qualities not so much in *either/or* as in *both/and* relations, that is, they use different, even conflicting, conceptions of media, media technology and practices of mediation productively.

In this context, literature's media ecologies come into play, and this opens up, we argue, the possibility for further investigations of the medial status of literature: media ecology highlights the fact that mediation is possible only as part of social practices, and that mediality constitutes itself only within complex cultural networks. This intricate interplay of media technologies and social practices is highlighted by Bernhard Siegert:

> The history of paper only turns into a media history if it serves as a reference system for the analysis of bureaucratic or scientific data processing. When the chancelleries of Emperor Friedrich II of Hohenstaufen replaced parchment with paper, this act decisively changed the meaning of 'power'. The history of the telescope, in turn, becomes a media history if it is taken as a system of reference for an analysis of seeing. Finally, a history of the postal system is a media history if it serves as the system of reference for a history of communication. That is to say, media do not emerge independently and outside of a specific historical practice. (2015, 5; see also Schüttpelz 2006)

A theoretical approach to literature informed by the concept of media ecology thus seeks to locate literature within a perpetually shifting field or network that consists of diverse materials, technologies, devices, practices and operations. Media ecologies of literature, then, observe these entanglements and their historical formation.

Media ecology

In a very general sense, one may define media ecology as the study of 'media formations as interrelations between human beings and their media environments in changing processes of medialization or "the history of mediation"' (Berensmeyer 2012, 330). Although of a rather recent date, this definition is still very much indebted to the historical origins of media ecology in theories of the Toronto school. Taking its cue from Marshall McLuhan and further developed by Neil Postman, traditional media ecology of the 1960s and 1970s looks at the medium within its environment, a theory deriving from the nineteenth-century roots of the term 'ecology'. Ecology in the dominant sense of the term stems from the field of biology and refers to the relationship of humans and their environment. Coined by Ernst Haeckel in the nineteenth century, the term denotes the following: 'By ecology, we mean the whole science of the relations of the organism to the environment [zur umgebenden Außenwelt] including, in the broad sense, all the "conditions of existence"' (qtd. in Stauffer 1957, 140). In the 1960s, this term was first used to describe media concepts. Based on his definition of media as 'extensions of man', McLuhan describes the media environment as a 'technological simulation of consciousness, when the creative process of knowing will be collectively and corporately extended to the whole of human society, much as we have already extended our senses and our nerves by the various media' (1994, 3). Within this vision of a technological expansion of the sensorial apparatus, human consciousness represents a relatively stable core, a position that is also supported by McLuhan's explanation in the *Gutenberg Galaxy* of 1962: 'My suggestion is that cultural ecology has a reasonably stable base in the human sensorium, and that any extension of the sensorium by technological dilation has a quite appreciable effect in setting up new ratios or proportions among all the senses' (32).

Around the turn of the millennium, a new understanding of media ecology started to emerge. In 2002, Ursula Heise criticized the rather static approach of the Toronto school, which she aptly summarizes as follows:

> Based on the assumption that media are not mere tools that humans use, but rather constitute environments within which they move and that shape the structure of their perceptions, their forms of discourse, and their social behavior patterns, media ecology typically focuses on how these structures change with the introduction of new communications technologies. (151)

Heise, instead, proposes a more dynamic definition of media ecology – not in opposition to the traditional concept but, rather, as a consequence of the productive tensions inherent in ecological thinking:

> Ecological concepts, in other words, are invoked either to drive home a systemic perspective on media technologies, or to propose an alternative to such a view. This opposition points to fundamentally different interpretations of what the notions of 'system' and 'environment' mean, in the study not only of technological, but also of natural habitats, and it thereby raises the question of how the role of the natural should be envisioned in the context of a technological 'ecology'. To put it somewhat differently, the rifts in the interpretation of media ecology allow one to bend the metaphor back to its literal context, and to investigate the

> interplay of technology and nature in a more broadly understood spatial ecology that encompasses both material and virtual habitats. (2002, 152)

Daniel Punday takes up this cue but otherwise still uses the concept of ecology in a very conventional manner, namely to investigate 'references to other media within the contemporary novel' (2012, 18). Such an approach is reminiscent of the theory of intermediality (see Wolf 2018) that is, in turn, influenced by intertextuality. Punday develops his theoretical framework in contradistinction to the terms 'field' – informed by Bourdieu's 1992 study *Les règles de l'art* – and 'system' – which Punday, perhaps surprisingly, traces back to Max Horkheimer (whom he does not mention) and Theodor W. Adorno's chapter on *Kulturindustrie* of their 1944 work *Dialektik der Aufklärung*. In the end, however, he comes to a conclusion very similar to Heise's, that is, a conception of the media as part of a dynamic system: 'The concept of the media ecology offers us, then, a flexible understanding of the environment in which the novel functions today' (Punday 2012, 14).

The more recent discussion on media ecology was mainly initiated and influenced by Matthew Fuller's book *Media Ecologies: Materialist Energies in Art and Technoculture* of 2005. This study bears little resemblance to the tradition going back to Postman and McLuhan, as it is much more indebted to Felix Guattari's *Les trois ecologies* (1985) as well as Guattari's and Gilles Deleuze's *Anti-Oedipe* (1972) and *Mille Plateux* (1980). Essentially, Fuller's approach to ecology deconstructs any dichotomy between culture or the human and nature. With reference to Deleuze and Guattari, Bernd Herzogenrath states: 'Categories such as "nature" and "man," "human" and "nonhuman," cannot anymore be grounded in an essentialist and clear-cut separation' (2009, 4), and he subsequently quotes the following passage from *Anti-Oedipus:*

> we make no distinction between man and nature: the human essence of nature and the natural essence of man become one within nature in the form of production or industry, just as they do within the life of man as a species. [. . .] man and nature are not like two opposite terms confronting each other – not even in the sense of bipolar opposites within a relationship of causation, ideation, or expression (cause and effect, subject and object, etc.); rather they are one and the same essential reality, the producer-product. (Deleuze and Guattari 1983, 4–5)

According to this tradition, there is no longer a centre to a medial network, and the whole set of connections is dynamic, ever-changing and performative: 'Within the multiplicities of these ecologies, complexity reigns supreme. Nonlinear, selforganizational, and transpositional systems behavior combine autopoietically at the intersection of media collisions' (Slayton

2005, x). Fuller himself defines his own approach in contradistinction to the 'environmentalism' of the Toronto School:

> Here [i.e. in Neil Postman's sense], 'media ecology' describes a kind of environmentalism: using a study of media to sustain a relatively stable notion of human culture. [. . .] Here, 'ecology' is more usually replaced with the term 'environment' or is used as a cognate term where the fundamental difference between the two concepts is glossed over. Echoing differences in life sciences and in various Green political movements, 'environmentalism' possesses a sustaining vision of the human and wants to make the world safe for it. Such environmentalism also often suggests that there has passed, or that there will be reached, a state of equilibrium: that there is a resilient and harmonic balance to be achieved with some ingenious and beneficent mix of media. Ecologists focus rather more on dynamic systems in which any one part is always multiply connected, acting by virtue of those connections, and always variable, such that it can be regarded as a pattern rather than simply as an object. (2005, 3–4)

When applied to the field of art in general or literature in particular, it is important to note that this conception of media ecology is in no way considered to be a philosophy or theory external to the field investigated but, rather, an integral part of the dynamic medial network it sets out to describe, as Michael Goddard and Jussi Parikka maintain:

> Media ecologies are quite often understood by Fuller through artistic/activist practices rather than pre-formed theories, which precisely work through the complex media layers in which on the one hand subjectivation and agency are articulated and, on the other hand, the materiality of informational objects gets distributed, dispersed and takes effect. (2011, §3)

Goddard and Parikka thus stress the performative and dynamic nature of the medium of art that can be approached with the help of media ecology:

> In this sense, artistic work, whether engaging with animal bodies, technological assemblages, or their combinations and relations, can be seen as an ecological – or even ecosophical – mapping of potential universes of enunciation as well as sensation. More than a question of interpretation, media ecology addresses the crucial question of activity; what do media do? (2011, §6)

In addition to this performative and dynamic dimension, Parikka also emphasizes yet another capacity of media ecology relevant to a media-theoretical approach to literature: its self-reflexive nature, since 'a media-ecological perspective relies on notions of self-referentiality and autopoiesis' (2005, n.p.).

Hence, the concept of media ecology, to return to the field of literary media studies, enables us to regard the literary and cultural media network as dynamic and performative, complex and ever-changing. Furthermore, since an individual investigation incorporates material media as well as non-material and performative elements, the question ultimately arises as to how these polar elements or constituents of a given media ecology and their respective relations are organized and processed. Here, *cultural techniques* and *remediation* come into play.

The theory of cultural techniques has a long-standing tradition in German cultural studies and in the field of media studies. It may help to underline the dynamic and performative nature of the historical formation of a given media ecology of literature. The term 'Kulturtechniken' comprises a wide range of meanings – from the nineteenth-century reflection on practices of transforming nature into culture by means of engineering to twentieth-century implementations of media competences such as watching television. As Sybille Krämer and Horst Bredekamp (2013), Bernhard Siegert (2015) and Geoffrey Winthrop-Young and Jussi Parikka (2013) have maintained, the concept of cultural techniques discloses a reflexive reference to cultural practices which bring forth technical media and artefacts in the first place (see Maye 2010, 121–2; Bayerlipp, Haekel and Schlegel 2018). In such an anti-ontological approach (Siegert 2015, 11), the medium appears as part of a dynamic system in which cultural techniques 'precede the media concepts they generate' (Siegert 2015, 58). According to such an understanding, a singular work is inextricably integrated in the production, dissemination and perception of meaning (Winthrop-Young 2013, 5–6). This, however, also implies that the technique itself escapes an immediate analysis; it can be made describable only as the difference between material manifestations. Hence, the direct environment of a medial manifestation and its partaking in cultural practices is central to an understanding of this medium itself. Elena Esposito's correlation of the media theory of cultural techniques with the idea of contingency is particularly fruitful in this context. Applying Luhmann's loose and flexible coupling of medium and form, she maintains that this conception of media is the necessary condition for an understanding of contingency: 'Media are only potentialities, and their fundamental function is to make contingent something that was formerly indispensable' (Esposito 2004, 7).

The investigation of literature in the light of cultural techniques accepts the ontological status of the medium of literature, and yet focuses on performative techniques such as reading, writing, production, distribution and critical reception. The outcome of such an analysis would establish the ecology of a given medium or a medial formation. The work of literature thus becomes conceivable as a material trace of a cultural technique which predates it and places it in the midst of a temporal and spatial network affecting its meaning and impact. The theory establishes links between all components involved, and also allows for a reconciliation of media-theoretical and traditional concepts of literature. The concept of narrative as a cultural technique takes on a key role here in that it connects writing, reading, memory and identity construction, thus serving as a link between the technical medium, text, production and reception. Meaning is no longer hidden in or behind a technological medium but, rather, created as part of a complex set of operations.

The second important concept incorporated in the theory of media ecology, remediation, as defined by Jay David Bolter and Richard Grusin in reference to the writings of Marshall McLuhan, considers 'the representation of one medium in another' (1999, 45; see also Grusin 2015). Formulated to describe the new digital media, remediation provides a methodology to describe media networks in general, combining an interest in media technologies and cultural techniques. It situates the individual medium in the midst of a dynamic and flexible system and discloses that 'media are not autonomous' but 'adapt, remodel and transcode the forms and practices of other media' (Straumann 2015, 254). James Brooke-Smith defines remediation as a way in which a 'dominant medium [. . .] acts as a filter through which residual media forms must pass' (2013, 234). Most importantly, for an analysis of literature as self-reflexive, '[r]emediation makes the medium as such *visible*' (Guillory 2010, 324; emphasis in the original). The term 'remediation' alludes to the much older term 'mediation'. The term 'mediation' signals the writings of Marx and Marxist theory (see Williams 1977, 98–100) while more generally figuring in a more neutral manner as 'a process whereby two different realms, persons, objects or terms are brought into relation' (Guillory 2010, 342).

The combination of these theoretical constellations – media ecology, cultural techniques and remediation – enables us to approach literature and literary theory while applying the whole range of media-theoretical concepts. In arguing for the importance of a media theory of literature, we focus on literature's capacity to create and reflect on its poetics and its ability to act as a medium between disciplines and discourses, especially between readers and the world. Jonathan Culler criticizes the fact that theory 'consists primarily of works originating in other, non-literary areas of endeavour' (2007, 5), and argues, together with a growing number of other critics, for a return to and refocusing on literature itself. Raman Selden, Peter Widdowson and Peter Brooker likewise maintain that 'it is explicitly literature and the literary which have been neglected. In particular, what has been sidelined is the self-reflexiveness of the literary text' (2005, 269). We follow this lead: it is the declared goal of this book to give literature its due, to distil its theory out of literature's potential for self-reflexion – in particular with regard to its mediality – and subsequently systematize this web of significance as a media ecology of literature.

Notes

1 We are aware that to use 'cultural turns' to refer to developments in literary and cultural studies is problematic. The linguistic turn is still the only development that initiated a revolution that affected the entire humanities, whereas other turns merely aim at propagating a new research project. That said, however, we believe that the transition from analogue to digital media will alter, though not challenge, the concept of literature fundamentally in the long run. Theory and the medial turn merely react to these deep-seated and essential changes.

2 In his *Literaturtheorie*, Jahraus writes: 'Literatur ist ein Medium. Aber diese Redeweise zielt weniger auf einen technischen Medienbegriff, weil man damit nur beim Buch ankommen würde.' (2003, 194).

References

Aragay, Mireia. *Books in Motion: Adaptation, Intertextuality, Authorship*. Amsterdam: Rodopi, 2005.

Assmann, Aleida. *Introduction to Cultural Studies: Topics, Concepts, Issues*. Berlin: ESV, 2012.

Bachmann-Medick, Doris. *Cultural Turns: New Orientations in the Study of Culture*. Trans. Adam Blauhut. Berlin: De Gruyter, 2016.

Bayerlipp, Susanne, Ralf Haekel and Johannes Schlegel. 'Cultural Techniques of Literature: Introduction.' *ZAA* 66.2 (2018): 139–47.

Berensmeyer, Ingo. 'From Media Anthropology to Media Ecology.' *Travelling Concepts for the Study of Culture*. Eds. Ansgar Nünning and Birgit Neumann. Berlin: De Gruyter, 2012. 321–36.

Birns, Nicholas. *Theory After Theory: An Intellectual History of Literary Theory from 1950 to the Early Twenty-First Century*. Peterborough: Broadview, 2010.

Bolter, Jay David, and Richard Grusin. *Remediation: Understanding New Media*. Cambridge, MA: MIT Press, 1999.

Brooke-Smith, James. 'Remediating Romanticism.' *Literature Compass* 10.4 (2013): 343–52.

Culler, Jonathan. *The Literary in Theory*. Stanford, CA: Stanford University Press, 2007.

Cunningham, Valentine. *Reading After Theory*. Malden, MA: Blackwell, 2002.

Deleuze, Gilles, and Felix Guattari. *Anti-Oedipus: Capitalism and Schizophrenia*. Trans. Robert Hurley, Mark Seem and Helen R. Lane. Minneapolis, MN: University of Minnesota Press, 1983.

Eagleton, Terry. *After Theory*. London: Allen Lane, 2003.

Esposito, Elena. 'The Arts of Contingency.' *Critical Inquiry* 31.1 (2004): 7–25.

Fuller, Matthew. *Media Ecologies: Materialist Energies in Art and Technoculture*. Cambridge, MA: MIT Press, 2005.

Gallie, Walter Bryce. 'Essentially Contested Concepts.' *Proceedings of the Aristotelian Society* 56.1 (1956): 167–98.

Giesecke, Michael. *Der Buchdruck in der frühen Neuzeit: eine historische Fallstudie über die Durchsetzung neuer Informations- und Kommunikationstechnologien.* Frankfurt a.M.: Suhrkamp, 1991.

Glaubitz, Nicola. 'Literaturwissenschaft.' *Handbuch Medienwissenschaft.* Ed. Jens Schröter. Stuttgart: Metzler, 2014. 427–34.

Goddard, Michael, and Jussi Parikka. 'Editorial: Unnatural Ecologies.' *The Fibreculture Journal* 17 (2011): 1–5.

Golding, Peter. 'Media Studies in the UK.' *Publizistik* 64 (2019): 503–15.

Griem, Julika, Ed. *Bildschirmfiktionen. Interferenzen zwischen Literatur und neuen Medien.* Tübingen: Narr, 1998.

Grusin, Richard. 'Radical Mediation.' *Critical Inquiry* 42.1 (2015): 124–48.

Guillory, John. 'Genesis of the Media Concept.' *Critical Inquiry* 36.2 (2010): 321–62.

Gumbrecht, Hans Ulrich. 'Medium Literatur.' *Geschichte der Medien.* Eds. Manfred Faßler and Wulf Halbach. München: Fink, 1998. 83–107.

Hansen, Mark B. N. 'Media Theory.' *Theory, Culture & Society* 23.2–3 (2006): 297–306.

Hayles, N. Katherine. *Writing Machines.* Cambridge, MA: MIT Press, 2002.

Hayles, N. Katherine. *Electronic Literature: New Horizons for the Literary.* Notre Dame: University of Notre Dame Press, 2008.

Heise, Ursula. 'Unnatural Ecologies: The Metaphor of the Environment in Media Theory.' *Configurations* 10.1 (2002): 149–68.

Herzogenrath, Bernd. 'Nature/Geophilosophy/Machinics/Ecosophy.' *Deleuze/Guattari & Ecology.* Ed. Bernd Herzogenrath. Houndmills: Palgrave, 2009. 1–22.

Iser, Wolfgang. *The Fictive and the Imaginary: Charting Literary Anthropology.* Baltmore, MD: John Hopkins University Press, 1993.

Jahraus, Oliver. *Literatur als Medium. Sinnkonstitution und Subjekterfahrung zwischen Bewußtsein und Kommunikation.* Weilerswist: Velbrück, 2003.

Jahraus, Oliver. *Das Medienabenteuer. Aufsätze zur Medienkulturwissenschaft.* Würzburg: Königshausen & Neumann, 2017.

Kittler, Friedrich. *Discourse Networks, 1800/1900.* Trans. Michael Metteer. Stanford, CA: Stanford University Press, 1990.

Krämer, Sybille. 'Friedrich Kittler: Kulturtechniken der Zeitachsenmanipulation.' *Medientheorien: Eine philosophische Einführung.* Eds. Alice Lagaay and David Lauer. Frankfurt a.M.: Campus, 2004. 201–24.

Krämer, Sybille, and Horst Bredekamp. 'Culture, Technology, Cultural Techniques – Moving Beyond Text.' *Theory, Culture & Society* 30.6 (2013): 20–9.

Luhmann, Niklas. *Art as Social System.* Trans. Eva M. Knodt. Stanford, CA: Stanford University Press, 2000.

Maye, Harun. 'Was ist eine Kulturtechnik?' *Zeitschrift für Medien- und Kulturforschung* 2 (2010): 121–35.

McFarlane, Brian. *Novel to Film: An Introduction to the Theory of Adaptation.* Oxford: Clarendon, 1996.

McLuhan, Marshal. *The Gutenberg Galaxy: The Making of Typographic Man.* Toronto, ON: University of Toronto Press, 1962.

McLuhan, Marshal. *Understanding Media: The Extensions of Man.* Cambridge, MA: MIT Press, 1994.

Middeke, Martin, and Christoph Reinfandt, Eds. *Theory Matters: The Place and Function of Theory in Literary and Cultural Studies Today.* London: Palgrave Macmillan, 2016.

Mitchell, W. J. T., and Mark B. N. Hansen, Eds. *Critical Terms for Media Studies*. Chicago, IL: University of Chicago Press, 2010.

Münker, Stefan, and Alexander Roesler, Eds. *Was ist ein Medium*? Frankfurt a.M.: Suhrkamp, 2008.

Nünning, Ansgar, and Jan Rupp, Eds. *Medialisierung des Erzählens im englischsprachigen Roman der Gegenwart*. Trier: Wissenschaftlicher Verlag Trier, 2011.

O'Malley, Tom. 'Media History and Media Studies: Aspects of the Development of the Study of Media History in the UK, 1945–2000.' *Media History* 8.2 (2002): 155–73.

Ouellette, Laurie, and Jonathan Gray, Eds. *Keywords for Media Studies*. New York: New York University Press, 2017.

Parikka, Jussi. 'The Universal Viral Machine: Bits, Parasites and the Media Ecology of Network Culture.' *Ctheory* (2005). <https://journals.uvic.ca/index.php/ctheory/article/view/14467/5309>. Accessed 1 April 2020.

Paulson, Sarah J., and Anders Skare Malvik, Eds. *Literature in Contemporary Media Culture: Technology – Subjectivity – Aesthetics*. Amsterdam: Benjamins, 2016.

Punday, Daniel. *Writing at the Limit: The Novel in the New Media Ecology*. Lincoln, NB: University of Nebraska Press, 2012.

Purdon, James. 'Literature – Technology – Media: Towards a New Technography.' *Literature Compass* 15.1 (2018): 1–9.

Reinfandt, Christoph. 'Literatur als Medium.' *Grenzen der Literatur. Zum Begriff und Phänomen des Literarischen*. Eds. Fotis Jannidis, Gerhard Lauer and Simone Winko. Berlin: De Gruyter, 2009. 161–87.

Schlegel, Johannes. 'By Way of Introduction. *Stoner*, Black Boxes, Institutions.' *The Institution of English Literature: Formation and Mediation*. Eds. Barbara Schaff, Johannes Schlegel and Carola Surkamp. Göttingen: V&R Unipress, 2017. 7–23.

Schüttpelz, Erhard. 'Die medienanthropologische Kehre der Kulturtechniken.' *Archiv für Mediengeschichte* 6 (2006): 87–110.

Selden, Raman, Peter Widdowson and Peter Brooker. *A Reader's Guide to Contemporary Literary Theory*. London: Pearson Longman, 2005.

Siegert, Bernhard. *Cultural Techniques: Grids, Filters, Doors, and Other Articulations of the Real*. New York: Fordham University Press, 2015.

Slayton, Joel. 'Foreword,' Matthew Fuller. *Media Ecologies: Materialist Energies in Art and Technoculture*. Cambridge, MA: MIT Press, 2005. ix–x.

Stam, Robert. *Literature Through Film: Realism, Magic and the Art of Adaptation*. Malden, MA: Blackwell, 2005.

Starre, Alexander. *Metamedia: American Book Fictions and Literary Print Culture after Digitization*. Iowa City: University of Iowa Press, 2015.

Stauffer, Robert C. 'Haeckel, Darwin, and Ecology.' *Quarterly Review of Biology* 32.2 (1957): 138–44.

Straumann, Barbara. 'Adaptation – Remediation – Transmediality.' *Intermediality: Literature – Image – Sound – Music*. Ed. Gabriele Rippl. Berlin: De Gruyter, 2015. 249–67.

Tabbi, Joseph, and Michael Wutz, Eds. *Reading Matters: Narrative in the New Media Ecology*. Ithaca, NY: Cornell University Press, 1997.

Valdivia, Angharad N. 'Introduction.' *A Companion to Media Studies*. Ed. Angharad N. Valdivia. Malden, MA: Blackwell, 2003. 1–16.

Williams, Raymond. *Marxism and Literature*. Oxford: Oxford University Press, 1977.

Winthrop-Young, Geoffrey. *Kittler and the Media*. Cambridge: Polity Press, 2011.

Winthrop-Young, Geoffrey. 'Cultural Techniques: Preliminary Remarks.' *Theory, Culture & Society* 30.3 (2013): 3–19.

Winthrop-Young, Geoffrey, and Jussi Parikka, Eds. *Cultural Techniques*. Special Issue of *Theory, Culture & Society* 30.6 2013.

Wolf, Werner. *Selected Essays on Intermediality (1992–2014): Theory and Typology, Literature – Music Relations, Transmedial Narratology, Miscellaneous Transmedial Phenomena*. Ed. Walter Bernhart. Amsterdam: Brill-Rodopi, 2018.

Wutz, Michael. *Enduring Words: Literary Narrative in a Changing Media Ecology*. Tuscaloosa, AL: University of Alabama Press, 2009.

PART I

Reading | Media | Theory

The first part of the collection explores media ecology as a tension between the materiality of the book or text and the immaterial practices and cultural techniques associated with handling this material medium – particularly the cultural technique of reading. This tension presents itself primarily as a theoretical problem, and, while focusing on the concept of mediation, the authors tackle, and aim at revising, the concept of reading from different angles.

Christoph Reinfandt's chapter 'From work to text revisited' discusses the productive tension between the material medium of the book, on the one hand, and the cultural practices and techniques involved in its reception, on the other hand. The chapter sets in with a close reading of the opening page of A. L. Kennedy's 2011 novel, *The Blue Book*. Kennedy's novel, Reinfandt argues, more or less explicitly acknowledges the basic coordinates of a more general theory of *text*: there is a world in which a text finds itself in its material form – in this case, a book made of paper. By explicitly addressing the reader, the material book evokes the topic of the act of reading, which is not directed at the actuality of the book as an object, but, rather, at the marks which are inscribed in the paleness of the paper pages of which it is made. His chapter demonstrates how 'reality' as we can know it comprises a complex interplay of signification and *signifiance*, of semantic and functional dimensions of meaning, of observation and operation, of appearance and abstraction. In order to tackle this complexity, Reinfandt proposes a reconceptualization of reading as a cultural technique within a multifaceted media ecology of literature.

In ‘Media theory as book theory’, Alexander Starre analyses the novel *S.* (2013), written by Doug Dorst and co-produced by writer-director J. J. Abrams, not as metafiction but as metamedium. Beginning with a critical and revisionary reading of the seminal theories by Marshall McLuhan and Friedrich Kittler, he focuses on what he calls the material embedding of content. The way the materiality fashions reading practice is, in a highly metareflective turn, itself thematized by the novel *S.* by advancing its own theory of the book. Through its lavish design, the novel radicalizes the classical concept of the editorial fiction and plays with the tension between the traditional book and the changing shape of literature in the digital age.

The subsequent chapter, Ralph Pordzik’s ‘The poetics of etcetera’, addresses George Orwell’s use of the literary list as an instrument to explore the boundaries of textuality and to counter classical realist narrative by arranging words and idioms for a dazzling and often unexpected outcome. Its main focus rests on the list or catalogue as a poetical device used to organize mental processes of storing, structuring and processing data as well as questioning the notion of a transparent discourse presenting only the raw or unmediated facts of reality and experience. Attention focuses in particular on Orwell’s techniques of selecting items from various orders of the fictional and the historically given and on his parading different semantic registers of objective or rhetorical use value. The chapter finds itself situated in a materialist-semiotic context of reading Orwell’s fiction not in terms of its critique of sociopolitical or class conflicts in Great Britain but in terms of its formative role in mapping out a new media ecology – new media frames and contexts in which any number of contingent items that provide its author with a powerful marking, mnemonic and recording device are absorbed. In Orwell’s writing, it is maintained, the list figures as a major literary device to strategically cut across various milieus of information production and accumulation, shaping its very own ecology of operative modes, perceptual patterns and structures of mentalities.

The final chapter in this first part, Rieke Jordan’s ‘Invisible thresholds’, explores the interplay of media ecologies that poetry and the novel create in Ben Lerner’s *Leaving the Atocha Station*. By way of close reading, she shows how the effects of the market and its forms and modalities influence both the writing and the reading of literature. One key argument places the emphasis on the reading experience as a specific expectation that essentially changes the works of literature itself – in the case of the novel, it is the experience of poetry at a public reading. Jordan argues for a careful assessment of the environs contemporary literature creates for itself, among them the literary market of the twenty-first century and the pressures it puts on its actors, media and writers alike.

1

From work to text revisited

'Reading' and the trajectory from literature to media theory

Christoph Reinfandt

Introduction: Reading a text

The opening of A. L. Kennedy's 2011 novel *The Blue Book* spells out explicitly (and self-reflexively) some of the frequently unspoken assumptions and prerequisites that are at work in all acts of reading:

> But here this is, the book you're reading.
>
> Obviously.
>
> Your book – it's started now, it's touched and opened, held. You could, if you wanted, heft it, wonder if it weighs more than a pigeon, or a plimsoll, or quite probably rather less than a wholemeal loaf. If offers you these possibilities.
>
> And quite naturally, you face it. Your eyes, your lips are turned towards it – all that paleness, all those marks – and you are so close here that if it were a person you might kiss. That might be unavoidable.
>
> You can remember times when kissing has been unavoidable. You are not, after all, unattractive: not when people understand you and who you can be.
>
> And you're a reader – clearly – here you are reading your book, which is what it was made for. It loves when you look, and then it listens and it

> speaks. It was built to welcome your attention and reciprocate with this: the sound it lifts inside you. It gives you the signs for the shapes of the names of the thoughts in your mouth and in your mind and this is where they sing, here at the point where you both meet.
>
> Which is where you might imagine, might even elicit, the tremble of paper, that unmistakable flinch. It moves for you, your book, and it will always show you all it can. (2012, 1)

Unlike many other texts, this text actually addresses its own status as an object (a book), which occupies a place in the world ('here this is'). It could be weighed against other animate or inanimate and more or less useful objects like pigeons, plimsolls or wholemeal loaves. At the same time, the text's very first words establish a somewhat precarious link to the world, hovering between continuity and interruption: why does it begin with 'but' and the somewhat unusual 'this' instead of just a confident and at the same time more casual 'here it is'? It could be argued that 'but' and 'this' make the opening stronger while a mere 'here it is' would just flag the book as a specific element in a world which is otherwise continuous; 'but' and 'this' acknowledge that something – the world – precedes the text, but they also stress the rupture created by the onset of the text in an act of reading which absorbs the reader's consciousness, turning the attention of the reader away from the actuality of the world and towards a different, textual or virtual register of existence. The book does not only exist as an object (as would be indicated by a mere 'it'), but also and more importantly, in this second dimension, which makes it an individual case ('this'): 'But here *this is*, the book you're *reading*' (my emphasis, CR). And with this we have obviously reached the topic indicated in the subtitle of this chapter: reading.

Let us begin to read, then: drawn into the unfolding text, a reader of the passage moves from the 'obviousness' of the world of objects in which s/he touches, opens and holds the book – these are all activities necessary for the act of reading – towards possible but unnecessary activities like comparing the weight of the book to the weight of other objects. This shift from actuality to virtuality is indicated not only on the level of content but also formally in a typical case of literary or even poetic overdetermination of language use: the deictic '*h*ere', which initially demarcates the position of the book in the world from the reader's perspective, is specified by the fact that the book is '*h*eld' by the reader – and the reader could then also choose to do other things with it, for example '*h*eft' it. This latter word does not only mark an unusual activity (at least with regard to books), but it is also a slightly unusual verb which is immediately replaced by its more frequent synonym '*w*eigh'. 'Weigh', however, is reached by way of '*w*onder', a verb which captures quite nicely what the text is doing by now: it enables the reader to create a virtual reality in which s/he may speculate on the weight of the book as compared to any old object, from '*p*igeon' to '*p*limsoll' to '*wh*olemeal loaf', without actually having to *do* it – and note that the '*wh*olemeal loaf' quite nicely combines the h-*sound* that echoes the world of activity outside the text so far ('*h*ere', '*h*eld', '*h*eft') with the *letter* w that demarcates the emergent virtual reality of the *w*ritten text ('*w*eigh', '*w*onder', '*w*holemeal loaf').

Once this point is reached, you, the reader, may be willing to acknowledge the possibility of further patterns in the text. In fact, p-words seem to proliferate and accentuate the gist of the opening passage: virtual objects ('*p*igeon', '*p*limsoll') reside in the potentiality ('*p*robably', '*p*ossibilities') opened up by the text ('all that *p*aleness, all those marks') that is carried by pages in the book ('the tremble of *p*aper') once a '*p*oint' is established where a '*p*erson' and a book meet in an intimate encounter of reading. This encounter is depicted as opening up the possibility of successful communication 'when *p*eople understand you and who you can be'. The book, it turns out now, is a special object which cannot only be touched, opened, held and hefted. It must also be faced and, in the equivalent of a kiss, *read*. This is 'what it was made for' and what animates it so that it can 'love' and 'welcome' the reader's attention, 'listen' to it and 'speak' to the reader. The reader's imagination renders the book dynamic and makes it move materially ('the tremble of *p*aper'), affectively ('for you, your book') and in terms of its semiotic potential: 'it will always show you all it can.'

While only a full reading of A. L. Kennedy's *The Blue Book* could support the legitimacy and adequacy of this kind of intense reading of its opening – and I will return to it at the end of this chapter – the observations so far shall, for the time being, serve only heuristic purposes. On the one hand, the beginning of *The Blue Book* seems to programmatically announce the status of the text as a literary *work* within the coordinates established by modern literary history from Romanticism to Modernism and beyond. On the other hand, however, it more or less explicitly acknowledges the basic coordinates of a more general theory of *text*: there is a world in which a text finds itself in its material form – in this case: a book made of paper. In this world there needs to be someone who can touch, open and hold the book in order to read it – in *The Blue Book*, this person, the reader, is explicitly addressed. The act of reading is not directed at the actuality of the book as an object, but, rather, at the marks which are inscribed in the paleness of the paper pages of which it is made. These marks let the book itself assume a kind of virtual agency: 'it lifts [the sound] inside' the reader by providing 'signs for the shapes of the names of the thoughts in [the reader's] mouth and [. . .] mind'. Here it becomes clear that what happens is not exclusively between the book and the reader: the 'names of the thoughts' are coded in language that, in turn, is coded in signs which, in turn, are coded in letters – and the close reading earlier has indicated that the text itself may draw attention to the significance of single letters ('h', 'w', 'p'), which can contribute to the semiotic potential of a text in various ways, that is, either by being conventionally subsumed into words or, as in this more specialized literary case, by establishing patterns in their own right.

The following observations will show that this seemingly specialized case of literary overdetermination can, in fact, be seen as a paradigmatic (if more intense) instance of what in principle applies to all media texts, that is, the anchoring of acts of reading in differentiable layers of materiality and mediality, which, in turn, establish the media ecology of literature. These layers bear traces of a text's place in the world in terms of both production and reception, and of its cultural pre-formation through not only genres and discourses but also, quite fundamentally, media formats. In what follows I will argue that Roland Barthes' famous essays 'From Work to Text' (1986, 56–64; first published in 1971) – and, to a certain extent, its less famous follow-up 'Theory of the Text' (1981; first published in 1973) – occupy a crucial transitional position in the trajectory from the paradigmatic status of literary communication in modern print-based culture (with the literary theories that come with it) to the multiplying media environments of the twentieth and twenty-first centuries (with the concomitant turn to media theory).

The work(s) of modern literature

Let us begin with the most famous catchphrase in Barthes' 'From Work to Text': 'The work,' Barthes writes, 'is held in hand, the text is held in language' (1986, 57). In the light of our reading of the opening of *The Blue Book* it seems that Barthes is aligning the term 'work' with the actuality of the book in hand, while the 'text' opens up the virtual realm of possibility and meaning. What is perhaps most striking about this laconic statement is that it runs counter to the most cherished assumptions of the hermeneutic/Romantic/Modernist/New Critical-Formalist tradition, which relies on the notion that it is the poetic or literary use of language that qualifies a 'text' for the status of 'work'. This special language use enhances the virtual dimension of a text and calls for reading techniques that map the rich connotative layers of meaning in such texts – and note that in the course of the trajectory of traditions indicated previously, these connotative layers of meaning are increasingly understood to be inscribed in the formal properties of a work in a development which re-actualizes virtuality, as it were. This shift relies on the circularity of the argument: in fact, the version of the argument presented earlier is already based on the outcome of the development. One could, of course, also argue that it is the specific reading technique that brings about the status of the work and not necessarily its formal features – as the pre-formalist versions of modern literary theory tended to do. But for all practical purposes of theory, this circularity is balanced with shifting emphases in what might be called the Romantic dimension of modern culture, which is predicated on a dynamic correlation between subjectivity, on the one hand, and linguistic and literary reflexivity, on the other.

In this understanding, a mere 'text' would be marked by 'normal', that is, denotative, non-literary language use and thus lend itself to 'normal' reading strategies determining the meaning 'behind' the text by reading 'through' it – note that the spatial metaphors employed here minimize the virtuality of meaning and replace it with a simulated or virtual actuality, too. This operation is at the heart of what might be called the enlightenment dimension of modern culture, which is predicated on objectivity and the idea(l) of transparency of discourse. 'This conception of the text,' Roland Barthes points out in 'Theory of the Text', 'is obviously linked to a metaphysics, that of truth' (1981, 33). And he also recognizes that this 'classical, institutional, and current conception' of text (1981, 33) *includes* the literary work. The work, according to 'From Work to Text', 'closes upon the signified' (Barthes 1986, 58) in a fashion which Nicholas Birns, following Paul de Man, has called the 'resolved symbolic', which 'raises the poem's meaning above ordinary life, making the text "symbolic" and metaphorical, and insists it has a coherent indissoluble meaning' that still makes 'the text determinate and "resolved"' (2010, 11–44, 15). What is special about the metaphysics of truth in literary works, then, is their subjective bent and their potential for a self-reflexive deconstruction of the metaphysics of truth through attention to form, which increasingly replaces the 'classical' arbiters of truth in both the objective/Enlightenment and subjective/Romantic sense (world and author, respectively) – first with the reader and then with the language of the text itself in a non-metaphysical sense.

My argument here is that it is the trajectory of modern literature itself more than the accompanying trajectory of literary theory from hermeneutics/Romanticism to Formalism/Modernism that leads up to Roland Barthes' argument in 'From Work to Text'. In terms of its meaning, a work of modern literature is just a special instance of text in the 'classical' sense, but what makes it special is that it 'closes upon the signified' within a particular frame (modern literature/Romanticism), while other texts 'close upon the signified' in different ways. With Niklas Luhmann, for example, one could argue that texts 'resolve the symbolic' in ways suggested by the symbolically generalized communication medium of the communication system in which they are processed (see 2012–13, 1:120–3 and 1:190–238), and the symbolically generalized communication medium of the system of modern art and literature is the 'work' as opposed to, for example, the 'publication' in the modern science system, which is framed differently. The crucial difference between modern literature and other contexts of communication is its specific reflexivity which is focused on form and language, while the reflexivity of modern science elides just this dimension and focuses on procedural problems, instead. It is this reflexivity of form and language which Roland Barthes transmutes into a notion of Text (with a capital T) that frames all texts (lower-case t) in the sense of a pervasive textuality.

A work, then, is merely 'the Text's imaginary tail', but it 'functions as a general sign' that 'represent[s] an institutional category of the civilization of the Sign', (Barthes 1986, 58–9), and as such it is perhaps the most overt symptom of the textual procedures through which the pervasive semiosis and dissemination constitutive of modern culture are appropriated for practical use. '[T]he Text,' on the other hand, 'does not stop at (good) literature' (Barthes 1986, 58). In fact, all symbolic generalizations established in modern culture turn the '*radically* symbolic' Text (capital T) into '*moderately* symbolic' texts whose 'symbolics runs short, that is, stops' at the boundaries of the system in which the respective symbolic generalization holds true (Barthes 1986, 59; original emphasis) – it is just that the works of modern literature are less moderately (or more radically) symbolic than others.[1]

So this is the work the works of modern literature perform: they provide traces of the inherent subversiveness of textuality. 'The Text,' Roland Barthes insists, 'is what is situated at the limit of the rules of the speech-act' that implement 'rationality, readability, etc.,' and it 'practices the infinite postponement of the signified' (1986, 58–9). With statements like this Barthes clearly articulates the move from structuralism to post-structuralism, which acknowledges that any text hovers between its domesticating context in which it aspires to the condition of the 'resolved symbolic' and its rootedness in the 'unresolved symbolic' of language *embodied* in textuality, both understood as 'structured but decentered, without closure' in 'a paradoxical idea of structure: a system without end or center' (Barthes 1986, 59). Any text can thus be 'restored to language' (Barthes 1986, 59), and as a general tendency in the context of 'the epistemological privilege nowadays granted to language' (Barthes 1986, 59; on the significance of the linguistic turn for the history of literary theory cf. Reinfandt 2020), this is what the mainstream of suspicious reading under the auspices of the New Historicism, Cultural Studies, Gender Studies and Postcolonial Studies has pursued on a post-structuralist/deconstructionist foundation to great effect (see Felski 2011b). The question which I want to pursue here, however, is whether closer attention to the media-historical dimension of Barthes' argument might not enable us to move away from the 'without end or center' emphasis of recent critical practice in order to refocus on the ends and centres of communication processes and their sedimentation into cultural patterns and practices.

Text(s) and media theory

More openly than in 'From Work to Text', Barthes pays attention to the material dimension of these processes in his 'Theory of the Text'. Here he points out that 'signification is not produced in a uniform way, but according to the material of the signifier' and that 'it is a practice' (1981, 36). Traditionally, this practice treated the text 'as if it were the repository of an objective signification [. . .] embalmed in the work as product', and both philology and interpretive criticism aimed to 'attribute a unique and in some sense canonical signification to a text' (37). Barthes, on the other hand, suggests that criticism should turn away from explicating 'signification' and acknowledge that it is participating in the never-ending process of textual 'signifiance' (37–8).[2] I would add, however, that while it is true that there is, as Barthes insists, 'no metalanguage' because '[n]o language has an edge over any other' (1981, 43), the differentiation of systems with their respective symbolic generalizations and discourses nevertheless creates diversified observer positions whose specific productivity should be used to gain an edge in the face of Barthes' notion of pervasive, non-differentiated textual 'productivity' (see 36–7). I would insist on this especially in view of the fact that the procedures predicated on symbolically generalized truth established in modern science would otherwise lose their systemic functionality *and* their particular horizons of meaning and productivity in larger contexts – and as of now I do not see any viable alternative for dealing with questions of truth (while acknowledging that there may be alternative 'canonical significations' in, say, literary or popular culture contexts).

What I would also want to insist on is another point not fully addressed by Barthes. It seems to me that the persistence of a belief in the possibility of 'objective signification [. . .] embalmed in the work as product' (37) is to a large extent an effect of the predominance of texts that can be individually 'held in hand' as most emphatically epitomized (and, paradoxically, at the same time potentially deconstructed) in the modern literary work. In other words, this belief is an effect of the regime of print and book culture. Book culture brings with it the doubling of *signification* and *signifiance* that Barthes diagnoses, and perhaps one can sharpen his insight that the 'theory of the text brings with it [. . .] the promotion of a new epistemological object: the reading' (42) in this respect: yes, an adequate understanding of reading should be, as Barthes puts it, based on 'the (productive) equivalence of writing and reading' (1981, 43). In fact, one could even argue that under modern conditions reading has supplanted writing in terms of authority, as Thomas Docherty has pointed out in his monograph, *On Modern Authority*:

> [T]he person normally thought of [. . .] as the 'reader' or audience is actually the one who, as master, is in the historical position of 'authority'; while the person dictating or rehearsing the text [. . .] is in the place of slave or servant or reader with no personal authority, and no ability to inaugurate or initiate the text or its lecture. (1987, 2)

While it is certainly necessary that people continue to write, the culturally significant connectivity is provided *exclusively* by readers, who, during the formative period of modern culture, encountered written texts in substantial numbers (on both sides) for the first time in the medium of print. And it is the medium of print which affords the 'simulated or virtual actuality effect' discussed earlier, which, in turn, translates into seemingly objective canonical *significations* easily. On the other hand, it is that very same medium of print which holds the potential for 're-actualising virtuality', in the sense discussed earlier, by preserving and laying open the formal properties of texts, which can then be conceptualized in terms of *signifiance*. Such readings will deconstruct on linguistic, literary, cultural, medial or other grounds the legitimacy and predominance of certain texts, readings and meanings which were naturalized and universalized as 'canonical significations' in/of specific contexts and periods.

Broadly speaking, then, *signification* is aligned with the enlightenment dimension of modern culture identified earlier, while *signifiance* is linked to the Romantic dimension. Unfortunately, however, this does not translate linearly into a clear affiliation with science and art/literature, respectively. Instead, there are uneasy combinations in both fields, which reflect upon and try to move beyond the predominance of *signification* in the lifeworlds of everyday life. Both these specialized fields of written (!) world observation acknowledge on principle that things are (even) more complex than they seem when experienced and observed at first-hand, and they try to describe this complexity without ever being fully able to escape their own mechanisms of complexity reduction. Both science and literature have their own 'canonical significations' (Barthes) and 'symbolic generalisations' (Luhmann), but they also programmatically employ modes of second-order observation which illuminate the blind spots of other observations – though not their own, or only partly so in the case of *earlier* observations, which, however, is *exactly* where the potential for a dynamics towards greater complexity resides, and it is again based on the observability of former observations facilitated by print.

So apparently, it is possible to 'see' more than meets the eye due to the differentiation and diversification of observer positions in modern society combined with the storage and distribution potential of printed texts, which in themselves implement a bias towards second-order observation by doubling the physical real with its virtual/textual representations (see Siskin 2007). And interestingly, the question sometimes seems to be which is which. For all practical purposes, *signification* seems to be more real than *signifiance*, for example, but from an academic, theoretical or even literary point of view, *signifiance* has increasingly been acknowledged as being more real in the humanities since the 1960s and 1970s. To a certain extent, this move seems to run parallel to developments in the natural sciences, as a quote from ecologist and object-oriented philosopher Timothy Morton illustrates: '[W]hen you take an evolutionary view of Earth, an astonishing reversal takes place. Suddenly, the things that you think of as real [. . .]

become the abstraction [. . .]. The real thing is the evolutionary process' (2011, 19–20). So this seems to be a new 'canonical signification' of our times – and the question is whether there are any clues as to why and how it came about.

First of all, it is striking that this inversion of reality and abstraction parallels the inversion of work and text introduced by Roland Barthes: what is really real is not what is 'held in hand' but the abstract principle which, quite literally, underwrites it, that is, Text (with a capital T) and not text (lower-case t) or work, *signifiance* and not *signification*, the evolutionary process and not things as they appear when they are directly observed or experienced. In a recent book which tries to provide an acute diagnosis of the current climate of pervasive disorientation for a non-academic reading public on a Luhmannian basis (but without the jargon), the German sociologist Armin Nassehi argues along parallel lines but adds a terminological and/or conceptual twist which provides an opening for the media perspective. He redescribes modern society as conceptualized by Niklas Luhmann (functional differentiation, autopoietic communication, etc.) in terms of 'distributed intelligence' ('*verteilte Intelligenz*', Nassehi 2015, 113–21). Under these conditions, the world still looks analogue (in the sense of 'representable in one-to-one correlations of identity or similarity or at least semblance'), but, in fact (!), Nassehi's reasoning goes, the complexity and pluricontextuality of modern society makes it necessary for it to operate on a more abstract level, transforming things as they are into countable data, less individual and more processible, in short: to digitalize them (see Nassehi 2015, 174 and his full elaboration of a 'theory of digital society' in Nassehi 2019). Pointedly heading a chapter with the question 'Is there analogue life in digitalized worlds?' (Nassehi 2015, 159), Nassehi basically suggests that

> the media revolution of the computer and the recombination of data it facilitates form a structural parallel to a society in which causalities and ascriptions can no longer be implemented in traditional analogue forms. Digital technology makes us surmise a network of connections behind visible reality which cannot be recuperated through analogue forms of observation. (200; my translation, CR)

And this, of course, is exactly the figure of thought which we saw earlier with Roland Barthes and Timothy Morton.

So one answer to the question of why and how this figure of thought came about is that in addition to the accumulation and decentring of knowledge implemented by print and subsequent dissemination media – which made Roland Barthes and others intuit the problem fairly early by relying on the evidence of modern literature as a paradigmatic case – the boost of digital technology finally makes visible and operationally (even) more feasible what has been the case all along, that is, an uneasy (for human beings) but highly effective (for modern society) doubling of digitalized (systemic) operation and analogue (human) observation, with the latter only slowly catching up with the first. So yes, there is analogue life in digitalized worlds, to answer Nassehi's question, but it is out of step with its environment. It takes highly specialized contexts of written and printed world observation in which analogue observations are transformed into systemic operations that ultimately yield descriptions that are sufficiently sophisticated to give us an *idea* of the unstable *signifiance* 'beneath' all *signification* – or of the evolution 'beneath' or 'behind' all reality, for that matter.

How can one address this fundamental digital divide theoretically? A first step would have to take into account the modern epistemological trajectory from ontology to constructivism. As Luhmann puts it in 'Cognition as Construction' (*Erkenntnis als Konstruktion*), while traditional ontological positions grappled with the problem of 'how [. . .] cognition [is] possible *in spite of* having no access to independent reality outside of it', 'constructivism [. . .] begins with the empirical assertion [that] cognition is only possible *because* it has no access to the reality external to it' (printed in Moeller 2006, 241–60; here 242). Why is this an *empirical* assertion? It is empirical because the operation of observation itself is empirically observable while the 'content' of the observation (as produced/construed by the observing system) emerges only in the descriptions produced on the basis of the observation and is as such already one step further removed from the world. Reading, for example, to return to my focus of interest, emerges as a 'real', that is, empirically observable operation that is culturally formative in the context of Luhmann's constructivist approach to cognition (*Erkenntnis*), which he defines as 'manufactured by operations of observing and by the recording of observations (descriptions). This includes the observation of observations and the description of descriptions' (245; for a fuller account of Luhmann's epistemology cf. Moeller 2012). The representations of the observed in language and text, on the other hand, remain categorically separate from the empirical level of operation, which is, of course, not to say that they are insignificant: all these representations are added to the world in one way or another and can thus, in turn, be observed. And what is more, they add a semantic layer to the functional layer of the world, which makes the latter astonishingly resilient to interruptions (due to the flexibility of complexity on this second layer which enhances connectivity).

The media, one could argue here, mediate between digitalized and analogue, or, in Luhmann's terminology, between functional dimensions of meaning (predicated on safeguarding the continuation of communication) and semantic dimensions of meaning (negotiating the relationship between actuality and potentiality; see Luhmann 2012–13, 1:18–28) – and as we have seen at the beginning of this chapter, this is exactly the difference that is articulated in texts, in hand and head, as it were. In fact, Luhmann's media theory with its basic distinction of medium and form as 'relative [terms]' depending 'entirely on the plane of analyses selected' (Wellbery 2010, 302), which are then traced in the foundational layers of meaning (in the sense outlined previously) and language, on the plane of storage and dissemination facilitated by writing, print and the electronic media and finally with regard to the (symbolically generalized) success media of modern culture which are counteracting the improbability of communication generated by writing and print by means of specialization and differentiation (see Luhmann 2012–13, 1:113–250; for a brief overview cf. Reinfandt 2012), provides an interesting framework for addressing the full complexity of the relationship between text(s) and media theory – and this is what I will try to do in my final section.

From work to text to practice

Texts, it emerges from what I have said so far, are 'recording[s] of observations' which Luhmann calls 'descriptions'. In the specialized fields of written world observation that we call (modern) science and literature, these textual descriptions rely heavily on 'the observation of observations and the description of descriptions' (in Moeller 2006, 245). For all practical purposes, they can be (more or less) held in hand in the sense that they are manifest in reality as objects (sheets of papers, books) or otherwise (on screen, for example): as works or texts like academic publications they do the cultural work of signification which establishes a virtual world of representations taken for real against the background of what Roland Barthes identified in the early 1970s as the 'classical, institutional and [then] current conception' of text 'obviously linked to a metaphysics [. . .] of truth' (Barthes 1986, 33). More recently, Sukanta Chaudhuri has called this *The Metaphysics of Text* itself:

> [T]he represented text [as] a conceptual, abstract being, separate from its material vehicle yet defining itself in material, even sensory terms: implicit locations, spaces, time-planes, relationships between the parties in the discourse (reader, purveyor, author et al.) – most basically the assumption of something spoken/heard or written/seen integral to any verbal exercise even in its most dematerialized and conceptual state (2010, 5)

– all this creates a 'reality effect' (a Barthesian term again, but used here in a different sense). It is, however, only an effect and not reality itself, which takes place 'beneath' this veil even in the very acts of reading which bring forth the veil. In Barthes' terminology of Text (capital T), Sign (capital S) and *signifiance*, this dimension remains fairly abstract and bound to the text(uality) paradigm itself in spite of the fact that he explicitly provides an opening for materiality and practice.

In recent years, however, this opening has been programmatically filled by theoretical endeavours which describe the media ecology of the literary system as establishing a network of converging materiality and practices. It is in this sense, for example, that texts can assume agency as non-human actors as suggested within the framework of Bruno Latour's Actor-Network Theory (see Felski 2011a, 581–8 drawing on Latour 2005). Such approaches seem to point to a new conceptualization of interpretation which avoids the metaphysics of truth (Barthes) and text (Chaudhuri) that underwrites traditional hermeneutics. In a recent attempt at bringing together *Hermeneutics, Actor-Network-Theory and New Media*, for example, David Krieger and Andréa Belliger plead for a description of 'the construction of meaning through *networking*' that involves 'action and artifacts'. They explicitly acknowledge 'that language is not purely cognitive, but an activity' which is socially and culturally situated and 'dependent upon media' (2014, 7; 8; 10). Even more succinctly, Steven Connor spells out the implications of this shift in his contribution to a 2014 *New Literary History* issue on *Interpretation and Its Rivals:*

> Now interpretation is part of a general practice of putting-into-practice [. . .]. This new, expanded form of interpretation does not say what things say, but shows how they work, which is to say, how they might be worked out [. . .]. The purpose of playing the game is not to show what the game means [. . .], but to explore what it makes possible [. . .]. Interpretation has been drawn into a general performativity, in which informing interacts with performing [. . .]. Interpretation is no longer to be thought of as the solving of a riddle, or the cracking of a code [. . .], but rather the playing out of a game, the running of a programme, the perfecting of a routine, the exploiting of a potential. (184–5)

Interpretation, Connor points out, thus no longer asks 'what does an object mean, but what are the implications of what it might mean – what does what it means *mean*?' (2014, 186) In his view, the results of this sophisticated second-order observation provide 'explication as part of the complex maintenance of systems through intensified self-referentiality' (2014, 192), and we should note that in a sense the difference between first- and second-order observation, between operation and observation, between functional and semantic dimension seems to be diminished or even elided here in a move that is later taken up by Rita Felski in her programme of 'Interpreting as Relating' (2020, 121–63).

Diagnoses like these alert us to the fact that late-, hyper- or postmodern culture's saturation with computer technology seems to increasingly rely on cultural practices of making sense (and meaning) beyond mere representation in a (for human beings) bewildering short-circuiting of analogue and digital dimensions of meaning. Krieger and Belliger, for example (and they are not alone), suggest that

> [a]lgorithms are the generalized symbolic media of the network age. Money, power, certification, knowledge, social capital, that is, the mechanisms of social integration are being mediated more and more by algorithms. We are entering a post-human world in which cognition, decision and action are the results of heterogeneous networks composed of human and non-human actors, where the conceptual work of generations of thinkers within the parameters of modernity no longer can guide us [sic], where long fought and hard won battles must be radically reinterpreted and seen from new perspectives. (Krieger and Belliger 2014, 12)

Within these networks, reading processes take place in various shapes and qualities: first of all, I assume that *human beings will continue to read texts* in a fairly traditional (i.e. hermeneutical, practical, pragmatic, analogue) sense. Beyond that, however, *texts will continue to read texts*, so to speak, in more specialized and elaborate contexts and discourses (modern literature and science, say), creating their own connectivity by implementing conventions and traditions, on the one hand, and innovations and new perspectives, on the other, governed by their respective symbolically generalized media of communication and continually establishing more or less canonical significations (for their respective spheres) in the process. One could argue that these contexts already minimize or compensate for what N. Katherine Hayles calls 'the costs of consciousness' (confabulation, slowness and the inability of the analogous modern self to fully come to terms with the complexity of the systems which it is made of and in which it is embedded; see Hayles 2014, 204–5) while at the same time drawing upon the rich resources of human consciousness. But finally, with *machines reading texts,* as made possible by the emergence of computer technology and the potentially all-encompassing archive of the web, what Hayles calls 'the cognitive nonconscious' fully comes into its own, though I would hesitate to say, as Hayles does, that '[f]or the cognitive nonconscious meaning has no meaning' (Hayles 2014, 199). In fact, this applies only to the semantic dimension of meaning, while the functional or procedural dimension of meaning in Luhmann's sense certainly persists. At any rate, her diagnosis suggests that we need to get used to an understanding of '"cognition" as a broader term that does not necessarily require consciousness but has the effect of performing complex modelling and other informational tasks' with its own brands of 'emergence, adaptation, or complexity' (as opposed to other 'material processes operating on their own rather than as part of a complex adaptive system'; Hayles 2014, 201. See also Hayles 2017).

As the moniker 'posthuman,' which is frequently employed in such contexts, indicates, the central question in all this is how human beings are supposed to interact with this complexity – what do algorithms want (see Finn 2017)? On the one hand, the new regime of mediation – besides nonconscious cognition, media convergence would be another important keyword – obviously boosts the processes of observation, description and communication in functionally differentiated systems – economy and science seem to profit immensely, for example, while literature seems somewhat reluctant, which leaves literary studies in a precarious position between close and distant reading, as it were. On the other hand, the principle of functional differentiation itself seems to be undercut to a certain extent, even to the point where Krieger and Belliger argue that the model of systems differentiation will have to be replaced by 'a new paradigm of open networks' (2014, 7), and Felski even goes beyond this and speaks of contingent 'work-nets', (2020, 143), which does not really make orientation any easier for human beings. And this at last brings me back to my opening example.

Postscript: Reading a Text

After all, and in spite of everything, one could say that a text offers stability and focus. At the end of the introduction to this chapter, we, the readers, had reached the point where *The Blue Book* began 'to show us all it can'; the next sentence (and actually the last sentence on the first page of the novel) is: 'And this is when it [the book] needs to introduce you to the boy' (Kennedy 2012, 1). The way this is put, the text clearly assumes full agency as a non-human actor in Latour's sense, and it does so by switching over from second-person to third-person narration while maintaining a certain degree of linguistic reflexivity:

> This boy.
> This boy, he is deep in the summer of 1974 and by himself and cutting up sharp from a curve in the road and climbing a haphazard, wriggling style and next he is over and on to the meadow, his purpose already set.
> No, not a *meadow*: only scrub grass and some nettles, their greens faded by a long, demanding summer and pale dust.
> So it's simply a field, then – not quite who it was in its spring.
> A field with an almost teenager live inside it.
> He is, taken altogether, a taut thing and a sprung thing [. . .]. (Kennedy 2012, 2)

I quote this at length again to illustrate how minutely Kennedy's writing continues to short-circuit representation and materiality (just as it did in its opening): the past of the boy is re-presented by the use of present tense. He is not climbing *in* a haphazard, wriggling style, but he *is* 'climbing *a* haphazard and wriggling style'. This style adjusts itself in terms of accuracy as it goes along: 'No, not a *meadow* [. . .] simply a field' – and it subtly confounds modes of existence: 'a field [. . .] not quite *who* it was in the spring'? 'He is [. . .] a [. . .] thing'? A casual reader will try to ignore these slight disturbances and go on reading in a realist fashion – this is a novel after all, a slightly odd one perhaps, but have we not reached by now a fairly conventional level of third-person narration whose reliability becomes manifest as it corrects itself in terms of accuracy of description?

If you read the novel like this (and ignore a lot in the process) you learn that the main protagonist, Elizabeth, boards an ocean liner with her fiancé Derek whom she expects to propose to her (he falls seasick though). Seemingly by accident she meets her former lover Arthur while queuing to board the ship. It turns out that she left Arthur some years ago because she could not cope with her role as Arthur's assistant in a séance/clairvoyance scam aimed at eliciting money from grieving or traumatized customers. This shared history is gradually evoked in the course of the narrative. At the same time, it also becomes clear that, ethically wrong as it may be, Arthur's talent for inhabiting other people's minds by reading their physiological and behavioural symptoms actually enables him to heal people (most strikingly and disturbingly in the case of a raped and traumatized woman from Ruanda, Agathe). What is more, Arthur's 'art' is also clearly presented as a parallel to the cultural function of narration which 'nourish[es] facts, [. . .] feed[s] them and let[s] them grow into usefulness', as the novel puts it (97) – and, by extension, as a parallel to the art of writing fiction (see Bennett 2015). Both practices are depicted as being intricately entwined with materiality, and when you reach the end of the book, it is clear that the outcome of the realist plot does not seem to, quite literally, matter much anymore (we kind of lose sight of seasick Derek in his cabin, and the future of Elizabeth's relationship with Arthur remains doubtful).

What matters, instead, is the book we are holding in hand, but not in the sense that we envisaged when this book seemed to be addressing us directly in the beginning. It turns out that there are two blue books: the one we, the readers, are holding in hand, and a second, fictional one which Elizabeth wrote for Arthur, imagining meeting him again and telling him in writing about why she left him and owning up to having kept from him the fact that he was a father until it was too late because the boy died.[3] So it turns out that our book is not our book after all but Arthur's. All the narrative techniques employed – in addition to the 'invisible' second- and third-person narrators mentioned so far there are extended first-person interior monologue/soliloquy-passages by Elizabeth in italics – are Elizabeth all the way down. It is Elizabeth who has carefully wrought the fictional object she intends to hand over to Arthur in the end (does she?), trying to transcend the boundaries of her representation into communication and practice: 'And, Arthur, this isn't a book. This is me and this is you and you were meant to see him [. . .]. I thought there'd be time' (Kennedy 2012, 371). The handing over of the fictional blue book, we see here, was meant to be a performative act, breaking down barriers and making good on the past, when Elizabeth and Arthur even shared an elaborate numerical code for secret communication during their séances, a code which is now inscribed in the book (both fictional and real) in the form of additional page numbers at the top of the page which veer into irregularity time and again to give Arthur additional secret messages about the content of the pages.

The actual object, on the other hand, the book we are holding in hand, which made us believe in the materiality of the existence of the narrated world, characters, ship, ocean and all, turns out to be what it *really* is, a fiction, and the potential immateriality of all that was presented *even* in the fictional world is extremely irritating for many casual readers and does not always provoke them into a different register of reading. When this different register of reading is deployed, however, the reader's attention is focused on *The Blue Book* as a material object, a novel authored and narrated by A. L. Kennedy, who inhabits Elizabeth's mind and body who inhabits Arthur's mind and body who inhabits Agathe's mind and body and so on. On the one hand, this object marks a special case in terms of its literariness and fictionality, and especially so with regard to its reflexive engagement with materiality. On the other hand, this special case demonstrates how narration, writing and print constitute *their* reality by explicitly staging *and* performing 'the interactivity, relational agency and "stickiness" that the new materialism ascribes to matter and the affective turn to affect' (Hotz-Davies 2016, 143). It will be one of the challenges of the near future to show how this might work in fully digitalized media environments, and for this we will need theoretical frameworks which manage to address the 'doublings of reality' (see Luhmann 2000, 1–9) induced by various media not only in terms of representation but also in terms of their material and practical conditionings and consequences. As I hope to have shown, 'reality' as we can know it comprises a complex media ecology, an interplay of signification and *signifiance*, of semantic and functional dimensions of meaning, of observation and operation, of appearance and abstraction. In order to tackle this complexity, a reconceptualization of reading as a cultural technique seems to be a promising starting point. As we have seen, reading by now comes in at least three dimensions (as outlined before: human beings reading texts, texts reading texts, machines reading texts), and in these various layers of situatedness transcends mere representation and 'the textualist bias of traditional cultural theory' (Krämer and Bredekamp 2013, 20). As such, it is one of the central cultural techniques for dealing with the complexity of perspectival differences that Armin Nassehi marks as both the problem and the solution under conditions of distributed intelligence without any focal point of integration (see 2015, 109–21). Never-ending mediation, it seems, is the only game in town – we just have to 'read' it.

Notes

1 At this point, the precarious relation between 'text' and 'Text' manifests itself in (the translation of) Barthes' essay when he writes 'the Text is *radically* symbolic: *a work whose integrally symbolic nature one conceives, perceives and receives is a text*' (Barthes 1986, 59, original emphasis).

2 Translator Ian McLeod points out that the French term '*signifiance*' is retained 'since no English word adequately invokes its sense of a continual process of signification' (Barthes 1981, 32).

3 And there is even an additional fictional blue book evoked here, the one formerly shared by Arthur and Elizabeth as a tool of their trade, that is, 'a record of both the general techniques associated with the craft of the medium and a record-book of details associated with a particular sitter, in order to aid the pretense of an accurate reading' (Bennett 2015, 173).

References

Barthes, Roland. 'Theory of the Text.' Trans. Ian McLeod. *Untying the Text: A Post-Structuralist Reader*. Ed. Robert Young. London: Routledge, 1981. 31–47.

Barthes, Roland. *The Rustle of Language*. Trans. Richard Howard. New York: Hill and Yang, 1986.

Bennett, Alice. 'Cold Reading *The Blue Book*: A. L. Kennedy's Critique of Mind Reading.' *Critique: Studies in Contemporary Fiction* 56.2 (2015): 173–89.

Birns, Nicholas. *Theory After Theory: An Intellectual History of Literary Theory from 1950 to the Early Twenty-First Century*. Peterborough: Broadview, 2010.

Chaudhuri, Sukanta. *The Metaphysics of Text*. Cambridge: Cambridge University Press, 2010.

Connor, Steven. 'Spelling Things Out.' *New Literary History* 45.2 (2014): 183–97.

Docherty, Thomas. *On Modern Authority: The Theory and Condition of Writing, 1500 to the Present Day*. Brighton: Harvester, 1987.

Felski, Rita. 'Context Stinks!' *New Literary History* 42.4 (2011a): 573–91.

Felski, Rita. 'Suspicious Minds.' *Poetics Today* 32.2 (2011b): 215–34.

Felski, Rita. *Hooked: Art and Attachment*. Chicago, IL: University of Chicago Press, 2020.

Finn, Ed. *What Algorithms Want: Imagination in the Age of Computing*. Cambridge, MA: MIT Press, 2017.

Hayles, N. Katherine. 'Cognition Everywhere: The Rise of the Cognitive Nonconscious and the Costs of Consciousness.' *New Literary History* 45.2 (2014): 199–220.

Hayles, N. Katherine. *Unthought: The Power of the Cognitive Nonconscious*. Chicago, IL: University of Chicago Press, 2017.

Hotz-Davies, Ingrid. 'When Theory Is Not Enough: A Material Turn in Gender Studies.' *Theory Matters: The Place of Theory in Literary and Cultural Studies Today*. Eds. Martin Middeke and Christoph Reinfandt. Basingstoke: Palgrave, 2016. 135–50.

Kennedy, A. L. *The Blue Book*. London: Vintage, 2012.

Krämer, Sybille, and Horst Bredekamp. 'Culture, Technology, Cultural Techniques – Moving Beyond Text.' *Theory, Culture & Society* 30.6 (2013): 20–9.

Krieger, David, and Andréa Belliger. *Interpreting Networks: Hermeneutics, Actor-Network-Theory & New Media*. Bielefeld: transcript, 2014.

Latour, Bruno. *Reassembling the Social: An Introduction to Actor-Network-Theory*. Oxford: Oxford University Press, 2005.

Luhmann, Niklas. *The Reality of the Mass Media*. Trans. Kathleen Cross. Stanford, CA: Stanford University Press, 2000.

Luhmann, Niklas. *Theory of Society*. 2 vols. Trans. Barrett Rhodes. Stanford, CA: Stanford University Press, 2012–13.

Moeller, Hans Georg. *Luhmann Explained: From Souls to Systems*. Chicago/La Salle: Open Court, 2006.

Moeller, Hans Georg. *The Radical Luhmann*. New York: Columbia University Press, 2012. 78–87.

Morton, Timothy. 'The Mesh.' *Environmental Criticism for the Twenty-First Century*. Eds. Stephanie LeMenager, Teresa Shewry and Ken Hiltner. New York: Routledge, 2011. 19–30.

Nassehi, Armin. *Die letzte Stunde der Wahrheit: Warum rechts und links keine Alternativen mehr sind und Gesellschaft ganz anders beschrieben werden muss*. Hamburg: Murmann, 2015.

Nassehi, Armin. *Muster: Theorie der digitalen Gesellschaft*. München: Beck, 2019.

Reinfandt, Christoph. 'Systems Theory.' *English and American Studies: Theory and Practice*. Eds. Martin Middeke, et al. Stuttgart: Metzler, 2012. 231–7.

Reinfandt, Christoph. 'Reading Texts after the Linguistic Turn: Approaches from Literary Studies and Their Implications.' *Reading Primary Sources: The Interpretation of Texts from Nineteenth and Twentieth Century History*. Eds. Miriam Dobson and Benjamin Ziemann. 2nd ed. Abington: Routledge, 2020. 41–58.

Siskin, Clifford. 'Textual Culture in the History of the Real.' *Textual Cultures: Texts, Contexts, Interpretation* 2.2 (2007): 118–30.

Wellbery, David. 'System.' *Critical Terms for Media Studies*. Eds. W. J. T. Mitchell and Mark B. N. Hansen. Chicago, IL: University of Chicago Press, 2010. 297–309.

2

Media theory as book theory

From the technologies of writing to the materialities of reading

Alexander Starre

Introduction

As he prepared *The Sound and the Fury* for publication in 1929, William Faulkner quibbled with his editor over typographical issues.[1] He thought it best to use 'colored ink' to indicate the abrupt time shifts that occur throughout the opening chapter, famously narrated in the tangled chronology of Benjy Compson's perspective. Having to settle for italicized printing, instead, Faulkner conceded in a letter: 'I think it is rotten, as is. But if you wont have it so, I'll just have to save the idea until publishing grows up to it' (qtd. in Polk 1993, 8). In 2012, the London-based Folio Society finally granted Faulkner his wish and put out a deluxe limited edition of the novel with fourteen different colours of ink. The existence of this lavish volume, of course, attests to the canonical status of this key work of American modernist literature. In their publication lists, institutions of fine printing have traditionally gravitated towards literary bestsellers, aiming to reduce economic risk and maximize impact in the somewhat conservative collectors' community. Besides colour printing, which does not factor into production costs as much as it used to, the Folio Society edition features specialty paper, a gilded top edge and a deluxe leather binding (Anon). Faced with such bibliophilic excess, we should not overlook the original impulse voiced in Faulkner's correspondence. Faulkner wished to use the visual features of typography to transport meaning and to counterbalance the temporal complexity of his narrative. He apparently did not quite expect that just this overcomplex opacity of the novel's opening section would ensure its canonization.

Recalling Faulkner's design ethos, a growing number of contemporary authors have started to integrate the printed artefact into their poetics, spawning novels and other literary works that form a challenge to the ingrained, text-centred methodologies of literary scholarship. While this development is tied to the perceived digital revolution of the past decades, it also forms another stage in the gradual coevolution of literary forms and material media, establishing a new media ecology of literature. Almost at the same time that computing became casual and affordable, the production mechanisms of literature completed a longer process of digitization that had started in the 1970s and 1980s. Innovations in typesetting and graphic design software as well as in printing technologies changed the modes of manufacture, rendering the production side of the book-based communications circuit electronic.[2] Afterwards, engineers and programmers concentrated on the reception side, developing the prototypes of reading machines whose most recent incarnations are the iPad and the Kindle. This instant became a crucial watershed of digital textuality as commercial developers now flocked to the emulative e-book model, effectively ending the brief flourishing of experimental hypertext environments. In the United States, a completely digitized environment for the production and distribution of books was in place in the late 1990s with the introduction of brands such as the Softbook and the Rocket Ebook. The commercial success of these devices was limited but their discursive significance for debates about the future of the book was immense. At this precise moment several authors, designers and publishers began to explore the ways in which post-digital print culture could foster literary expression.

My book *Metamedia* departs from this moment of media shift and explores a group of literary works published around the turn of the millennium, all of which share an unprecedented degree of bibliographic reflexivity. Supplementing postmodernist metafiction with an artistic embrace of the book medium, novelists Mark Z. Danielewski, Jonathan Safran Foer, Dave Eggers and others built on the new media ecology of literature and thus helped to shape a metamedial form of narrative. In essence, metamedial narrative is context sensitive: its discursive content knows about its medial frame and freely communicates about this.

In our current conversations on the relevance of media theory for literary studies, the social and aesthetic function of the codex book – including its recent digital reincarnations – deserves increased attention.[3] The focus of much media-theoretical work has been on inscription and production technologies, fostering the tendency to treat books not as medial artefacts but as mere discursive tropes. Through a critique of Kittlerian media theory and an accompanying close reading of a recent American novel, this chapter aims to shift the thrust of medial literary analysis from 'writerly' accounts centred on technologies of production to a more 'readerly' appreciation of the bibliographic dimensions of literature. Using the novel *S.* by J. J. Abrams and Doug Dorst (2013) as a tutor text, I explore the aesthetic trajectory of metamedial American writing now that unconventional typography, multimodal elements and expressive book design have gained considerable traction in mainstream literature. *S.* incorporates several crucial challenges of post-digital print culture and attests to the ways in which the aesthetics of embodied texts mobilize differential, but sometimes antagonistic, modes of reader engagement. Through its design and its material form, the novel invites both 'forensic' and 'aesthetic' modes of reading, yet it eventually fails to meaningfully connect and balance these two poles of signification.

Literary medialities within and beyond Kittlerian media theory

In academic parlance, 'literature' itself is often held to be a medium.[4] Yet, even if we aim for more phenomenal specificity and start from the premise that literature is a form of art produced and consumed *with* and *through* specific media, we hardly arrive at a unified media concept. The theoretical archive of European and Anglo-American media studies gives us such a broad array of definitions that it appears increasingly hard to imagine what is *not* a medium. Media scholars Stefan Münker and Alexander Roesler list some of the best-known instantiations of media: 'a chair, a wheel, a mirror (McLuhan), a class of schoolchildren, a football, a waiting room (Flusser), the electoral system, a general strike, the street (Baudrillard), a horse, a camel, an elephant (Virilio), gramophone, film, typewriter (Kittler), money, power and influence (Parsons), art, religious faith, love (Luhmann)' (2008, 11; my translation, AS). From this theoretical grab bag, what is the literary scholar to choose? Friedrich Kittler's work – closely associated with literary history as it is – appears to be one of the most viable candidates for a sufficiently *literary* media theory and has accordingly influenced much recent scholarship. But whereas Kittler seems to write quite extensively about the book as a medium, the material codex itself has relatively little relevance for his general outlook.

Judging from recent surveys of media studies, many scholars appear to doubt the political or ethical viability of Kittlerian media theory. Even critics sympathetic to technological approaches have attached the label 'antihumanist technological determinism' to Kittler's brand of literary and media studies (Mitchell and Hansen 2010, 13–14). With his poignant aperçus and his knotty scholarly jargon, Kittler, indeed, appears as an easy target for such critique. Yet, the apparent taboo surrounding technological determinism often works more like a red flag than a sound argumentative rejoinder. Along these lines, Geoffrey Winthrop-Young writes that the use of this label says more about the speaker than about the addressee:

> To label someone a technodeterminist is a bit like saying that he enjoys strangling cute puppies: the depraved wickedness of the action renders further discussion unnecessary. There is no shortage of critics – many of whom appear to lack either the talent or the time to specify what exactly they mean by technodeterminism – who are not interested in pursuing the matter any further; they just want to make the label stick and move on. (2011, 121)

John Durham Peters likewise holds that the demonization of technology-centred arguments 'not only underestimates the power of devices, but also overestimates the power of people' (2015, 88). Instead of merely putting Kittler in a box and moving on, I wish to follow his reasoning and inquire into what kinds of literary readings it affords.

In various publications, the German theorist professes strong affinities between his method and that of Marshall McLuhan.[5] While Kittler shares the most fundamental premise of medial determinacy with McLuhan, he diverges in most other regards. The human senses were the focal point of the McLuhanite idea of media as the extensions of man. Kittler, who doubts the very existence of the human subject as a discrete entity, is less interested in the human sensorium: 'Only McLuhan, who was originally a literary critic, understood more about perception than electronics, and therefore he attempted to think about technology in terms of bodies instead of the other way around' (Kittler 2010, 29). Kittler's most provocative, yet also most suggestive, thesis holds that, apart from being art, literature is furthermost a storage medium. In his understanding, the entire combination of the alphabet, paper, bookbinding and handwriting or printing techniques forms – along with a host of cultural practices – an encompassing 'discourse network' (*Aufschreibesystem*), which determines the potential of a given historical society to store and process data.

As far as writing and print are concerned, Kittler does not situate their emergence as a discourse network with the invention of letterpress printing, as McLuhan did. In this important sense, he is, indeed, not a strict technological determinist in that he surmises that 'the monopoly of writing' (Kittler 1999, 9) could not simply emerge on the basis of a new technology. It needed an entire media ecology, including a new set of cultural protocols to achieve large-scale relevance. The decisive shift came about through various social developments around the turn of the nineteenth century, ushering in the era of 'discourse network 1800'. When the book was the single medium that could preserve content over time, it possessed an absolute status hardly imaginable today: 'Aided by compulsory education and new alphabetization techniques, the book became both film and record around 1800 – not as a media-technological reality, but in the imaginary of readers' souls. As a surrogate of unstorable data flows, books came to power and glory' (9). In the discourse network 1800, no alternative for representing experience was available, which required every communication that was to extend beyond the immediate context of interpersonal exchange to pass through 'the bottleneck of the signifier' (Kittler 1999, 4) so as to be set down either in print or in handwriting.

For McLuhan the fall from sensory grace came with the advent of typography. 'Typographic man' lost his audile-tactile abilities because he was confronted with linear, uniform books. For Kittler, sensory fragmentation is not directly connected to typography. Against the unidirectional argument of McLuhan, Kittler's discourse networks surround predominant media technologies with institutions and practices.[6] While Kittler employs an analytical method akin to Michel Foucault's knowledge archaeology, he argues that media have to be entered into the equation in order to extend the Foucauldian framework beyond the writing monopoly of the nineteenth century (1999, 5). Based on this premise, Kittler conceives of media as technologies of inscription. English translations of his works have somewhat obscured the fact that inscription systems (*Aufschreibesysteme*) hold the prime position in Kittlerian media theory and inform his account of the discourse networks 1800 and 1900.

Around 1800, printed books were still able to initiate quasi-magical meanings: 'As long as the book was responsible for all serial data flows, words quivered with sensuality and memory. It was the passion of all reading to hallucinate meaning between lines and letters: the visible and audible world of Romantic poetics' (Kittler 1999, 10).This experience becomes intelligible only if the common practices of writing at the time are taken into account alongside the printed book itself. Readers who are schooled in the subjective art of cursive handwriting, argues Kittler, will be able to permeate the mechanized surface of the typeset book and 'hallucinate' a reiteration of their own inscriptive performance on a papery surface. They will thus be able – to use a bit of Kittlerian techno-vocabulary – to reverse-engineer the Gutenberg book, choosing to perceive, instead, an instantiation of individualized communication. The prototypical genre for this period is the epistolary novel, which, like Goethe's *Werther*, 'surreptitiously turn[s] the voice or handwriting of a soul into Gutenbergiania' (1999, 10).

The key role of technology in discourse networks becomes even more prevalent in Kittler's account of the advent of electric alternatives to the storage monopoly of print. By the end of the nineteenth century, Western society possessed two alternatives to the inscription technology of print. Film stores visual data, while phonography transfers the audible world into grooves on records. For the composition of texts, the typewriter enters discourse network 1800 as a disturbing machine in the hallucinatory garden of handwritten communication. Kittler uses the metaphor of the 'discursive machine-gun', likening the function of the typewriter keys to the operation of the 'ammunitions transport in a revolver and a machine-gun' (1999, 191). This militarization of media technology is typical of Kittler's overall fixation on war as a catalyst for innovation. He produces evidence from a number of turn-of-the-century literary writings, in which authors point out the similarity between the typewriter and a weapon. Yet, formulating the function of the typewriter in this manner appears to prescribe what writers will be able to achieve with this new technology.

His idea of current computational technologies reiterates this technological bias. As a truly dystopian counter-vision to McLuhan's electric paradise, the Kittlerian image of digitization promises little solace:

> Before the end, something is coming to an end. The general digitization of channels and information erases the differences among individual media. Sound and image, voice and text are reduced to surface effects, known to consumers as interface. Sense and the senses turn into eyewash. [. . .] And once optical fiber networks turn formerly distinct data flows into a standardized series of digitized numbers, any medium can be translated into any other. With numbers, everything goes. Modulation, transformation, synchronization; delay storage, transposition; scrambling, scanning, mapping – a total media link on a digital base will erase the very concept of medium. (1999, 2)

This eminently quotable portrayal of the digital future follows the same logic as his account of the discourse network 1900: the emergence of new writing machines reorganizes the entire medial ecosystem. Overcoming the analogue mapping of sight and sound onto film stock and vinyl, digitization returns society to the 'bottleneck of the signifier' that was already present during the monopoly of writing. Yet at this point, the signifiers have left the intelligible realm of alphabetical language behind; instead, text has become encoded information in the form of binary digits.

In most cases, Kittler uses the term 'media' in a concrete, technological sense. In the earlier quote, however, he holds that the 'digital base' of contemporary technology will erase the 'concept of medium' itself. This should not be seen as a blanket statement to the effect that digitality will wipe out all other media.[7] Instead, the different material media that still exist have been degraded to marginal attachments of this underlying digital network; they merely serve the function to provide visible interfaces, from which humans can take a glimpse at the computing processes (see Winthrop-Young 2011, 75). Thus, while we may still have books, movie theatres and radios, the importance of their medial differences has supposedly dwindled now that all their data streams can be processed by computers.

Where does this leave media studies? For Kittler, the answer is clear: if technology is the driving force of history, hermeneutics as the logocentric method of inquiry into meaning is not qualified to provide insight into the mediality of literature. Instead, he argues for a type of neo-Foucauldian discourse analysis that takes into account the 'standards of the second industrial revolution' entailed by new processes of automation and information storage (1990, 370).[8] In order to achieve this, literary and cultural scholars need to become well versed in information science and technological history, in the historical media ecology of literature. If we, instead, wish to extend hermeneutics to the material text, Kittlerian media theory holds both problems and potentials. Merging the spheres of production technologies and (artistic) medial carriers, it rather too readily subsumes the agency of the material text under the encompassing reach of a technological apparatus. On the valuable side, however, Kittler's interpretive practice extends roughly the same investigative care to the content of artefacts as to their medial embedding, thus opening a media-ecological perspective for literary scholars used to the method of textual close reading.

Behind Kittler's media-theoretical framework and his insistence on the psychological effects of inscription technologies nevertheless lurks the danger of an interpretive bias, which I have elsewhere termed the 'technological fallacy' (see Starre 2015, 53–4). In their classic essay 'The Intentional Fallacy' (2001 [1946]), William K. Wimsatt and Monroe C. Beardsley fiercely criticized the formerly predominant method of analysing literary works with recourse to communicative ambitions of their authors. In their core proposition, Wimsatt and Beardsley point to the following problem with intentionalist readings:

> How is [the critic] to find out what the poet tried to do? If the poet succeeded in doing it, then the poem itself shows what he was trying to do. And if the poet did not succeed, then the poem is not adequate evidence, and the critic must go outside the poem – for evidence of an intention that did not become effective in the poem. (2001 [1946], 1375)

Intention-based criticism works with the assumption that the authors' experiences, thoughts and motives constitute the key to their work. To this basic formula, Kittler adds a new dimension: inscription media. In his short readings in the 'Typewriter' section of *Gramophone, Film, Typewriter*, he accordingly cites letters in which Mark Twain reflects on the composition process of *Tom Sawyer* and T. S. Eliot on his usage of a typewriter while writing *The Waste Land*. Kittler thus assumes that once scholars have thoroughly investigated an author's use of technology and the wider embedding in a specific media ecology, they will be able to see the 'deep' meaning of a work, instead of merely looking at its surface. The analyses of such individual 'cases', as Kittler fittingly terms the objects of his study, read quite mechanical. When he addresses the social consequences resulting from his quasi-experimental set-up, he often closes with offhand remarks like 'But that's how it goes' (1999, 209) or 'And so it happened' (1999, 208).

Even though Kittler is often labelled a post-structuralist, his method effectually resembles much more traditional types of author-centred criticism. In order for Kittler's investigative logic to make sense, one not only has to accept the notion that writing technologies affect the thoughts of authors – which may well be true, yet hardly verifiable through methodologies used in the humanities. One would also need to agree that an author's technologically manipulated psyche controls the work and the range of its possible interpretations. This deductive method dismisses several decades of narratological scholarship and reader-oriented criticism; it furthermore attempts to elevate Kittlerian media studies to the status of a higher-order technoscience that debunks the work of other disciplines in the humanities as metaphysical 'eyewash' in view of larger media-psychic predeterminations.

The valuable aspects of Kittlerian media analysis for media-centred literary studies appear less in his anti-hermeneutic accounts of the author/technology nexus. As one of his biggest merits, Kittler has helped to reformulate McLuhan's central assertions in a theoretically more advanced, media-ecological outlook on literature. Accordingly, Winthrop-Young speculates on the 'Kittler effect' in literary and cultural studies: 'The battle cry "media determine our situation" is reduced to the tacit agreement that scholars should pay some attention to media formats after having paid none at all for decades' (2011, 146). Subtracting the technology- and author-centred bias that informs Kittler's work still leaves a repertoire of suggestive insights on the relationship of the book to other storage media. As such, Kittler's method of close medial inspection may be used to illuminate the phenomenal differences between screen reading and paper reading. It also asks us to probe beyond the similar surface visuality of e-book and print book to the respective production chains and institutional networks that need to be in place for the final product to end up in the reader's hands. The communicative domain of literature is bound to hard facts, such as the flows of capital between graphic designers and database administrators, bookbinders and computer manufacturers, or struggling publishing houses and oligopolistic internet corporations. Reading does not take place in a transmedial sphere filled with endless neutral content.

As we have seen, Kittlerian media theory accords an inferior position to the readers' aesthetic experience vis-à-vis the authorial scene of writing. In this context, the book as artefact figures merely as an index that points to the writing machines that produced it. Digital humanities scholars have embraced this technological reasoning, claiming that any and all print books in the present are subject to an overarching regime of digital technologies. Matthew Kirschenbaum and Sarah Werner, to give just one example, recently concluded that Jonathan Safran Foer's experimental work *Tree of Codes* (2010) 'turns out to be a book which, despite its flagrant bookishness, could not have been created [. . .] without the employment of sophisticated digital technologies' (2014, 446). This is quite a trivial observation and tells us little about the meaning of Foer's work, let alone the signification of the manipulated codex within it.[9] But for many analyses in emerging fields such as media archaeology or platform studies, the notion that the computer determines print already figures as *quod erat demonstrandum*.

This tendency to accord much value to production technologies while bracketing the effect of the book is a staple feature of media theory in general.[10] Practising media theory in this form will continue to take us away from the material. Yet, despite its seeming inertia, the printed codex has the potential to be as disruptive a category of analysis as media technology has been in the past. 'Attention to the book,' writes Andrew Piper in *Dreaming in Books*, 'does not aim to reproduce a textual stability and singularity that were in fact never there [. . .]. Instead, it foregrounds the multiple and dynamic material identities that constitute any literary work' (2009, 9). If we are seriously looking for a media theory of the book, we cannot ignore the ways in which the literary system itself reflects on the affordances of book mediality within a larger media ecology. A usable theory of the book's agency in literary communication may emerge only from places where texts act on books and vice versa.

The forensic and the aesthetic in the book of *S.*

The first decade of the new millennium saw a flourishing of metamedial writing in American literature, feeding into an 'aesthetic of bookishness' that Jessica Pressman (2009) perceives as a cultural response to the ongoing media shift. As one of the most recent additions to this emerging genre, J. J. Abrams and Doug Dorst's novel *S.* attempts to join the narrative pleasures of a layered mystery plot with a profound meditation on the tenuous relationship between identity, memory and storage media. *S.* meets the reader in a black slipcase sealed on the fore-edge with a paper strip. This external layer identifies J. J. Abrams and Doug Dorst as authors of the book, with further biographical information and the publisher's logo printed on the back cover. Once readers cut the seal, they enter the first level of *S.*'s diegetic ontology through the outer shape and form of the codex book that emerges, supposedly a copy of the 1949 edition of the novel *Ship of Theseus* by the Czech author V. M. Straka. The prefatory matter frames Straka as a prolific writer, with no less than eighteen novels to his name prior to *Ship of Theseus*. As in its obvious intertextual inspiration, Danielewski's *House of Leaves*, the text of the novel is channelled through a layer of editorial intervention, in this case by F. X. Caldeira, Straka's long-time English translator who admits in her preface that she filled in parts of the incomplete final chapter.

On the same ontological level but with a lag of over fifty years, the rediscovery of *Ship of Theseus* unfolds. A student named Eric Husch picks up the book from his high school library on 14 October 2000, reads it, writes a number of pencil annotations into the margins and then never returns it. All of this is depicted in the endpapers of the book, as well as on the spine, which bears a library sticker with a plausible Dewey decimal classification number. Another ten years later, we are led to believe, the book resides in a workroom in the library of Pollard State University among Eric's research materials. Eric, by now a PhD student of literature, has turned his youthful fascination with V. M. Straka into a professional pursuit, aiming to uncover the true identity of the historical figure behind the author's name. The undergraduate library assistant Jen eventually finds the book while shelving and writes a note on the title page to Eric. Departing from here, a conversation conducted entirely in handwriting evolves in the book's margins.

Eric and Jen turn out to be characteristic practitioners of what television scholar Jason Mittell has termed 'forensic fandom'.[11] Faced with the many mysteries and riddles in *Ship of Theseus*, they collect an astonishing array of information and evidence to corroborate their theories about the plot. *Ship of Theseus* itself revolves around the strange journey of a protagonist named S., who travels on board a fantastic vessel through mythical, timeless settings and has to deal with severe amnesia while witnessing a workers' revolt and uncovering an unlikely worldwide conspiracy contrived by a weapons manufacturer. One could deliberate at length about the finer points of the plot, yet progressing along with Eric and Jen, readers are swiftly spoon-fed a particular interpretation. The marginal annotations reveal that *Ship of Theseus* functions as a *roman à clef*, encrypting the story of a clandestine writer's collective – the eponymous 'S.' – within its baroque narrative apparatus. The S. collective is rumoured to have instigated a number of early twentieth-century labour unrests, espionage attempts and kidnappings. Each of its members has an avatar in Straka's novel, and as the two young researchers begin to untangle this web of references, they catch the attention of some active associates who begin to intimidate them and sabotage their search.

Like the TV series *Lost*, the other major mystery narrative co-produced by J. J. Abrams, *S.* posed a challenge to the online community of fans through its narrative gaps and riddles. Engaged readers collectively went to work, posting the results of their fan labour on a number of wikis and forums, some of which now originate from college courses devoted to the book. In the final count, however, the reading experience of *S.* reveals its conceptual shortcomings. Despite its commercial success, the novel garnered mixed reviews that faulted the authors for erecting an overcomplex narrative apparatus without adequate closure. Regarding the story, such evaluations appear justified, as the romance plot of the novel chafes against and ultimately undermines its mystery component: at the very end, both ontological levels converge as the respective couples S. and Sola and Eric and Jen deem the fate of the enigmatic V. M. Straka insignificant when measured against the power of their mutual affection.

Far more consequential for the cultural work of *S.* are the two divergent modes of reading mobilized by the book. These modes, which I will term the 'forensic' and the 'aesthetic', complicate rather than complement each other. In its material and commercial presentation, *S.* actively calls for forensic analysis. Abrams's production firm Bad Robot expertly used the new tools of 'spreadable' content production in the age of social media.[12] A trailer that 'leaked' months before the book's publication promised a new J. J. Abrams franchise without explicitly referencing its medial form. Among growing internet buzz, the company also put up corresponding websites and dispersed further pieces of evidence through Twitter and Tumblr. When the book finally appeared, a decentralized online ecosystem was in place to harness the detective effort of readers. Yet, the recursive mechanisms of today's digital media ecology complicate the situation: *S.* cannot only be *decoded* with the tools of hyperlinking, data retrieval and encyclopaedic research; the creators also used these technologies to map out the complex character constellations and the numerous historical references in the book. The result feels like a battle in which each side ignores the other's arsenal. Dorst's prose often merely points to mythologies and loaded symbols without engaging them. In the same manner, the entries on sites like the *S.*-Wiki mostly extract these references from the book and enhance them with links to other pertinent pages or to Wikipedia entries.

Running against the forensic impulse, the aesthetic form of *S.* encourages readers to ponder the narrative significance of identity, embodiment and inscription. Yet, the novel does not allow this mode and its concomitant reading practice to interfere with the central mystery in any consequential form.[13] The pieces of this metamedial narrative are dispersed throughout the book. Travelling on the mythical ship, the character S. spends long days scratching letters and words into the walls of his cabin and later discovers a hidden room full of ink and paper in which he finds solace: 'the words appearing on the page are the ones he has intended to put there, the images match the scenes in his mind, the sensations the very ones that warm his chest, prickle his scalp, push against his eyes' (296). At the very end of the plot, S. considers the ethical imperative to store writing: 'All that ink, all that pigment, all that desperate action to preserve that which had been created – it is valuable because story is a fragile and ephemeral thing on its own, a thing that is easily effaced or disappeared or destroyed, and it is worth preserving' (450–1). On the ontological level of the marginal annotations, Eric and Jen likewise discover the value of revisiting an unchanging artefact after a lapse of time. As in Faulkner's design scheme for *The Sound and the Fury*, their marginal annotations use coloured ink to indicate the passage of time: they write in black and blue when they first start swapping the book; as their relationship unfolds, this is followed by combinations of green and yellow and red and purple, before converging in black. The most heavily annotated pages therefore contain an intricate layering of chronologies staged through visual design and material placement.

The forensic and the aesthetic modes of reading operate on divergent premises concerning the nature of documents: for the forensic reader, a paragraph of text, a chart, a map or a photograph are mere signs. They are pieces of evidence from or access points to an imaginary storyworld and the events that take place in it. For the aesthetic reader, conversely, a shred of paper is not only a means of storytelling but also an end of it. Just as traditional literary theory has conceived the literariness of writing based on style – that is, how something is said, instead of simply what is said – metamedial fiction tries to extend its stylistic reach to encompass material design. In passing, then, *S.* teaches us that our understanding of the media ecology in the present remains incomplete unless we embed the ecology of paper within it.[14]

Paper, indeed, occupies a tenuous position in theoretical discussions premised on new technical media. Building on Kittler's media-historical conceptions of discourse networks 1800 and 1900, Alan Liu has outlined a potential structure of the emerging 'discourse network 2000'. Liu argues that the digitized communication structure of the present consists of 'three functionally independent strata, each comprising a set of functions enacted by a variable assemblage of machines, programs, people, and institutional support structures' (2004, 56). These strata comprise the management of content, transmission and reception in an all-digital circuit. Focusing specifically on the implicit ideology of XML (extensible markup language), Liu writes that discourse network 2000 privileges formal flexibility and visual malleability while divorcing content from material instantiation. When digital data traffic evolved into a standard form of communication, the status of material carrier media became precarious: 'Material embodiment – in the substrate of a work and the bodily practices of the artisanal artist both – was now immaterial to the full, independent expression of content and form' (2004, 80). Liu's essay displays the rhetorical effect of a Kittlerian framework: the 'substrate' or 'material' of an artwork is bracketed from the sphere of mediality. Liu, in fact, casts physical carriers like paper, book and body as the heroic antagonists of media, instead of presenting them as media in and of themselves. With regard to contemporary literature, however, the relationship between digitality and materiality appears less characterized by antagonism than by coevolution.

In a book like *S.*, we see this coevolution at work. As a display medium, the screen has become the window through which contemporary culture perceives the world and the mirror in which it sees itself. As technologies of production, however, computers and graphic design software foster new alliances of writers and designers and deploy new networks of production such as the one behind *S.* Beyond the authors, this network institutes a media ecology which includes the production firm Bad Robot, the printing specialist Melcher media, the graphic design studio Headcase and its chief designer Paul Kepple, as well as the outsourced printing plants in China.[15] On the other side of the communications circuit, the physical book demands readerly activities that are markedly different from standard cognitive processing of text. It asks for a leap of faith, fuelled by what Andrew Piper in his work on romantic literature has called 'the bibliographic imagination' (2009). When Jen asks Eric to read a confessional letter that she wrote and then tucked into the book (Abrams and Dorst 2013, 376), readers need to pretend that this writing and tucking has actually taken place – in the same functional sense that the plot has actually taken place. Similarly, they will have to fantasize that the letterhead paper stock stems from the front desk of the fictional library where Jen works. As Julia Panko writes: 'to believe in S. as "real" is to take the pleasure of temporarily, and knowingly, entertaining the notion that the fiction really happened, rather than actually mistaking the novel's ontological status' (2020, 14).[16]

Such an immersive mode of reading smacks of complacency and passivity, especially when measured against the sharing and commenting practices of forensic readers. As we have seen, Abrams and Dorst distrusted the aesthetic readers to such an extent that they framed their creation as a problem to be solved, not as an artwork to be appreciated. All the while, the supposedly resistant and disruptive activities of forensic readers have increasingly come to resemble the marketable skill-set of today's information worker.[17] The careful design and the probing exploration of material surfaces in metamedial print narratives are also, therefore, always attempts to counteract ascendant notions of reading as mere information processing. It is a peculiar historical twist that the very electronic technologies that Kittler associated with the death of literary enchantment now fulfil the ambition of romantic authors: to create perfect simulations of handwritten lovers' discourse on the printed page. Words may no longer quiver with sensuality, as Kittler claimed, but the physical page will make an aesthetic difference so long as literary texts endow it with meaning. Depending on the future path of post-digital print culture, *S.* will likely one day appear as retrograde kitsch or as a visionary experiment in the mediality of literary expression.

Notes

1 I wish to thank Julia Panko for her feedback and suggestions based on a draft of this essay.

2 On the printed communications circuit as a foundational concept for book historical scholarship, see Darnton (2006).

3 On the lack of theoretical work on the book as a medium, see Stanitzek (2010).

4 Publications from the field of intermediality studies, for example, commonly use the phrase 'literature and other media'. For a critique of intermediality theory premised on the materiality of media, see Gumbrecht (2003).

5 In the first chapter of *Optical Media* (2010), Kittler praises McLuhan's theoretical stance and takes German media studies to task for following a comparatively insignificant path over the course of the late decades of the twentieth century. On the affinities of McLuhan and Kittler, see Winthrop-Young (2011, 120–4).

6 See his short definition in the afterword of *Discourse Networks*: 'The term discourse network [. . .] designate[s] the network of technologies and institutions that allow a given culture to select, store, and process relevant data.' (1990, 369).

7 In his essay 'The History of Communication Media', he categorically holds, 'New media do not make old media obsolete; they assign them other places in the system.' (1993, 72) This thesis is well established since Wolfgang Riepl's 1913 dissertation on communications networks in ancient Rome. In media studies, the premise contained in Kittler's statement has also been dubbed 'Riepl's Law'.

8 Sven Grampp holds that Kittler never genuinely employed the post-hermeneutic method he proposes. Grampp sees in Kittler's work a thesis-driven narrative based on the results of hermeneutic inquiry into various textual artefacts (2009, 146–7).

9 For an extended reading of *Tree of Codes*, see Starre (2015, 244–52).

10 Ursula Rautenberg diagnoses the same tendency in a number of standard handbooks of German media studies (2010, 52–3). Sven Grampp (2010) furthermore argues that several major theorists have referenced the book exclusively as a rhetorical trope. Surveying the works of Marshall McLuhan and Jacques Derrida, Grampp perceives a 'figurative jargon' ('Jargon der Uneigentlichkeit') vis-à-vis bibliographic forms. Instead of addressing mediality directly, McLuhan casts the book as a synecdoche for typographical civilization while Derrida employs it metaphorically to represent the obsolete idea of textual closure.

11 With regard to *Lost* and other complex television series, Mittell holds that 'viewers find themselves both drawn into a compelling diegesis (as with all effective stories) and focused on the discursive processes of storytelling needed to achieve each program's complexity and mystery' (2015, 52). With regard to the material form of *S.*, the term 'forensic' takes on additional significance.

The codex book and its many loose-leaf inserts are imbued not only with storytelling capacities, but also with the aura of evidential traces. Readers are supposed to pretend that the proximity between their own life and the fictional ontologies is not merely rendered through semantic and visual indexicality. Rather, the 'real' readers and the 'fictional' readers Eric and Jen share the experience of the same textual object. In the end result, the book bears physical witness to the existence of these characters.

12 On spreadability as a production strategy growing out of participatory culture, see Jenkins, Ford and Green 2013.

13 See also Jessica Pressman's assessment of the reading experience triggered by the novel (2020, 95–103). *S.*, Pressman holds, 'reads more like an imitation of a novel with complex narrative ideas than a novel with complex ideas of its own' (100).

14 For suggestive work in this direction, see Müller (2014); Gitelman (2014).

15 See Berman (2013) for a detailed report on the designers and printers involved in producing *S.*

16 See also Gibbons (2017) who has explored reader engagement with the novel using empirical methods.

17 This narrative mode is also reminiscent of the audience engagement demanded by Abrams's series *Lost*. As Frank Kelleter has recently noted, active audiences increasingly perform fandom like labour: 'In this fashion, the current generation of TV series requires and stages a labor-like type of dedication that corresponds well with a communicative environment in which people are supposed to be at work at all times, in all places. This is entertainment for a new age of capitalist stress indeed, and *Lost* knows it, its cognizance evident in the way it tells stories about driven individuals forced to become temporary team-players, and in the way it collectivizes viewers into restlessly committed and connection-friendly peer communities.' (2015, 76)

References

Abrams, J. J., and Doug Dorst. *S.* London: Canongate, 2013.

Anon. 'Faulkner, William. The Sound and the Fury.' <https://www.manhattanrarebooks.com/ pages/books/1942/william-faulkner/the-sound-and-the-fury?soldItem=true> Accessed 26 October 2021.

Berman, Aaron. 'The Most Complex Project of 2013?'. <https://www.paperspecs.com/caught-our-eye/s-by-jjabrams-complex-project/> Accessed 26 October 2021.

Darnton, Robert. 'What Is the History of Books?' *The Book History Reader*. Eds. David Finkelstein and Alistair McCleery. London: Routledge, 2006. 9–26.

Gibbons, Alison. 'Reading *S.* across Media: Transmedia Storyworlds, Multimodal Fiction, and Real Readers.' *Narrative* 25.3 (2017): 321–41.

Gitelman, Lisa. *Paper Knowledge: Toward a Media History of Documents*. Durham, NC: Durham University Press, 2014.

Grampp, Sven. *Ins Universum technischer Reproduzierbarkeit: Der Buchdruck als historiographische Referenzfigur in der Medientheorie*. Konstanz: UVK, 2009.

Grampp, Sven. 'Das Buch der Medientheorie: Zum Jargon der Uneigentlichkeit.' *Buchwissenschaft in Deutschland*. Ed. Ursula Rautenberg. Berlin: De Gruyter, 2010. 105–30.

Gumbrecht, Hans Ulrich. 'Why Intermediality – If at All?' *Intermédialités* 2 (2003): 173–8.

Jenkins, Henry, Sam Ford and Joshua Green. *Spreadable Media: Creating Value and Meaning in a Networked Culture*. New York: New York University Press, 2013.

Kelleter, Frank. '"Whatever Happened, Happened": Serial Character Constellation as Problem and Solution in *Lost*.' *Amerikanische Fernsehserien der Gegenwart: Perspektiven der American Studies und der Media Studies*. Eds. Christoph Ernst and Heike Paul. Bielefeld: transcript, 2015. 57–87.

Kirschenbaum, Matthew, and Sarah Werner. 'Digital Scholarship and Digital Studies: The State of the Discipline.' *Book History* 17 (2014): 406–58.

Kittler, Friedrich. *Discourse Networks 1800/1900*. Trans. Michael Metteer. Stanford, CA: Stanford University Press, 1990.

Kittler, Friedrich. 'Geschichte der Kommunikationsmedien/The History of Communication Media.' *On Line. Kunst im Netz*. Ed. Helga Konrad. Graz: Steirische Kulturinitiative, 1993. 66–81.

Kittler, Friedrich. *Gramophone, Film, Typewriter*. Stanford, CA: Stanford University Press, 1999.

Kittler, Friedrich. *Optical Media: Berlin Lectures 1999*. Cambridge: Polity Press, 2010.

Liu, Alan. 'Transcendental Data: Toward a Cultural History and Aesthetics of the New Encoded Discourse.' *Critical Inquiry* 31.1 (2004): 49–84.

Mitchell, W. J. T., and Mark B. N. Hansen. 'Introduction.' *Critical Terms for Media Studies*. Eds. W. J. T. Mitchell and Mark B. N. Hansen. Chicago, IL: University of Chicago Press, 2010. 7–22.

Mittell, Jason. *Complex TV: The Poetics of Contemporary Television Storytelling*. New York: New York University Press, 2015.

Müller, Lothar. *White Magic: The Age of Paper*. Malden, MA: Polity Press, 2014.

Münker, Stefan, and Alexander Roesler, Eds. *Was ist ein Medium?* Frankfurt a.M.: Suhrkamp, 2008.

Panko, Julia. 'Auratic Facsimile: The Print Novel in the Age of Digital Reproduction.' *The Novel as Network: Forms, Ideas, Commodities*. Eds. Tim Lanzendörfer and Corinna Norrick-Rühl. Cham: Palgrave-Springer, 2020. 229–49.

Peters, John Durham. *The Marvelous Clouds: Toward a Philosophy of Elemental Media*. Chicago, IL: University of Chicago Press, 2015.

Piper, Andrew. *Dreaming in Books: The Making of the Bibliographic Imagination in the Romantic Age*. Chicago, IL: University of Chicago Press, 2009.

Polk, Noel. 'Introduction.' *New Essays on The Sound and the Fury*. Ed. Noel Polk. Cambridge: Cambridge University Press, 1993. 1–21.

Pressman, Jessica. 'The Aesthetic of Bookishness in Twenty-First Century Literature.' *Michigan Quarterly Review* 48.4 (2009): 465–82.

Pressman, Jessica. *Bookishness: Loving Books in a Digital Age*. New York: Columbia University Press, 2020.
Rautenberg, Ursula. 'Buchwissenschaft in Deutschland: Einführung und kritische Auseinandersetzung.' *Buchwissenschaft in Deutschland*. Ed. Ursula Rautenberg. Berlin: De Gruyter, 2010. 3–64.
Riepl, Wolfgang. *Das Nachrichtenwesen des Altertums mit besonderer Rücksicht auf die Römer*. Leipzig: Teubner, 1913.
Stanitzek, Georg. 'Buch: Medium und Form – in paratexttheoretischer Perspektive.' *Buchwissenschaft in Deutschland*. Ed. Ursula Rautenberg. Berlin: De Gruyter, 2010. 157–200.
Starre, Alexander. *Metamedia: American Book Fictions and Literary Print Culture after Digitization*. Iowa City: University of Iowa Press, 2015.
Wimsatt, William K., and Monroe C. Beardsley. 'The Intentional Fallacy.' *The Norton Anthology of Theory and Criticism*. Ed. Vincent Leitch. New York: Norton, 2001. 1374–87.
Winthrop-Young, Geoffrey. *Kittler and the Media*. Cambridge: Polity Press, 2011.

3

The poetics of etcetera

A materialist-semiotic reading of George Orwell's literary lists

Ralph Pordzik

> *I think I could make out at least a preliminary list of the people who would go over [if the Germans got to England].*
> (George Orwell 1942)[1]

Becoming mollusc: The resolute incompleteness of the list

George Orwell has mostly been viewed as a writer obsessed with argumentative clarity and verbal directness, with the notion of a transparent discourse presenting only the raw or unmediated facts of reality and experience (see Eagleton 1970; Hitchens 2002; Bowker 2003; Bluemel 2004). His sharp criticism frequently concerns public language used improperly, its staleness of imagery and lack of precision. The writer's well-known aversion to the habitual mixture of hackneyed English prose and 'foolish thoughts' (Orwell 1968[4], 128) is reflected in his consistent use of a minor literary form whose full aesthetic impact Orwell himself never appears to have become aware of: the list. Lists and enumerations are recording or notation systems as described by Friedrich Kittler in his influential study of modern media, *Discourse Networks 1800/1900* (Kittler 1990). They are meaningful as networks of diverse semantic and material contexts, all connected by their exploring the boundaries of textuality in modern discourse, its material and technological roots and power to organize mental processes of storing, structuring, comparing and reprocessing data. Twisting words and items out of their original contexts and substituting associative paradigmatic selection for syntagmatic array, the list serves a variety of aesthetic and mediating purposes, suggesting infinitude and open-endedness, achieving simplification and a higher degree of abstraction at the same time.

In many of Orwell's essays, novels and shorter prose pieces, the enumerative, poetical or literary list figures as a privileged means of structuring reality, of arranging distinctive signifieds and referents for a dazzling outcome. Catalogues, lexicons, inventories, rubrics, litanies, registers and other means of accumulation and classification inscribe distinctions into the solid realm of realist narrative that have striking effects on composition and knowledge formation, disrupting readerly expectation and subverting the expressive system they primarily seem to enforce. A preliminary example may suffice to introduce an attractive facet of literary technique in Orwell's oeuvre not yet sufficiently tackled by critics:

> To say 'I accept' in an age like our own is to say that you accept concentration camps, rubber truncheons, Hitler, Stalin, bombs, aeroplanes, tinned food, machine-guns, putsches, purges, slogans, Bedaux belts, gas-masks, submarines, spies, *provocateurs*, press censorship, secret prisons, aspirins, Hollywood films and political murders. Not only those things, of course, but those things among others. (1968[1], 499–500)

The lexemes are curious for their having been selected from various orders of the fictional and the historically given as well as for their parading different registers of objective and rhetorical use value. In this short extract from his seminal essay 'Inside the Whale' (1940), Orwell connects the notion of political acquiescence current among British and American writers of the 1940s, their 'mystical acceptance of the thing-as-it-is, [. . .] of tyranny and regimentation' (1968[1], 499), with a repertory of terms distinctly chosen for their potential to confuse and irritate the reader. Words selected for their alliterative proximity appear alongside climactic ('rubber truncheons, Hitler, Stalin') and anti-climactic strings of terms ('purges, slogans, Bedaux belts') so as to let the sequence in its entirety appear as one grand metaphor summarizing the century of persecution and annihilation in a variety of catchwords, symptoms and stigmatizing icons.

In materialist terms, this list deserves to be read as paradigmatic of a sublime pattern of modern literary representation manifesting *horizontalized* ways of knowing and classifying a defamiliarized and technologically saturated world.[2] It suspends realist excesses of narration and verisimilitude, putting in their place a resolute incompleteness as part of a larger strategy geared towards disassociating objects and object-relations and triggering a variety of rhetorical effects derived from the unlimited expandability of text formation and seriation. Interrogating the economization of the narrative voice and appropriating the list as a counterforce to syntagmatic closure, Orwell encodes a modern recording practice that translates the concept of inclusivity and expansive accretion into material networks of meaning at once lateral and planar, implying priority – or seniority – in running from left to right, but also allowing for horizontal displacements and startling locational shifts. In contradistinction to writers using the technique of enumeration and cataloguing merely to suggest the unitary significance of the real,[3] Orwell untiringly returns to the list as a spatial framework for experiential and sense-conceived objects transmuting into a system of equivalences the plenitude and ineffability of existence. Permanently operating or keeping in readiness the material potentiality and inexhaustibility of the world at large, his lists inscribe into realism the concepts of dispersion, anti-teleology and transversal communication. Instead of retrieving a preselected homogeneity of items or rendering graspable a catalogue of disconnected objects perfunctorily drawn together by a *shifter* or first-person pronoun ('I think' or 'I accept'),[4] they strive to replace the aesthetic finality of established narrative discourse with a strong concern for the temporal and the immediate, with a discourse that can absorb any number of contingent items and thus provide author and reader with a powerful marking, mnemonic and recording device. Reordering and refining words and the objects and experiences they refer to, making possible a different kind of inspection by removing them from the body of the single sentence or phrase, they set aside verbal units in a decontextualized and often media-sensitive and poetic or even delightfully chaotic context.

The following guided tour through some of Orwell's impressive catalogues and lists of words will shed some light on a notable facet of this writer's art as yet strangely under-represented in critical accounts and essays alike.

Disquieting epiphanies: How to fall in love with a heteroclite list

As opposed to simple object-related or lexical lists,[5] the literary list may be defined in terms of an apparent paradox, namely that of excising fragments of referential or descriptive discourse (noun or proper name) and fixing them within a new verbal frame, but in such a way that the excision functions as a disruptive force opening up a far more ample reality – a dynamic and flexible arrangement of elemental units that transcends the narrowly defined field of description embraced by the narrative voice. As Orwell himself once argued in view of the limitations of veristic art: 'A writer [. . .] can do very little with words in their primary meanings. He gets his effect if at all by using words in a tricky roundabout way, relying on their cadences and so forth, as in speech he would rely upon tone and gesture' (1968[2], 5). This claim holds true particularly for his literary catalogues or lists. In their most elementary form, they appear as simple chains or series of names, objects, devices, utensils, lexemes, clauses and figurative terms arranged in such a way as to interconnect with one and the same topic, field or category. Their centre of reference or 'theme' (pantonym) is usually provided for and defined by a code, understood as a set of rules or conventions navigating the flow of information in semiotic transactions. In Orwell's unique way of selecting and arranging words to lump together or pin down meanings and classificatory schemas, these series frequently morph into (anti-)encyclopaedias challenging the expectations and habitual responses of modern readers. Waves of illustration and enumeration follow upon each other, retarding the narrative flow, yet amplifying its satirical and accusatory undercurrent. At the beginning of his fourth novel, *Coming Up for Air* (1939), for instance, suburban prosperity is efficiently ridiculed without taking recourse to a single pejorative or explicitly dismissive term:

> [The god of building societies] would carry an enormous key [and] a cornucopia, out of which would be pouring portable radios, life-insurance policies, false teeth, aspirins, French letters and concrete garden rollers. (Orwell 1990, 11)

All objects enumerated in this list are related metonymically, evoking semantic features that connect the slickness and staleness of modern life ('life-insurance policies,' 'French letters') with the drudgery of middle-class professionalism and the rampant fear of ageing without having lived up to one's full potential ('false teeth, aspirins'). The list never cares to switch levels, substituting an abstract for a contiguous term, for instance, or surprising its readers with an apparently incoherent or even disjunctive element. By and large, the figuratively homogeneous series assumes a conjunctive function, reaching its full impact by relying on the 'anchoring' function of nomenclature (see Barthes 1991, 28), including some minor gaps and deliberate omissions to heighten its overall rhetorical effect.

Frequently, Orwell's epic inventories are extended to include utterances and gnomic statements[6] that amass to a strikingly powerful set of verbal items parallel or similar in construction:

> I am back in Lower Binfield, and the year is 1900. [. . .] Uncle Ezekiel is cursing Chamberlain. [. . .] The drunks are puking in the yards behind the George. Vicky's at Windsor, God's in heaven, Christ's on the cross,

> Jonah's in the whale, Shadrach, Meshach and Abednego are in the fiery furnace, and Sihon king of the Amorites and Og the king of Bashan are sitting on their thrones looking at one another – not doing anything, exactly, just existing, keeping their appointed places[.] (1990, 31)

In this sample, the accumulative method adds not only sardonic mockery but also plenitude and rhythm to the syntactic sequence, giving each utterance the force of a maxim and thus allowing more imaginative latitude. That a considerable number of phrases has been selected from Scripture only enhances the ferocity of the scene in which Orwell contrasts the wretchedness of streamlined modernity with the relative merits of the 'good world' (1990, 31) his juvenile narrator affects to have grown up in. His deceptive sense of nostalgia quickly catches up with the protagonist's frustrating experiences as a modern salesman returning to his hometown of Lower Binfield to recover long-forgotten childhood feelings of contentment and ease.[7] In the end, the conscripted voices of his enemies all collaborate to thwart his secret escape plans – a paranoid fantasy expressed in a series of anaphoric clauses emphasizing practices of confinement and intimidation enforced in a Puritan context of sexual anguish and moral repression:

> They were all on my track. It was as if a huge army was streaming up the road behind me. [. . .] Hilda was in front, of course, with the kids tagging after her, and Mrs Wheeler driving her forward with a grim, vindictive expression, and Miss Minns rushing along in the rear[.] And Sir Herbert Crum and the higher-ups of the Flying Salamander in their Rolls-Royces and Hispano-Suizas. And all the chaps at the office, and all the poor down-trodden pen-pushers from Ellesmere Road and from all such other roads[.] [. . .] And all the soul-savers and Nosey Parkers [. . .], the Home Secretary, Scotland Yard, the Temperance League, the Bank of England, [. . .] Hitler and Stalin on a tandem bicycle, the bench of Bishops, Mussolini, the Pope. (Orwell 1990, 182–3)

None of the parallel statements assembled here is superfluous or dysfunctional in relation to structure and meaning; in fact, in their semantic coherence they constitute a very strong index of character and atmosphere and so can ultimately be read as serving the larger aim of raising issues of classification and pushing at the frontiers of classical realist narrative. The self-contained, unified meaning of the bourgeois novel tradition is refuted by cutting up its sequential, readerly flow into small segments and catchy verbal miniatures. Taken together, these miniatures stand startlingly opposed to the discursive flux and connectedness of literary realism as defined by 'the very absence of the *signified*, to the advantage of the *referent* alone' (Barthes 1989, 148, emphasis added). A striking facet of Orwell's chequered form of satiric portrayal, the notations reveal ingenious arithmetic in their rendering of a polysyndetic sequence of written hypograms and appear as separable, yet internally related, bits of 'actual' speech set to work in a vivid but decidedly anti-ekphrastic context.

In modern literature, lists and catalogues abound.[8] Understudied models of recording, composition and contextualization, their significance for conceptual thinking and cognitive processes cannot be denied. Indeed, far from being simple enumerations in consecutive prose, lists should, rather, be regarded as formative elements in the organization of the semantic fabric of modern culture, forging connections between contents that did not exist prior to the act of listing. They assert the materiality of the print object itself as a locus for social relations and as a site for the construction of power and meaning. The few examples extracted from his writing so far have shown that Orwell's lists are rather elaborate in this respect, acting as a syncretic record of social and literary phenomena, even though their narrative or descriptive element is limited. It is curious to note that some of these records deal with items or topics so profane at first sight that one is inclined to ask why they should deserve the writer's attention at all. This is the case with books, for instance, objects of everyday use and distraction and as such lending themselves to treatment within the usual frames of data organization, such as listing in (private) libraries or archives, but also to being enjoyed with a certain amount of critical reserve. The way Orwell takes them centre stage shows quite clearly that his own techniques to arrange, catalogue and rubricate proceed from *two* different list poetics, depending on his ideological stance or strategic interest.[9] Constitutive of epistemology, they operate according to a dual notation system that divides the excising and concatenating enthusiasm of the literary traveller from the precise and systematic knowledge of the list or catalogue as a sorting device or resource of reference and information. In 'Books and Cigarettes,' for example, the number of books owned by the writer is carefully gathered and recorded in order to establish a relationship between the purchase price of books and the value of reading them. A simple chart assumes the role of proving that reading is unmistakeably one of the 'cheaper recreations' in a cultural environment where the 'ordinary man spends more on cigarettes than an Indian peasant has for his whole livelihood' and thus warrants sustained institutional support:

Bought	251
Given to me or bought with book tokens	33
Review copies and complimentary copies	143
Borrowed and not returned	10
Temporarily on loan	5
Total	442 (Orwell 1968[4], 95, 93)

The assumption the list is supposed to confirm is refuted at the end of the essay, when the writer admits, quite unexpectedly, that reading is possibly a 'less exciting pastime' than 'going to the pictures or the pub,' thus disputing the probative value of his record along with his initial assertion that the purchase of books is 'beyond the reach' (Orwell 1968[4], 92) of the average factory worker. Orwell's use of the list in this case clearly manifests a subverting of stereotypical meaning and of the unquestionable signifieds of list-making. His inventory of books accumulated over '15 years' (Orwell 1968[4], 93) makes a mockery of the list as inscription and instrument of knowledge, as an established way of framing and organizing serviceable or productive data. Simply put, its constitutive elements are not a bit operative in empirical time or space but, on the contrary, employed to support a practical joke; they draw a red herring across those readers' tracks who go on in the good belief that the table serves the attempt to streamline and economize relevant material clues. Instead of removing redundant data or compressing useful information within the bounds of the given medium and thus acting in support of the writer's argument, the essay, underpinned by enumerations, lists and tables, gleefully exposes the scientific naivety of those who confide in verifiable results and reasonable arguments logically deduced from observed fact. A long tradition of listing connected to observation, calculation and archival notation is revealed as insipid cultural stereotype and put in its place through the ironic layout of the essay form.

In a related manner, yet propelled by a different poetics regarding lists, the issue reappears in Orwell's novel *Keep the Aspidistra Flying*, where the narrator's critical exposure of the social import of books is captured in a startlingly brusque figure of speech:

> Gordon turned away from the door and back to the bookshelves. In the shelves to your left as you came out of the library the new and nearly-new books were kept – a patch of bright colour that was meant to catch the eye of anyone glancing through the glass door. Their sleek unspotted backs seemed to yearn at you from the shelves. 'Buy me, buy me!' they seemed to be saying. Novels fresh from the press – still unravished brides, pining for the paperknife to deflower them – and review copies, like youthful widows, blooming still though virgin no longer, and here and there, in sets of half a dozen, those pathetic spinster-things, 'remainders,' still guarding hopefully their long-preserv'd virginity. (1989, 6)

In this passage, the listing of the different works takes place not by category, price or quality but by metaphor, subsuming the various classes of books to an entirely different matrix of combination and valuation. The chosen register is not that of a common feature but that of an isotopy based on partial matches of *semes* (basic traits) all of which concern attributes frequently assigned – within the discursive bounds of the period – to the female body:

'sleek' or 'unspotted', 'unravished', 'virgin', 'deflower', 'spinster-things' and the like. These attributes can be read either metaphorically, as referring to books savoured or rejected one way or another, or, more concretely, as related to the social and corporeal features of women stigmatized by their not enjoying the respect and social weight of a married wife. At any event, the misogynist attitude of the focalizer transpiring in this passage depends on the compiling of books/females as items for trade and commerce to convey its degrading message. Evoking a potentially unlimited series of properties based on an absurdly outrageous comparison, it ironically unmasks all classifying patterns as arbitrary and objectifying in relation to whatever textual medium contains them – shows as utilizing and economizing the methods in which phenomena are defined and turned into means of control and calculation.

This is not to argue that all of Orwell's poetical lists may be interpreted freely or continued at random beyond their conceptual limits, being justified by no finality of addition or combination. On the contrary, some lists are of a strikingly simple form, not a few of them relating to the writer's lifelong struggle with material and economic issues. Characters worrying about money problems or ending up in financial difficulties can be found in practically every fictional text he wrote after *Down and Out in Paris and London* (1933) and *Burmese Days* (1935). His less well-known second novel *A Clergyman's Daughter* (1935), for instance, features a whole variety of simple to-do or 'memo lists' (Orwell 2000, 2) recording the privations and hardships of mundane life in the 1930s: 'Tea, coffee, soap, matches, candles, sugar, lentils, firewood, soda, lamp oil, boot polish, margarine, baking powder – there seemed to be practically nothing that they were not running short of' (Orwell 2000, 29). Despite their few gaps, compilations of this sort ultimately engender the impression of referential closure, making notation the untrammelled encounter of a real-life object and its naked expression. Poor but essential with reference to the particular features of lack and deprivation they call attention to, their enumerating can do little more than enlisting words as objects, single speech acts encoding and justifying a referential illusion. Structurally superfluous – as enumeration is only a 'narrative luxury' (Barthes 1989, 141) embodying the resistance of the real to socially produced meaning – supply lists like these cannot but demonstrate an emphatic interest on the narrator's part to name a quantity of solid items wanted in a situation of penury and need: as though the incantation of an object's name itself could already conjure up the thing in question and the act of invocation remedy the experience of misery and distress explored in his narrative.

In semiotic terms, one is thus dealing with two distinct kinds of lists: referential and significatory. About the latter type one could argue that it provides more rewarding insights into Orwell's technique of writing, having recourse to a larger supply of lexemes that exceeds the limits of empirical or realist verisimilitude. Nothing in a practical or supply list is calculated to suggest it may continue forever beyond its 'natural' scope of reference, the *ordre des choses* it is limited by and supposed to reproduce in a given text. A crude inventory like the one mentioned previously is rarely highlighted against the totality of a semantic field that could be extended beyond a restricted number of imaginable or related objects; nothing in a shopping list of this kind would make us think that what we read is only an extract from a catalogue of items whose number is infinite and hard to calculate. This is in stark contrast to lists of a significatory arrangement, however – lists transcending the referent's exactitude and constative manner and placing before the readers catalogues meant to encourage them to step into the production of autonomous meaning, to overstep the limits of the instrumental series. Like other novels in the Orwellian canon, *The Clergyman's Daughter* features enumerations that are unique because they hint at a broader canvas of meaning, an abundance of items or properties of which they are only a random example:

> Compared with the ordinary scandalmonger of a country town, [Mrs Semprill] was as Freud to Boccaccio. From hearing her talk you would have gathered the impression that Knype Hill with its two thousand inhabitants held more of the refinements of evil than Sodom, Gomorrah and Buenos Aires put together. Indeed, when you reflected upon the lives led by the inhabitants of this latter-day City of the Plain – from the manager of Barclay's Bank squandering his clients' money on the children of his second and bigamous marriage, to the barmaid of the Dog and Bottle serving drinks in the taproom dressed only in high-heeled satin slippers, and from old Miss Channon, the music-teacher, with her secret gin-bottle and her anonymous letters, to Maggie White, the baker's daughter, who had borne three children to her own brother – when you considered these people, [. . .] you wondered that fire did not come down from Heaven and consume the town forthwith. (Orwell 2000, 45–6)

Here, the narrating voice employs the list as specimen, example or indication of something larger, potentially continuable or maybe unlimited. By and large, the composition attains an effect of verbal abundance, of the plenitude of variation suggested, listing residents along with their wheelings and dealings that represent the inexhaustible diversity of what is thinkable under the conditions of moral bankruptcy and decline afflicting the community of Knype Hill. Unable to enumerate all the culprits brought to life in Mrs Semprill's quirky almanac, the text deliberately subordinates the list as recording device to the sheer pleasure and ecstasy of making it, attempting a register of local eccentricities in which the unlimited possibilities of description and characterization are still embryonically visible.

The broad canvas graspable in these few examples alone suggests aesthetic potential for the list as yet largely unacknowledged in Orwell criticism. Ranging from catalogues embracing the names of English novelists – some arranged alphabetically – in a manner that sums up as well as subverts a wholesale tradition of popular middlebrow literature ('Arlen, Burroughs, Deeping, Fell, Frankau, Galsworthy, Gibbs, Priestly, Sapper, Walpole. Gordon eyed them with inert hatred') to lists of cultural clichés and labels ('the gifts of Scotland to the world, [. . .] golf, whisky, porridge') and advertised goods which elaborate the consumer society's deep entanglement with British colonialism ('QT Sauce, Tru-weet Breakfast Crisps [. . .], Kangaroo Burgundy, Vitamalt Chocolate, Bovex'),[10] Orwell's enumerations owe much to the formal constraints of the discourse that essentially contains them: realism and the denotative speech act. This is not to argue, however, that he invariably and strictly adheres to the elementary rules of verisimilitude and factuality. Quite the contrary – irrespective of the individual pragmatic list that may refer to objects and properties of the real world or those of his own epic world, he deftly manages to pass on 'from a list concerned with referents and in any event with the *signified*, to a list concerned with sounds, the phonic values of the list, in other words with *signifiers*' (Eco 2012, 118). A bizarre listing of women's illustrated papers in *Keep the Aspidistra Flying* shows quite clearly the degree to which Orwell was aware of the dimension of the sign and its semiotic versatility. Drawing on a variety of magazines, his narrator pontificates about 'cosmetic advertisements' in the 'twopenny weeklies' at one point, such as 'Whiterose Pills for Female Disorders, Your Horoscope Cast by Professor Raratongo, The Seven Secrets of Venus, The Truth about Bad Legs, Drink Habit Conquered in Three Days, and Cyprolax Hair Lotion Banishes all Unpleasant Intruders' (Orwell 1989, 55). The listing confers order, and hence a hint of literary form, to an otherwise arbitrary set of items and products epitomizing, in a nutshell, the complexity and confusion of a modern economic environment gradually surrendering itself to vicarious consumption and planned obsolescence. It is also no more than a *possible* list, composed into a consecutive series of titles and slogans neither expected nor due.[11] Inscribing silences and adumbrating the semiotic significance of intentional omissions, it hints at the ubiquitous presence of linguistic habits that delimit innovative thought and the opportunity to think outside the archive. It is at this juncture, therefore, that poetical lists reveal their true potential for dialogic intervention into the rigid patterns of realist portrayal.

In the case at hand, the progression of examples comes with a sharp and dazzling amplificatory precision, forcing the reader to confront *le malaise moderne* by highlighting only those of its aspects that show the true scale of consumer deception, materialism and waste. As this also takes place with recurrence to profane language, to modes of the grotesque and the carnivalesque, it may well be read as a critique of the monologic tradition of moderate realist discourse and the chronicling, authorial voice of its narrator. The congeries quoted earlier is curious for marshalling slogans that all refer to the same conceptual field, saying something *more* or with greater intensity, while simultaneously being rendered homogenous by the single universe or, rather, the discourse of modern advertising it radiates. It presents us with a world crammed full of individual desires, sharing, competing and clashing over different ways of speaking. As it parodies and transforms existing modes of speech, it presupposes and reinforces other formulas, perceptual clichés and opinions, forcing the reader along a circuitous and unpredictable path. Permeated with viewpoints and idiomatic traces, the list serves at least *two* speaking voices at the same time – the narrator and the surrounding world of business discourses and marketing strategies – and therefore expresses divergent intentions impossible to unify or harmonize. What makes the congeries particularly disquieting is the fact that, among the elements it classifies, it includes those already classified through frequent, *heteroglossic* use. It alerts the reader to the 'already read', foregrounding the descriptive and interpretive systems continually actualized in the dialogic universe of everyday speech and communication. Gluing together a whole array of jingles and catchwords within a sprawl of utterances, the list thus raises important questions about the nature of the different classes or categories of slogans in the very act of joining them together.

In *Keep the Aspidistra Flying*, a related, though more radical, case is made in a breathtakingly contemptuous enumeration that affects to rubricate the 'secret despair' hidden away behind the 'frightful emptiness' of capitalist urban life:

> The great death-wish of the modern world. Suicide pacts. Heads stuck in gas-ovens in lonely maisonettes. French letters and Amen Pills. And the reverberations of future wars. Enemy aeroplanes flying over London; the deep threatening hum of the propellers, the shattering thunder of the bombs. (Orwell 1989, 16)

In this enumeration, the focalizer unrolls a varied series of dreadful events referring to the near future or to nothing existent at all.[12] Like an ancient chronicle, the list is virtually open-ended, rooted in social experience as well as imaginative freedom and declaring no incident or observation too ignoble or plebeian to be part of its synopsis. Written for the sheer enjoyment of iteration and voraciously putting layer upon layer of shocking remarks and observations, the catalogue sporadically verges on the mordant (to the point that it can permit itself the luxury of relative brevity), containing trifles of modern life such as 'French letters' and 'Amen Pills' but also sheltering Freud's controversial concept of the death-drive, forcefully magnified into a collective desire that envelops the destructive and suicidal tendencies of a world slowly drifting to global war. The list thus reveals, among other things, the essential contingency of associative thoughts, presenting a 'glossary' of unorthodox impressions grafted onto one another in surprising and often confounding ways. Where traditional realist narratives self-assuredly hierarchize the past and omit undesirable voices, events and histories, Orwell's embedded list disrupts realist views on temporality by conjuring up a grotesque series of parallel (or correlated) events, spatially juxtaposing the near and remote, the trivial and the solemn, the popular and the high-minded. Realism as a literary genre has been exploded by this idiosyncratic use of the list form: a means of tabulation and enumeration that significantly affected the (scientific) logic of modernity, has attained new honours as a medium clearing the space for thinking and writing differently, for provoking disjunction instead of flow and unveiling the structures of narrative prose by rupturing, puncturing and perforating them. Ruins of expandability, of copiousness and creative excess, Orwell's lists have remained greedy and chaotic until today, maps and mazes circumscribing and exceeding the possibilities of text, offering an embarrassment of choices as well as provoking thought, amazement and wonder.

Modernist mirabilia: List poetics or, the map is the territory

Many of Orwell's lists run counter to the linear modes of writing established in the canon of realist fiction, exhibiting a marked interest in the semiophoric and ontographic[13] qualities of the single object and transcending the singularity of the item listed along with the economic-cumulative effect of mere enumeration. Denying the order or regularity many readers assume they will provide, they momentarily take them out of the narrative and invite them to marvel at the textuality of the medium containing it, the minutiae of depiction and its power to conjure up by naming, laying out and arranging reality. Inviting diversions, contradictions and reversals, they intrude upon and break up the homogenous temporality of narrative and critical prose alike. Given the apparent power of the catalogue to short-circuit thematic motifs, character arcs and compelling plot twists, it comes as no slight surprise, therefore, to see that the use of lists drops considerably in Orwell's later works. The aesthetic potentials of the inventory are increasingly sacrificed to the so-called 'virtues' of formulaic social commentary and futuristic extrapolation (*Nineteen Eighty-Four*, 1949), linear storytelling and allegorizing (*Animal Farm*, 1945), and the manifest early interest in contrasting the cohesion of narrative against the disjunction and montage technique of the list disappears. A possible reason for this dwindling commitment to the list may lie in a growing sense of its poetical shock-effect having worn off gradually; since not even the stylistic treasures of the poetical list can be varied forever, new registers and modes of combination need to be wrested from literary discourse in an endless process of testing, grafting and compiling – a practice the ailing writer may have grown tired of after so many years when, having finished the manuscript of what in the end was to become his last and most famous novel, he questioned his success as a writer of fiction, declaring that he never was 'a real novelist anyway' (Orwell 1968[4], 422) and casually taking up his earlier conclusion that 'every book is a failure' (Orwell 1968[1], 7). Before he embarked on crafting his most prolific work of fiction, Orwell brought himself to appreciate the fact that, along with similar styles of formal experimentation, the list had served its time as a definite spatial framework for verbal concepts and an essential tool of composition. Scraps of discourse or fragments from forgotten poetry and prose that, for all their humour and 'perversion of logic', once may have expressed 'a deeply pessimistic view of life', no longer harboured that kind of 'amiable lunacy' (Orwell 1968[1], 44–45) he now sought fit to equip an ambitious literary work meant 'to make political writing into an art' *and* to express an 'aesthetic experience' (Orwell 1968[1], 6). Lists and catalogues, boundless yet periodic, consisting of both 'conjunctive' or 'disjunctive enumerations' and making their readers wonder if they are 'based on the *signified*' or 'on the *signifier*' (Eco 2012, 321; 324), become very rare in his later writings. Bold forays into poetical experiments with the list, like one memorable example specified in *Keep the Aspidistra Flying*, slowly subside or remain the exception:

> They think of rent, rates, season tickets,
> Insurance, coal, the skivvy's wages,
> Boots, school-bills, and the next instalment,
> Upon the two twin beds from Drage's. (Orwell 1989, 71)

The practice of enumeration, temporarily transferred to the realm of poetry, brings to it a touch of perverted logic by means of soberly archiving and administering a disenchanted urban elite's social failures and anxieties, and thus interrogates the poetical mode itself. Divesting poetry of its traditional imagery and music, the sequence or stanza is a mere simulacrum of a poem, erecting a barrier through the inclusion of words according to a structure of metonymic combination. Embedded within it is a challenge to the literary form it imitates and to the knowledge formation it sets up as an alternative to it, observable in its formal attributes and the features and objects listed to render the portrayal of modern city dwellers (including the narrator) persuasive. The list 'poem', in other words, occupies a semantic space not due to it; as a catalogue of modern trifles in an idyllic verbal environment, it makes the setting unfamiliar and helps remove the automatisms of literary reception. Its mediatizing potential thus lies in the capacity to 'interrupt' a culturally established 'system of exchange' (Harari and Bell 1982, xxvi) and in the intensification created by new, as yet untried, relations and combinations taking place in a constantly shifting milieu of (inter-)media options. Liam Young has revealed the essential feature of the device by suggesting that the list be seen as 'something that moves in, through, and across various media, as something that gives us a sense of the "mediality" of any given media environment' (Young 2017, 37). Maybe one could even go one step further by regarding the list as a cultural 'parasite' or 'intercepter' (Serres 1982, 11), the proverbial 'fly in the ointment' making possible communication between different media frames and arrangements in the first place. In the terminology of French science historian Michel Serres, what lies between or frames the elements of a communicative situation is itself asymmetrical and volatile, an unstable ground or milieu enabled to block or hamper the accustomed flow of information. A media-ecological focus on the literary list thus requires us to see it as a kind of third- or interspace, a cross-over or membrane, rendering possible but also impinging on the actual exchange between operative modes, patterns of perceptions and structures of mentalities. All data flows, in the words of Friedrich Kittler, have to 'pass through the bottleneck of the signifier' (Kittler 1999, 4), and in this enforced passage the list or catalogue serves as a kind of custodian monitoring the variegated processes of mediation and translation determining our techniques, accounts and archival regimes.

Orwell's creative absorption, since at least 1943, in 'a novel about the future – that is, [. . .] in a sense a fantasy' (1968[4], 329) may have contributed further to his increasing neglect of lists and enumerations as defamiliarizing devices. A mode confronting the empirical world with a speculative realm that arises out of an alternative historical hypothesis, science fiction presents a whole cornucopia of representational discontinuities with those few single facts in life that truly can be known. Despite the strength of its nihilism and claustrophobia, *Nineteen Eighty-Four* owns a capacity for transformation and for reinventing literary space reminiscent of the radicalism of the list. No longer feeling the urge to write 'novels with unhappy endings, full of detailed descriptions and arresting similes, and also full of purple passages in which words were used partly for the sake of their sound' (Orwell 1968[1], 3), Orwell recognized the perceptual alternatives available to him within the speculative framework of a genre totally different from those he had worked in until that time without resounding success. What the multiple occasions and facilities of lists did for him in the 1930s – 'illuminating the contours of modern epistemologies' (Young 2017, 150), demonstrating that secret connections are discoverable and in principle decipherable, and that the world is acquirable and collectable – now quickly passed into the orbit of influence of an archetypal dystopian fiction *en route* to becoming one of the most famous and influential works ever published. It is owing not least to the remaining success of *Animal Farm* and *Nineteen Eighty-Four* that Orwell's inspiring and versatile lists have faded into obscurity.

Notes

1 Quoted in his 'London Letter' to the *Partisan Review* in 1942 (Orwell 1968[2], 183). The phrase 'Orwell's list' has gained wider currency since the publication, in 2002, of a catalogue of names of writers and intellectuals Orwell considered unsuitable to defending Britain's interests in the post-war order of democratized Europe.

2 The difference is crucial in view of the fact that the earliest lists known to us – administrative and nominal ones mostly – were quite different in purpose and organization, frequently making use of *vertical* placement of information in a column. In classical lists, the vertical hierarchy is more compelling than 'horizontal differentiation' (Goody 1977, 130), unilineal ranking being regarded as the most convenient form of spatial ordering. It remains open to debate, however, if horizontal listing also has more 'grammatical continuity' (Belknap 2004, 23).

3 Detlev Schumann saw the list raised to 'cosmic rank' (1942, 176) in the works of some late-nineteenth- and early-twentieth-century writers such as Franz Werfel and Rainer M. Rilke. Created in reference to the great 'ensemble of the world' (1942, 176), these poets' catalogues marked an epistemological shift from materialism to idealism, assuming a divine immanence and universal force in all things and thus drawing up lists of properties and objects with special regard to their metaphysically and ontologically conjunctive function.

4 For a detailed analysis of the shifter function in narrative writing, see Fludernik (1991).

5 For a whole plethora of historical and anthropological knowledge about the substantive usages of non-literary lists, see Goody (1977, 80–93) and Belknap (2004).

6 Derived from the Greek word for 'opinion' or 'judgement', *gnome* is commonly defined as a 'short pithy statement of a general truth; [. . .] a maxim or aphorism' (Cuddon 1991, 379).

7 For a critical account of the early Orwell as a sardonic parodist attacking the nostalgic values and predispositions of the Edwardian generation, especially H. G. Wells, see Fink (1973) and Hunter (1980).

8 For more information on lists in European and American literature, see Barney (1982), Buell (1968), Eco (2012), Jullien (2004) and von Contzen (2016; 2017; 2018); on the list in a specifically German and British literary context, see Cotten (2008), Merbitz (2005) and Pordzik (2017).

9 In this regard, Orwell's politics of making (and merging) lists and compilations dovetails with Robert Belknap's distinction between 'pragmatic' and 'literary' types of list – the latter serving the 'creation of meaning, rather than merely the storage of it' (Belknap 2004, 3).

10 Orwell 1989, 3; 39; and 4. Concise lexicons of authors are frequent in Orwell's writings, often compiling reputed artists with no further reference to their works or actual merits and achievements as artists. These lists are mostly elliptical; they rarely comply with contextual pressure, serving, instead, the

purpose of denigrating a literary movement by leaving out certain evocative names but including others: 'the extinct monsters of the Victorian age, [. . .] quietly rotting. Scott, Carlyle, Meredith, Ruskin, Pater, Stevenson,' or: 'Eliot, Pound, Auden, Campbell, Day Lewis, Spender. Very damp squibs, that lot' (Orwell 1989, 7; 12). In theory, these recitals might be continued interminably; their sardonic tone alone suggests that Orwell does not want these lists to have an end.

11 I am, of course, well aware of the fact that consecutiveness is not inherent in the array of said cosmetic products themselves and that it should be seen as a mere effect of linear structure. Essentially a horizontal form, the modern literary list frequently refrains from clarifying whether its elements are to be sorted in ascending/descending order or if they represent a framework of words arranged in parallel lines and textures. This shows very plainly that literary lists raise important questions about the nature of opposites, analogies and relations, challenging the realist ideal of narrative along with its empiricism, unifying sensibility and authorial intention.

12 Which is to concede only partially and conditionally the possibility that the dire events thrown together in this catalogue may have occurred somewhere at some point. Quite apparently, their recital primarily serves to satirically exploit the political chaos and the injustice people endured in the 1930s.

13 Relating to the 'nature' and 'essence' of things and to seeing things and their properties as subjects of their processual relations with the surrounding world – not representing it, that is, but *making it visible* in the first place, as means or instances of 'world-making and world-sustaining' (Lynch 2013, 444) cultural and material practices. In a wider sense, ontography – a figure of thought within the recent 'material turn' in the Humanities – concerns the issue of what may count as phenomenal identity and 'nature' in specifically defined settings and practical contexts.

References

Barney, Stephen. 'Chaucer's Lists.' *The Wisdom of Poetry: Essays in Early English Literature in Honor of Morton W. Bloomfield*. Ed. Larry Dean Benson and Siegfried Wenzel. Kalamazoo, MI: Western Michigan University Press 1982. 189–223.

Barthes, Roland. 'The Reality Effect.' *The Rustle of Language*. Trans. Richard Howard. Berkeley and Los Angeles, CA: University of California Press, 1989. 141–148.

Barthes, Roland. 'The Rhetoric of the Image.' *The Responsibility of Forms: Critical Essays on Music, Art, and Representation*. Trans. Richard Howard. Berkeley and Los Angeles, CA: University of California Press, 1991. 21–40.

Belknap, Robert E. *The List: The Uses and Pleasures of Cataloguing*. New Haven, CT: Yale University Press, 2004.

Bluemel, Kristin. *George Orwell and the Radical Eccentrics: Intermodernism in Literary London*. New York and Basingstoke: Macmillan, 2004.

Bowker, Gordon. *George Orwell*. London: Little, Brown, 2003.
Buell, Lawrence. 'Transcendentalist Catalogue Rhetoric: Vision Versus Form.' *American Literature* 40.3 (1968): 325–39.
Contzen, Eva von. 'The Limits of Narration: Lists and Literary History.' *Style* 50.3 (2016): 241–60.
Contzen, Eva von. 'Die Affordanzen der Liste.' *Zeitschrift für Literaturwissenschaft und Linguistik* 3 (2017): 317–26.
Contzen, Eva von. 'Experience, Affect, and Literary Lists.' *Partial Answers* 16.2 (2018): 315–27.
Cotten, Ann. *Nach der Welt. Die Listen der konkreten Poesie*. Wien: Klever, 2008.
Cuddon, John Anthony. *A Dictionary of Literary Terms and Literary Theory*. 3rd ed. Oxford: Blackwell, 1991.
Eagleton, Terry. 'George Orwell and the Lower Middle-Class Novel.' *Exiles and Émigrés: Studies in Modern Literature*. New York: Schocken Books, 1970. 71–107.
Eco, Umberto. *The Infinity of Lists: from Homer to Joyce*. Trans. Alastair McEwen. London: MacLehose Press, 2012.
Fink, Howard. 'Coming Up for Air: Orwell's Ambiguous Satire on the Wellsian Utopia.' *Studies in the Literary Imagination* 6.2 (1973): 51–60.
Fludernik, Monika. 'Shifters and Deixis: Some Reflections on Jacobson, Jesperson and Reference.' *Semiotica* 86 (1991): 193–230.
Goody, Jack. 'What's in a List?' *The Domestication of the Savage Mind*. Cambridge: Cambridge University Press, 1977. 74–111.
Harari, Josué V., and David F. Bell. 'Introduction: Journal à plusieurs voies.' Michel Serres, *Hermes: Literature, Science, Philosophy*. Ed. Josué V. Harari and David F. Bell. Baltimore and London: The Johns Hopkins University Press, 1982. ix-xl.
Hitchens, Christopher. *Why Orwell Matters*. New York: Basic Books, 2002.
Hunter, Jefferson. 'Orwell, Wells, and "Coming Up for Air".' *Modern Philology* 78.1 (1980): 38–47.
Jullien, François. *Die Kunst, Listen zu erstellen*. Trans. Ronald Voullié. Berlin: Merve, 2004.
Kittler, Friedrich. *Discourse Networks 1800/1900*. Trans. Michael Metteer with Chris Cullens. Stanford, CA: Stanford University Press, 1990.
Kittler, Friedrich. *Gramophone, Film, Typewriter*. Trans. Geoffrey Winthrop-Young and Michael Wutz. Stanford, CA: Stanford University Press, 1999.
Lynch, Michael. 'Ontography: Investigating the Production of Things, Deflating Ontology.' *Social Studies of Science* 43.3 (2013): 444–62.
Merbitz, Anja. 'The Art of Listing: Selbstreflexive Elemente in Nick Hornbys *High Fidelity*.' *Self-Reflexivity in Literature*. Ed. Werner Huber et al. Würzburg: Königshausen & Neumann, 2005. 179–94.
Orwell, George. *A Clergyman's Daughter*. London: Penguin, 2000.
Orwell, George. *Burmese Days*. London: Penguin, 2009.
Orwell, George. *Coming Up for Air*. London: Penguin, 1990.
Orwell, George. *Down and Out in Paris and London*. London: Penguin, 2001.
Orwell, George. *Keep the Aspidistra Flying*. London: Penguin, 1989.
Orwell, George. 'Why I Write.' *The Collected Essays, Journalism and Letters of George Orwell. Vol. I: An Age Like This, 1920–1940*. Ed. Sonia Orwell and Ian Angus. New York: Harcourt, Brace & World, 1968[1]. 1–7.

Orwell, George. 'Inside the Whale.' *The Collected Essays, Journalism and Letters of George Orwell. Vol. I: An Age Like This, 1920–1940*. Ed. Sonia Orwell and Ian Angus. New York: Harcourt, Brace & World, 1968[1]. 493–527.
Orwell, George. 'New Words.' *The Collected Essays, Journalism and Letters of George Orwell. Vol. II: My Country Right or Left, 1940–1943*. Ed. Sonia Orwell and Ian Angus. New York: Harcourt, Brace & World, 1968[2]. 3–12.
Orwell, George. 'Nonsense Poetry.' *The Collected Essays, Journalism and Letters of George Orwell. Vol. IV*: In *Front of Your Nose, 1945–1950*. Ed. Sonia Orwell and Ian Angus. New York: Harcourt, Brace & World, 1968[4]. 44–8.
Orwell, George. 'Books vs. Cigarettes.' *The Collected Essays, Journalism and Letters of George Orwell. Vol. IV*: In *Front of Your Nose, 1945–1950*. Ed. Sonia Orwell and Ian Angus. New York: Harcourt, Brace & World, 1968[4]. 92–6.
Orwell, George. 'Politics and the English Language.' *The Collected Essays, Journalism and Letters of George Orwell IV: In Front of Your Nose, 1945–1950*. Ed. Sonia Orwell and Ian Angus. New York: Harcourt, Brace & World, 1968[4]. 127–40.
Orwell, George. 'Letter to Julian Symons.' *The Collected Essays, Journalism and Letters of George Orwell IV: In Front of Your Nose, 1945–1950*. Ed. Sonia Orwell and Ian Angus. New York: Harcourt, Brace & World, 1968[4]. 421–3.
Orwell, George. 'Letter to F. J. Warburg.' *The Collected Essays, Journalism and Letters of George Orwell IV: In Front of Your Nose, 1945–1950*. Ed. Sonia Orwell and Ian Angus. New York: Harcourt, Brace & World, 1968[4]. 448.
Pordzik, Ralph. 'Poesie der Liste. Sammelleidenschaft und Sprachkritik in der modernen deutschen Lyrik.' *Sammeln. Eine (un-)zeitgemäße Passion*. Ed. Martina Wernli, Würzburg: Königshausen & Neumann, 2017. 207–30.
Schumann, Detlev W. 'Enumerative Style and its Significance in Whitman, Rilke, Werfel.' *Modern Language Quarterly* 3.2 (1942): 171–204.
Serres, Michel. *The Parasite*. Trans. Lawrence R. Schehr. Baltimore and London: Johns Hopkins University Press, 1982.
Young, Liam C. *List Cultures: Knowledge and Poetics from Mesopotamia to BuzzFeed*. Amsterdam: Amsterdam University Press, 2017.

4

Invisible thresholds

Ben Lerner's *Leaving the Atocha Station*

Rieke Jordan

Introduction

This article discusses Ben Lerner's 2011 debut novel *Leaving the Atocha Station* with particular attention to how the novel links media ecologies, shifting poetry in what the protagonist calls 'the virtual' (2011, 45) towards the actual and immediate. I understand this shift as a passing through invisible thresholds that Adam, the protagonist, encounters in different areas of his artistic and personal life. Adam hovers between two genres of literature (the novel and the poem), the two experiences they evoke and the ecologies that unfold for the two genres. *Leaving the Atocha Station* challenges literature's media ecologies in ways that outline that literature and its reception are ambivalent and multidirectional, allowing for ambiguity of meaning. This calls for an analysis of environments that literature creates *for* literature, and, to explore this, I would like to discuss and analyse the self-referentiality and self-understanding of literature in Lerner's novel. The literary text is, in the capacity that I discuss it, equally interested in what Jonathan Culler calls a 'non-literary area' of its own endeavour – and I see the market as one such area, as one such ecology – as well as in the potentials that open up for poetry once shifted into such surprising, non-literary areas (2007, 5). Adam's experiences with the pitfalls of producing and experiencing art (and poetry) are discussed by way of the possibilities of the genre of the novel.

Born in 1979, Ben Lerner entered the literary field as a poet, and in his first novel he explores questions pertaining to the experience *of* experience, chronicling a young poet's year abroad and the experiences fiction and art afford him. It is a smart, self-reflexive novel that can be subsumed within the genre of what Paul Crosthwaite has coined 'market metafiction' (2019, 38). *Atocha Station* discusses the negotiations of medium and literary market within the poetic form, and in regard to Lerner's second novel *10:04* (but applicable to *Leaving the Atocha Station* as well), Crosthwaite points out that the 'incompatible pressures – from fellow writers, from critics, from publishers, and above all from the market itself – [. . .] cause the novel to be constructed in the way it is' (2019, 195). These tendencies can be seen in Lerner's first novel already: the forms, the genres, the tone the text takes on are all catering to a diffuse understanding of how poetry should *be* – reflecting, for instance, the immediate political and economic conditions of a country (i.e. the bombing of the Atocha station in Madrid in 2004).

Writers such as Ben Lerner, Tao Lin, Sheila Heti, Rachel Cusk or Carmen Maria Machado reflect on the pressures on writers/artists to be marketable and 'supportable'. They challenge the boundaries of fiction and the market – and how these boundaries are permeable. These authors enjoy high currency in the field of contemporary literature as smart, unruly, metafictional voices that cleverly bend the form of the novel towards and away from the market. And notably, they reflect not only on the torturous writing processes, but also on the locales and the temporalities of being creative. Rachel Cusk, for instance, in her groundbreaking *Outline* trilogy portrays an author who hosts writing workshops or attends readings and literary fairs. As literary scholars and avid readers, we need to care for/about – and be careful of – such spaces that open up where protagonists produce texts and in which venues literature appears – particularly in the experimental and self-reflexive form that Lerner chooses.

The protagonist of Ben Lerner's novel is Adam Gordon, a young American poet who receives a prestigious stipend (equivalent to a Fulbright that Lerner received in real life) and moves to Madrid for a year. He faces the dilemmas of his artistic practice, poetry, which he calls the 'deadest of all media' (Lerner 2011, 25), while actually entangled and kept alive in all sorts of (digital) environments, such as chat messages. At the same time, while Adam is working on his own poems and translations, he increasingly wonders in what way concepts of performance, experience and translation relate to one another and how these three components dictate his time abroad in Spain. Adam, because of his anxiety and disillusionment, retains an ironic distance.

Leaving the Atocha Station can be described as a neo-picaresque novel, and Lerner transplants a self-conscious, neurotic American into the genre's country of origin, Spain. Shelley Godsland remarks about the neo-picaresque[1] how 'aspects and facets of the picaresque myth can be deployed to respond to a particular social or socio-political reality' by way of the 'narration of the life story of a character who bears a resemblance to the picaro' (2015, 265). In his review for the website *Poetry Foundation*, Adam Plunkett writes about *Leaving the Atocha Station* that it is 'a picaresque of poet-protagonist Adam Gordon moving to Madrid on the equivalent of a Fulbright, lying his way through the city, and realizing that his sense of his own fraudulence is fertile ground for his poetry' (2014, n.p.). These circumstances that Lerner creates for his protagonist – privilege and distance, the literary market and its agents – underline the metatextual angle of the novel on its own literary production. In this way, Lerner brings the picaresque and the literary market in close proximity. The protagonist is faced with the inability to penetrate the socio-economic realities (of the literary market, of his class position) he is part of – and has to come to terms with his position towards the dead and barren ecologies of his genre, poetry.

The editors of this volume use a helpful and illuminating definition of media ecology, namely as an angle to understand 'the ways in which a literary text is interwoven in its material, technical, performative, praxeological, affective, and discursive network and which determine how it is experienced and interpreted' (see Bayerlipp, Haekel and Schlegel 2022, 1). The theoretical approach of media ecology and Culler's idea of 'non-literary areas' help unlock such experiences and interpretations to be legible. Lerner's novel transplants the experience and production of the literary text into a manifold of ecologies that are interwoven with affective and performative dimensions. This approach helps sharpen my reading of *Atocha Station,* namely which spheres, environments, areas – ecologies – Lerner imagines for the production and reception of literature and its genres. I propose that Lerner uses thresholds of fiction and metafiction to instigate environs for the genesis and reception of poetry and fiction.

By way of turning to different spheres of literary reception, the thresholds of fictional and metafictional, as well as an instant message exchange and an alienating poetry reading, I explore the question of how Lerner chooses and discusses spaces for the literary in the twenty-first century. These spaces differ greatly from one another, and I see this plethora of spaces that first seem to be non-literary areas (to refer back to Culler) to test out the invisible thresholds of Lerner's writing. I will argue for a vantage point on spaces created *for* literature – in Lerner's case the novel genre, the literary market, Spain, the virtual and invisible thresholds, among others, helps entering Lerner's novel by way of asking about meta-reflections on the textual production and the production of environs for texts. In *Atocha Station* the reader explores ecologies for poetry by way of the form of the *novel*, and in the following, I will discuss how Lerner's forms of literature celebrate their coming into being particularly by their self-aware and self-conscious style –

Lerner chooses poetry, social media, the novel to initiate such conversations about the environments for literature *in* literature.

Poetry and prestige

> It was clear Rufina was going to ask me what kind of poetry I wrote. 'What kind of poetry do you write?'
>
> 'What kinds of poetry are there?' I was pleased with this response and made a mental note to use it from then on.
>
> 'Bad and worse,' Rufina said with mock derision. [. . .]
>
> 'I too dislike it,' I said in English.
>
> 'You must come from money,' Rufina said, ignoring me again. (Lerner 2011, 58)

As outlined previously, Adam spends a year abroad in Madrid on a prestigious fellowship that affords him to do research on the literary heritage of the Spanish Civil War. He plans to write a long poem about it. Instead, he is wasting a fair amount of time doing nothing, hanging out with friends, or taking language classes. The conditions of his fellowship remain unclear to Adam, and the picaresque quality of the novel picks up here in order to underline a protagonist at odds with his environment. While his art should bring him closer to Spain (working through the cultural heritage of literature), he remains alienated and isolated. At the beginning of the novel, Adam is oftentimes alone but also condescending and hostile towards his peers.

Adam experiences, therefore, being a bit at odds with his own art and the mandates of his stipend, eschewing his fellows (he does not even read the emails from the foundation anymore) and smoking too much pot and going to the Prado, instead. In American literary history, this environment for literature, the foreign country for a privileged expat, was notably explored by Ernest Hemingway, who in *The Sun Also Rises* (1926) also portrays life in Spain for a young American. Lerner inverts the literary tradition of Americans abroad in Europe. Nonetheless, Adam *applied* to spend a year in Madrid and, consequently, applied to become a part of the larger machinations of a privileged ecology of prestige in this environment, attempting to continue a long literary history that was initiated by Hemingway and his modernist peers in Europe. Adam is sent within the market logics of a prestigious stipend to represent a cultural elite of the twenty-first century that smoothly transitions in and out of countries.

In a larger context, in American literary history[2] fellowships and residency programmes are imbued with ideas of productivity and prestige, allowing for established and young writers to appear on the literary field.

Such residencies create both temporal communities and a certain visibility in the field. Such programmes can be understood, almost tongue-in-cheek, as cultural 'incubators' (or Plunkett's 'fertile ground'), a term that I borrow from Kathryn Roberts, that support promising young writers. Kathryn Roberts explains that residency programmes and colony models in American literary history 'were compelling to writers not only because it respected the values of the art world, but also because it solved the problem of intellectual loneliness' (2019, 401). Lerner's novel is built on a similar premise – the isolation and loneliness that a young man faces in an artistic environment and how it affects his ways of communication and commitment to the fellowship.

Throughout the five chapters (which correspond to the five phases of his research trip) the protagonist fashions his isolation and difficulties to engage authentically with his surrounding *as* prestige and privilege – his intellectual loneliness is self-chosen, marked by way of his alleged inability to speak Spanish fluently or to connect meaningfully with the people around him. Because, even during his residency, the bubble of privilege and isolation is tended to by market forces – Adam faces the challenges of 'selling himself' during gallery openings or lectures in a certain way to the audience and to the programme director of his fellowship – he actually avoids interacting with his peers and his work.

Ironically, as lost as Adam feels, he is among the selected few to enjoy the privilege and prestige of residing in Madrid, and yet, he never fully arrives but lives as a 'typically pretentious American' (Lerner 2011, 50). The protagonist experiences the 'rapid fragmentation of your so-called personality' (Lerner 2011, 17), unable to penetrate the experience that is unfolding before him, and lamenting the imprecision of meaning that Adam experiences when being faced with art, such as poetry, paintings and novels. This cliché of the privileged expat who is a bit too cool to engage also becomes his shtick; he grooms his illiteracy in Spanish to remain aloof, cultivating an aura of prestige and profundity.

James English writes in *The Economy of Prestige* how the awarding of literary prizes and fellowships involves fundamentally the question of art's relationship to money, to politics, to the social and the temporal:

> It involves questions of power, of what constitutes specifically cultural power, how this form of power is situated in relation to other forms, and how its particular logic and mode of operation have changed over the course of the modern period. It involves questions of cultural status and prestige. How is such prestige produced, and where does it reside? (In people? In things? In relationships between people and things?) What rules govern its circulation? It involves, indeed, questions about the very nature of our individual and collective investments in art – questions of recognition and illusion, belief and make-belief, desire and refusal. (2005, 3)

This longer quote explains the ambivalences of market fictions in more detail; English's argument outlines the contradictions and paradoxes Adam experiences in the novel that pertain to both the embeddedness and remoteness that he experiences in his environs – the confusion and privilege of *not* understanding, of conversational bits and pieces that Adam links with 'or', not 'and'. Adam explains that he 'understood in chords, understood in a plurality of worlds. [. . .] This ability to dwell among possible referents, to let them interfere and separate like waves, to abandon the law of excluded middle while listening to Spanish – this was a breakthrough in my project, a change of phase' (Lerner 2011, 14). Often lost in translation and not yet entirely proficient in Spanish (though better than he thinks), Adam pieces together fragments of conversation that link different possibilities of reality, of communication that potentially leads into many different directions.

His prestigious situation finds him isolated and ill-equipped to deal with everyday life, and Eric Bennett emphasizes that protagonists such as Adam 'share a consciousness of communicative inadequacy with the texts that constitute them. They are miserable and render this misery beautiful, annoying, transfixing, and pathetic' (2017, 378). I support this assessment, for it links the idea of prestige and privilege to that of language and translation – and ultimately communication, a factor that media ecology as a theoretical field is particularly invested in. This emphasizes Elizabeth Dickey's analytical perspective of Lerner's novel and the relationship between art and its socio-economic factors. According to Dickey, these ambivalences of prestige and marketability are an 'understanding in chords, in simultaneous possibilities listed out, all existences all at once – unfurled' (2015, n.p.). She continues to ask: 'What is it about the anxiety of possibility and the possibility of creative work that seems so inherently linked?' (Dickey 2015, n.p.; i.e. linking sentences with 'or'). The repeated list of possibilities linked with 'or' also marks the prestige and privilege of not *fully* understanding, of leaving the intersubjective spaces of experience ambiguous and contradictory and anxious.

Invisible thresholds

In terms of his status as an anxious expat who fails to communicate in the language of the country, Adam wonders about 'how long I could remain in Madrid without crossing whatever invisible threshold of proficiency would render me devoid of interest' (Lerner 2011, 51). I establish this point about the privilege afforded by the stipend and his status as an expat who remains on the outside because it reveals to him 'invisible thresholds', a term that can be applied to the narratological and poetic strategies of Lerner's novel. Such thresholds that he can and cannot cross to remain interesting help understand the dynamics of the novel and its efforts at being interesting (a debut novel that should perform well on the market) and being interested in its own genesis (its metatextual reflectivity). In this way, the invisible threshold can arguably be a media ecology that *Atocha Station* embeds itself in – the ambivalence of crafting and the reception of contemporary literature in the twenty-first century.

Ben Lerner reflects upon these facets in his second novel *10:04* more directly. *Atocha Station* already hints at the self-awareness of this character towards his own art and the distance he feels from it. Adam equally acknowledges the challenges of the specific conditions and 'modes of production' – by way of financial status and by way of artistic practice. As Paul Crosthwaite states about *10:04*: 'On the one hand, this means highlighting the forms of "privilege" that allow such a novel to be constructed at all, such as the narrator's – and Lerner's – (relatively) affluent Brooklyn lifestyle, college teaching post, literary world contacts' (2019, 195). The flipside of this lifestyle is the aimlessness and emptiness that Adam oftentimes experiences and that he tries to fill with ironic distance and drugs. Here, Lerner acknowledges the contradictions of (market) pressure and attention, and, similarly, how these pressures shape the form of the novel, equally self-aware and self-conscious.[3]

Adam understands that he does not have to build a meaningful life in Spain, that he is there for a year only and can hover between groups of friends and commitments. For Adam, the year in Madrid is an awkward time:

> there were months and months of my fellowship left, it had only just begun; but the fellowship wouldn't go on too long – I would be returned to my life at such and such a date, a little more interesting to everyone for my time abroad, thinner probably, otherwise unchanged. I didn't need to establish a life in Madrid beyond the simplest routines; I didn't have to worry about building a community, whatever that meant. (Lerner 2011, 15)

The time in Madrid feels fraudulent, unreal and fake (just like the foreign currency of the European Union seems fake to Adam, as he explains again and again, because he is used to American dollars). Following Lerner's poetic logic, we might want to ask when alienation is prestigious, and when prestige is alienating. Adam's first months in Spain are marked as those of an onlooker and of a flaneur, a rather prestigious situation of the 'preposterous image of a Bohemian poet supported by his psychologist parents' (Lerner 2011, 60). In this case, prestige and access are modes of production that are marked with social powerlessness, as Sianne Ngai observes quoting Adorno's *Aesthetic Theory*: 'bourgeois art's reflexive preoccupation with its *own* "powerlessness and superfluity in the empirical world" is precisely what makes it capable of theorizing social powerlessness in a manner unrivalled by other forms of cultural praxis' (2005, 2). Well aware of his futile efforts to connect and to explore, Adam understands the powerlessness of his endeavour (writing poetry), yet understands his socio-economic privilege by way of his class position (he can afford to loaf around for a year).

These tensions lie at the centre of the conundrum that Adam is faced with, namely performance and performativity versus an authentic experience and how this affects the life around him. He often finds himself, rather, playing the role of a poet than actually writing poetry. In this way, Adam explains that 'the closest I'd come to having a profound experience of art was probably the experience of [. . .] distance, a profound experience of the absence of profundity' (Lerner 2011, 9). This, in turn, is reflected on the metalevel of the creation of texts, the dislocation of the protagonist into a different culture and the temporal and spatial boundlessness that Lerner's protagonist experiences. For Lerner's novel shows how these factors are all filtered by way of an 'experience of experience sponsored by my fellowship' (2011, 68). After all, the reader is set out to witness, or hopes to witness, the creation of poetry.

The novel outlines the inability of engaging with and removing from experiences on different levels – media, by language barriers, or by drugs. These different barriers hold the protagonist at bay. This is to say that the novel is well aware of this invisible threshold, too. Referring back to the idea of the making of poetry, Johannes Voelz understands Lerner's novels pertaining to the genre of postmodern self-referentiality that Voelz coins the '*making-of* novel', which narrates its own genesis and refers to an existing presence that is hard to deny for its readership (2019, 327). Ironically, the reader does not really witness the making of poetry, but the interaction of fiction and real-life events. Hence, both the reader and Adam find themselves confronted with the problem of entering an authentic experience while being thrown off by references to real-life events.

Referring to Lerner's second novel, *10:04,* but already outlined in *Atocha Station*, Voelz writes that its 'aim [is] to create the impression that their (semi-)fictions form a part of the reader's real world. Not because they are presented realistically, but because they are inscribed by, and refer back to, really existing presences' (2019, 327). The novel 'hover[s] between the fictional and the non-fictional', (2019, 327) and includes events such as the bombing of the Atocha station or the references to the politics of the presidency of George W. Bush, to make references to really existing presences, narrated almost in real time (i.e. the bombing of the Atocha Station that Adam witnesses). These multiple meanings and combining of real-life events locate 'the possibility, and not just the complicity, in letting things be what they are' (Huehls 2016, ii). After all, letting things be as they are might be 'another compromise between formal play and the concerns of real people', breaking down the barriers among the characters and the implied reader and implied author (Smith 2015, 32).

This goes to say that Lerner is well aware, in the poetics of *Atocha Station*, of the tensions and environments he creates. These contacts of real-life events with a quest to immerse the self fully in the fictional (as Adam again and again tries) are governed and structured by what Voelz calls 'hover', hence an invisible threshold. In this sense, Dena Fehrenbacher subsumes *Leaving the Atocha Station* among the genre of the *künstlerroman*. Fehrenbacher explains that '[t]he *künstlerroman*, however, has never been the genre of the immature beginner, but the opposite: a genre of the successful, the established, the authoritative, the serious' and links this to the theoretical concept of 'punchline aesthetics' (2021, n.p.). Both a punchline and a making-of need a set-up, and Adam's fellowship and the prestige it grants him and the circles it opens up to him (the bourgeois Bohemian circles of Madrid) are embedded into a new mode of production that follows its own temporal and spatial logistics.

Since *Atocha Station* draws such strong attention to its own mediality and its own coming into being, Lerner tests out different venues for poetry – choosing the novel as one of them. In the following, I will turn to these ideas in more detail and think them together with the ideas established previously – that of the ways of remediating poetry. Maybe, then, poetry can offer another invisible threshold for profound experiences after all, and move away from questions of marketability that I outlined earlier towards other environments to connect with other humans by way of art and poetry.

Experiencing the deadest of all media

> There's nothing sentimental about a machine, and: A poem is a small (or large) machine made of words. When I say there's nothing sentimental about a poem I mean that there can be no part, as in any other machine, that is redundant. (William Carlos Williams 1988, 54)

In the 'Introduction to *The Wedge*', William Carlos Williams likens poetry to a machine made of words[4] – Lerner borrows this image for the protagonist's musings on the machinations of poetry for the virtual and the actual. David Wellbery reminds us in his foreword to Friedrich Kittler's *Discourse Networks* that mediality is 'the general condition within which, under specific circumstances, something like "poetry" or "literature" can take shape' and that we are 'dealing with media as determined by the technological possibilities of the epoch in question' (1990, xiii). Lerner, in turn, explores the interdependency of mediality and poetry, and terminology of the machine further links and likens poetry to technology in the epoch of the 'United States of Bush' (2011, 36). These technological possibilities, for Adam, include chat messages or live updates on newspaper websites, while the real event happens outside of his window. Lerner's novel wonders about the media ecology for poetry in the twenty-first century – what kind of technological possibilities can poetry find or shun in order to establish networks of affective and social dimensions?

Yet, the powerlessness that Adam feels pertains to that of his privilege as well. Is prestige not to engage with what Adam describes as the deadest of all media, poetry? Might poetry, so dead yet so alive, actually alleviate market forces experienced by the author, because it just does not sell? In the following passage, the protagonist reminds us:

> I tried hard to imagine my poems' relation to Franco's mass graves, how my poems could be said meaningfully to bear on the deliberate and systemic destruction of a people or a planet, the abolition of classes, or in any sense constitute a significant political intervention. I tried hard to imagine my poems or any poems as machines that could make things happen, changing the government or the economy or even their language, the body or its sensorium, but I could not imagine this, could not even imagine imagining it. And yet when I imagined the total victory of those other things over poetry, when I imagined, with a sinking feeling, a world without even the terrible excuses for poems that kept faith with the virtual possibilities of the medium, without the sort of absurd ritual I'd participated in that evening, then I intuited an inestimable loss, a loss not of artworks but of art, and therefore infinite, the total triumph of the actual, and I realized that, in such a world, I would swallow a bottle of white pills. (Lerner 2011, 44–5)

Here, we can detect not only a threshold but also an interface. Interfaces must be seen as zones of aesthetic gravity that allow for 'new methodologies of scanning, playing, sampling, parsing, and recombining' (Galloway 2012, 29). To combine Alexander Galloway's ideas about interface with my argument about the media ecologies of literature discussed in Lerner's novel, I would like to pick out terms that the protagonist uses, such as 'triumph of the actual', 'virtual possibilities of the medium', 'poems as machines' or 'sensorium'. These terms exemplify in the internal logics of the novel the relation of virtual and actual experiences in *Atocha Station.*

As I established earlier, experiences are linked with either an 'and' or an 'or', creating, in turn, multiple possibilities of interpretation. Poetry, too, can, in reference to Galloway, 'remix' experiences (such as referring back to Voelz's idea of the making-of novel, the inclusion of actual and fictional events in the novel). Yet, poetry holds a special form of experience in store that is difficult to negotiate for Adam. Adam brings mediality and machine into proximity. He struggles to draw lines between his art and social and mass media, stating: '"The language of poetry is the exact opposite of the language of mass media," I said, meaninglessly' (Lerner 2011, 50). Yet, a text like *Atocha Station* expresses an 'interest in preserving the formal gains achieved under the modernist and postmodernist dominants of the twentieth century while reconnecting with the personal in such a way that might be appealing to a larger group of potential readers, such as those who find narrative sustenance from television rather than books' (Smith 2015, 32).

This 'personal' experience is, drawing back on Johannes Voelz's point about the making-of novel, located exactly on the cusp of real experience and its fictionalization. Combining this with Rachel Greenwald Smith's comment quoted earlier, that this mediality now recombines and reconnects readers with 'the personal' that would otherwise, according to Greenwald Smith, be found in television, we might wonder in what way the experience of poetry *and* the novel in *Atocha Station* draws on that of mass and social media – that pertains to meaningless, self-effacing and oftentimes ridiculous experiences. Such media ecologies, affecting the social and affective networks that Adam is embedded in, and yet removed from, is first and foremost visible in his (self-)effacement, as he explains:

> I tried my best not to respond to most of the e-mails I received as I thought this would recreate the impression I was offline, busy accumulating experience, while in fact I spent a good amount of time online, especially in the late afternoon and early evening, looking at videos of terrible things. (Lerner 2011, 19)

With the internet and its consistent stream of information offering diversion, Adam is able to hide away from the actual and turn to the virtual. This is reflected in the reader's experience with the novel as well, for you 'don't have to invest yourself, and can observe at arm's length Adam's experience of coming to understand and write poetry and his experience of life as poetic, overlapping sentences on Instant Messenger–like line breaks of verse and imprecise translations of Spanish like lines with multiple meanings' (Plunkett 2014, n.p.).

In a particularly moving moment of the novel, Adam chats with his friend Cyrus in Mexico. Cyrus and his girlfriend have witnessed a woman drowning. The dialogue, delayed and interrupted due to bad internet connections, underlines the intermingling of virtual and actual as well, for the girlfriend, as Adam's friend laments, was looking for an authentic, real experience (similarly to Adam). Lerner consciously renders this in the form of the chat dialogue, reminiscent of the line breaks and pauses in poetry, or even verse drama:

> ME: you there? what's up in xalapa
> CYRUS: Yeah. Went on a kind of trip this weekend. Planned to camp
> ME: i was going camping here for a while

ME: hello?
CYRUS: I remember. It's hard to imagine you camping, I must say. Anyway, we drove to the country to see some pueblos, walk around
ME: cool
ME: what did you see
CYRUS: There was a bad scene there
ME: you mean a fight with jane?
CYRUS: No. Although we're fighting now, I guess
ME: stressful to travel together if you haven't before
CYRUS: Well we were walking
ME: still there?
CYRUS: along a river and
CYRUS: I'm still here, yes. Jane wanted to swim, but I was a little worried about the current. Not to mention the water did not strike me as particularly clean
ME: my brother once picked up a parasite swimming in a lake and was sick for a month
CYRUS: Right. And Jane launched into this speech about - half joking - about how I was afraid of new experiences or something, how I was always happier as a spectator. Not a fight, just teasing, albeit
ME: i hate new experiences (2011, 68–9)

The chat continues for a number of pages, and Cyrus's account of the traumatizing scene cumulates in his telling Adam ('ME') about seeing a woman, whom they had encouraged to enter the wild river, drown. Seeing the woman float lifelessly down the river traumatized the couple and caused a rift in their intimate relationship. For Adam, this might be a cautionary tale regarding his own quest for authenticity. Lerner embeds, or rather invites, the chat dialogue as a legitimate poetic form(at), and in this exchange, I appreciate the conversation about new experiences, with Adam self-consciously admitting that he hates new experiences.

The novel is, additionally, interested in the immediate and intimate ecologies of poetry and the affective dimensions it explores – in the experience of poetry at a reading. At the beginning of his time in Madrid, Adam is invited to participate in a reading and watches a fellow panellist, a Spanish poet, dramatically performing his work. Adam smirks that 'this poem was totally intelligible to me, an Esperanto of clichés: waves, heart, pain, moon, breasts, beach, emptiness, etc.; the delivery was so cloying the thought crossed my mind that his apparent earnestness might be parody' (Lerner 2011, 37). But when Adam looks at his friend, Arturo, 'his face implied he was having a profound experience of art', so Adam tries to 'listen *as if* the poem were unpredictable and profound, as if that were given somehow, and any failure to be compelled would be exclusively my own. The intensity of my listening did at least return strangeness to each word'

(Lerner 2011, 37; emphasis in the original). He feels the pressure to 'perform absorption in the face of what they knew was an embarrassing placeholder for an art no longer practicable for whatever reasons, a dead medium for whose former power could be felt only as a loss' (Lerner 2011, 37). The question of performing absorption and predictability comes to the fore, for Adam's experiences are held at bay by an ironic distance and his take on poetry as a machine – predictable and accurate.

Here, we might come back to the question of the picaresque, with the protagonist at odds with his environment, yet Dena Fehrenbacher would posit that the self-effacement is part of the grander poetics of Lerner's novel. Lerner's narrator resolves his 'embarrassing desperation to be appreciated [. . .] by having [his] reading audience laugh at [his] desperation and the ridiculous narrative turns it produces' (Fehrenbacher 2021, n.p.). Still the audience is earnest and listens to the 'Esperanto of clichés' with appreciation and awe, which alienates Adam from his contemporaries even more. To build upon this failure of – or resistance to – being absorbed, the narrator chooses the following description: 'the poems would constitute screens on which readers could project their own desperate belief in the possibility of poetic experience, whatever that might be, or afford them the opportunity to mourn its impossibility' (Lerner 2011, 38). If they constitute screens, for Adam, this screen is broken and blank. Adam observes, at a different moment in the novel:

> reading poetry, if reading is even the word, was something else entirely. Poetry actively repelled my attention, it was opaque and thingly and refused to absorb me; its articles and conjunctions and prepositions failed to dissolve into a feeling and a speed; you could fall into the spaces between words as you tried to link them up; and yet by refusing to absorb me the poem held out the possibility of a higher form of absorption of which I was unworthy, a profound experience unavailable from within the damaged life, and so the poem became a figure for its outside. (Lerner 2011, 20)

In his isolation – in the experience of (cliché-ridden) poetry – Adam fails to see that one component of poetry blossoms during these beautiful evenings at readings, namely in the absorption of the audience. He looks for it in the 'thingly', as he says, in the material, while for others it might lie in the effacement of the immediate to that of the immersion into the world of the poet. We can now return to the challenges of the invisible thresholds, of language impenetrable for Adam. On this, Eric Bennett writes: 'In its intractable resistance to credulous reception, language is a broken medium whose breakage provides the final trace of the human. Insight into the dynamics of signification lead, in Lerner's hands, to isolation rather than to the romantic emancipation of consciousness' (2017, 378). It is the imprecise experience that renders life poetic and unpredictable – the deadest of all media, the broken machine, now emerges as a possibility to break down the ironic distance Adam so carefully cultivates.

Conclusion

Leaving the Atocha Station shows the reader a metatextual angle on the literary production and experience *about* the pitfalls of producing and experiencing of art by way of an outsider in a foreign country. Poetry, the novel initially implies, is a genre, an ecology, that does not necessarily help Adam Gordon overcome the spatial and temporal illusions and disillusionments that the year abroad affords him. Lerner, in the case of *Atocha Station,* chooses the mediality, the thingliness, but also the affects of poetry as environment to explore the contours of the novel and, ultimately, its marketability. My article first asked about the environments – the ecologies – of different forms of literature by way of Lerner's *Atocha Station* and how the novel is self-reflexively entangled in its own becoming. This coming into being is first governed by way of drawing attention to organizational (market) forces – competitiveness, cohorts, creativity, for instance – but also to individuality and isolation, (un)marketability and prestige.

How should the novel be, then, if the literary market and its cultural, economic and personal pressures defy an immediate experience with the artwork that Adam longs for, but formulate it alongside of market values? In what way does the market construct and form the novel, how do tone and form construct an environment of market forces, and not so much of plot? In the course of the novel, it becomes clear that Lerner tests out different environs that make both Adam and the novel itself hover in invisible thresholds. I began my analysis by asking the question of prestige, privilege and intellectual isolation that established a distance for Adam, of not really ever being in the moment. I coined this the 'invisible thresholds' of the virtual and the actual – the cultural and the socio-economic conditions of life of an American expat in Madrid at the beginning of the twenty-first century. I arrived at the challenges of forms of remediation, the medium within the medium, that creates new ecologies for poetry by way of Adam's experiences with language in different venues, such as the instant message chat or the reading. Surprisingly, it is the genre of the novel that points towards a multidirectional, overdetermined agency of meaning-making in poetry. Both genres draw attention to themselves by way of language and literariness.

Literariness here also includes knowing how to navigate the terrains of poetry and novel, as the market dictates. It is here that *Atocha Station* blends genre conventions and expectations with the actual. Ultimately, the pathos and power of listening to poetry as if for the first time surprises

Adam, and underlines the volatility of experience, far away from Adam's contestation that poetry functions as a machine. The end of the novel shifts its tone significantly: Adam actually sits down and engages with an audience, with his surroundings, in the here and now – no language barrier, no ironic distance can pollute his experience.

The ironic veil of isolation and privilege is torn and reveals authenticity and immediacy, the experience Adam yearned for and facilitates, now, by way of his art, and not by way of his aloof, privileged sneering. Authenticity here is a concept and immediacy a media effect – and Lerner brings those two concepts, namely, effects in proximity. Yet, by way of his aloof and privileged expat protagonist, Lerner juxtaposes the effect of authenticity and immediacy with an impenetrable intellectual snobbery and a naïve 'feeling' for poetry. Adam sneers that poems 'aren't about anything' (Lerner 2011, 54). Yet, Ben Lerner *makes* them about something and locates them in the invisible thresholds. These thresholds might be ones of the ecologies that *Atocha Station* offers, and it surprisingly leads us away from the market to the personal, immediate, idiosyncratic experience of language and life.

Notes

1 Another characteristic of the picaresque is that is has little or no plot, and Adam Plunkett explains that, '[y]et the story lacks the consequentiality of plot, the sense of things happening to characters in response to their decisions and of characters changing in kind. The novel makes a joke out of hinting again and again that Gordon's decisions will matter only to show that they don't, as he caroms between women who take him around Spain and let him know that he's better than he thinks he is at speaking Spanish and writing poetry.' (2014, n.p.) While I do not aim to analyse *Leaving the Atocha Station* through the lens of the picaresque in more detail, I do think it is worthwhile to point out these formal parallels to the Spanish picaresque tradition and Lerner's debut. Adam Gordon, nonetheless, enjoys thumbing through his bilingual edition of Cervantes' *Don Quixote* to pass the time.

2 Ben Lerner's novel *Leaving the Atocha Station* in particular tests out these tensions of loneliness and what Kathryn Roberts postulates as, paradoxically, 'anti-communitarian communities' (2019, 399) – this, she explains, means that colonies 'provide an effective way of negotiating the art-community tension. They are a solution to the loneliness of writers in a dispersed, democratic nation—or at least they were once conceived to be (2019, 399). Roberts' article explores the cultural and historical dynamics of Thornton Wilder's *Our Town* vis-à-vis residency programs and further links the tension between public and private in that specific example – an important angle when we want to consider what literature does *not* want to be, but ultimately is: exclusive and exclusively prestigious.

3 This self-awareness differs from academic interest in writing programmes, such as McGurl's work on the programme era and the institutionalization of creative writing programmes at universities. Here, we turn to recent literary criticism that asks about literary institutions – Mark McGurl's influential study *The Program Era* argues that Creative Writing programmes stand among the most important events in postwar literary history. Yet, residency programmes offered by Yaddo and MacDowell draw, as I would argue, from a long(er) history of utopian communities of the United States in the nineteenth and early twentieth centuries; as such, they precede the academic incorporation of fiction writing 'to be learned' but offer(ed) a creative space outside educational institutions. As artistic enclaves, they offer stipends to artists and writers and a repose from the stressful day-to-day and embed individuals into a temporary community of fellow minds.

4 Stephanie Burt in her article 'The New Thing' explains that 'The new poetry, the new thing, seeks, as Williams did, well-made, attentive, unornamented things. It is equally at home (as he was) in portraits and still lifes, in epigram and quoted speech; and it is at home (as he was not) in articulating sometimes harsh judgements, and in casting backward looks. The new poets pursue compression, compact description, humility, restricted diction, and – despite their frequent skepticism – fidelity to a material and social world.' (2009, n.p.)

References

Bayerlipp, Susanne, Ralf Haekel and Johannes Schlegel. 'Introduction: The Media Ecologies of Literature.' *Media Ecologies of Literature*. Eds. Susanne Bayerlipp, Ralf Haekel and Johannes Schlegel. London: Bloomsbury, 2022. 1–14.

Bennett, Eric. 'Creative Writing, Cultural Studies, and the University.' *American Literature in Transition, 2000–2010*. Ed. Rachel Greenwald Smith. Cambridge: Cambridge University Press, 2017. 370–84.

Burt, Stephanie. 'The New Thing – The Object Lessons of Recent American Poetry.' *Boston Review*. 1 May 2009. <http://bostonreview.net/poetry/new-thing>. Accessed 20 July 2021.

Crosthwaite, Paul. *The Market Logics of Contemporary Fiction*. Edinburgh: Edinburgh University Press, 2019.

Culler, Jonathan. *The Literary in Theory*. Stanford, CA: Stanford University Press, 2007.

Dickey, Elizabeth. 'On Blind Spots.' *Michigan Quarterly Review*. 20 May 2015. <https://sites.lsa.umich.edu/mqr/2015/05/on-blind-spots/>. Accessed 1 July 2021.

English, James. *The Economy of Prestige: Prizes, Awards, and the Circulation of Cultural Value*. Cambridge, MA: Harvard University Press, 2005.

Fehrenbacher, Dena. 'Punchline Aesthetics: Recuperated Failure in the Novels of Ben Lerner and Sheila Heti.' *Post45*. 20 July 2021. <https://post45.org/2021/07/punchline-aesthetics/>. Accessed 21 July 2021.

Galloway, Alexander. *The Interface Effect*. New York: Polity, 2012

Godsland, Shelley. 'The Neopicaresque: The Picaresque Myth in the Twentieth-Century Novel.' *The Picaresque Novel in Western Literature: From the Sixteenth Century to the Neopicaresque*. Ed. J. A. Garrido Ardila. Cambridge: Cambridge University Press, 2015. 247–68.

Greenwald Smith, Rachel. *Affect and American Literature in the Age of Neoliberalism*. Cambridge: Cambridge University Press, 2015.

Huehls, Mitchum. *After Critique: Twenty-First-Century Fiction in a Neoliberal Age*. Oxford: Oxford University Press, 2016.

Lerner, Ben. *Leaving the Atocha Station*. London: Granta Publishing, 2011.

Ngai, Sianne. *Ugly Feelings*. Cambridge, MA: Harvard University Press, 2005.

Plunkett, Adam. 'Ovid and Marty McFly.' *poetryfoundation.org*. 14 September 2014. <https://www.poetryfoundation.org/articles/70150/ovid-and-marty-mcfly>. Accessed 3 July 2021.

Roberts, Kathryn. 'Our Town, the MacDowell Colony, and the Art of Civic Mediation.' *American Literary History* 31.3 (Fall 2019): 395–418.

Voelz, Johannes. 'The American Novel and the Transformation of Privacy: Ben Lerner's *10:04* (2014) and Miranda July's *The First Bad Man* (2015).' *The American Novel in the 21st Century: Cultural Contexts – Literary Developments – Critical Analyses*. Eds. Michael Basseler and Ansgar Nünning. Trier: Wissenschaftlicher Verlag Trier, 2019. 323–37.

Wellbery, David. 'Foreword.' Friedrich Kittler. *Discourse Networks 1800–1900*. Trans. Michael Metteer and Chris Cullens. Stanford, CA: Stanford University Press, 1990. vii–xxxiii.

Williams, William Carlos. 'Author's Introduction to *The Wedge*.' *The Collected Poems of William Carlos Williams: Volume II 1939–1962*. Ed. Christopher McGowan. New York: New Directions, 1988. 53–5.

PART II

Material | Designs | Techniques

With its emphasis on both concrete materiality and the techniques deployed in its handling, design and circulation, Part II picks up several key concerns of the previous section. While the contributions to Part I focus on semiotic processes of reading and the (necessarily) self-referential operations of the construction of meaning of texts, the three chapters assembled here address materiality as something that not only precedes, but also serves as the *sine qua non* of any signification in the first place. It is precisely for this reason, the chapters argue, that media ecologies of literature enable us to transcend the all too narrow boundaries of the 'culture-as-text' metaphor and to see how 'webs of significance' are spun by the circulation, not – at least not only – of abstract, ultimately intangible social energy, but also of concrete, material objects.

At the heart of Mirna Zeman's 'The cyclography of literature' is a plea to re-evaluate literary history in light of such cycles and circulations. She suggests three categories that challenge traditional historiographies of literature – namely, a cyclography of fashions, a cyclography of forms and a cyclography of things. The approach presented in this chapter allows for tracking processes, networks and fluid formations, and thus establishing a framework to describe an epistemologically self-reflective branch of contemporary media ecologies of literature. One example, Zeman claims, is the agglomeration of stories told from the point of view of an object as it circulates through human hands and in production- and economic cycles, occurring in seventeenth-century German and eighteenth-century English literature, and consequently repeating itself throughout the nineteenth century in many different national literatures. The literary device, the 'circulating object narrator', while autobiographically reflecting its own life cycle, belongs to a heterogeneous formation of techniques, methods and technologies, winding its way through the history of media, science and literature.

The sensory, haptic and tactile aspects of concrete cultural practices of reading – 'Flipping, flicking, turning' – are investigated by Sabine Zubarik. The chapter aims to analyze page-turning as a material activity as well as a cultural technique in three concrete examples: B. S. Johnson's *The Unfortunates* (1969), Alan Ayckbourn's British theatre play *Intimate Exchanges* (1982) and Mark Z. Danielewski's experimental novel *Only Revolutions* (2006). These works, Zubarik argues, engage in very different necessities of page-turning, but all three put an emphasis on the activity itself and mark the readers' option to use, abuse or deny it. Thus, digital technology highlights an aspect characteristic of contemporary media ecology: it rests on and absorbs residual aspects of traditional techniques and technologies of mediation. Structurally reflecting the materiality of the literary medium, the investigated works of literature reinforce the significance and potentiality of the very core techniques of paper-print media.

Finally, Balazs Keresztes's chapter 'Craftsmen versus dandies' turns to the Victorian period, which witnessed a renaissance not only of practices of decoration, but during which the concepts of craft and design also emerged. By concentrating on the works of Joris-Karl Huysmans, Oscar Wilde and William Morris, this chapter shows how their works attest to the decorative practices that shaped them by referring to their crafted and designed books as well as by reading portions of their work side by side. Thus, the chapter demonstrates how media theory is able to restructure literary historiography by showing that what is separated on an ideological level (decadence versus arts and crafts) is tightly interwoven on the level of practices and materials.

5

The cyclography of literature

Mirna Zeman

Each single thing that you see or hold in your hands has a long and interesting life. During its life that thing was passed from hand to hand, came in contact with many people, underwent many transformations. We just need to get it to talk about itself.
(Tret'iakov 1972, 87, my translation, MZ)

Introduction

Throughout the history of literature, there are repeatedly accounts of 'life cycles' or 'life histories' of things: efforts to narrate the trajectories of artefacts in socio-economic cycles, which *in toto* elude observation and remain imperceptible (see Tischleder 2014). The basic assumption here is that a constantly shifting formation of devices, methods, techniques, genres, aesthetic forms and 'hard' technologies has been winding its way through histories of literature, science and media until the present day, responding to the need to overcome the imperceptibility and opacity of circulation and life cycles of artefacts. I propose to call this formation 'cultural cyclography of things'.[1] In effect, this cyclography takes the form of a metareflection on the media ecology of literature, a parable of the material dimension of the book that yet, through its power of mediation, retains agency and semantic energy.

Historically, the literary tradition of this cyclography of things reaches back at least as far as the Early Modern period. In the following, I will first outline the origins of the theoretical framework of the cyclography of literature in the tradition of Russian formalism, before giving a sketch of the different historical formations in a backward chronology. Ultimately, it is the aim of this first section to outline a typology of the literary cyclography of material objects. In the second section, I will correlate thing-cyclographic narratives from the seventeenth and eighteenth centuries with theoretical models proposed within the disciplines of the history of the book and contemporary German literary and media theory, and take a look at some cycles that are constitutive of literature. Considering models of book-life cycles developed by Robert Darnton (1982) as well as Thomas R. Adams and Nicolas Barker (1993), and drawing on cyclological-materialist concepts and approaches to culture, literature and media, formulated and pursued in the works of Jürgen Link (1983; 1990; 1998; 2015), Rolf Parr (2013) and Hartmut Winkler (2004; 2015), I will argue that the sphere of cultural production, (sub)system or practice commonly called literature can be described as 'cyclological' (Link 1983), that is, as a series or an ensemble of intercoupled and more or less strongly mutually intertwined cycles. After pointing at some of the many circular processes constitutive of the materiality and mediality of literature, this chapter will – in its third and final part – briefly focus on what tentatively could be called epistemological cycles, which structure the knowledge, writing and pedagogy of literary history.

The cyclography of things – a typology

The media ecology of literature described in this volume has an important precursor in early twentieth-century literary theory: Russian formalism. A return to the formalists' writings of the 1920s – particularly of Sergei Tret'iakov and Victor Shklovsky – serves to illuminate the roots contemporary media theory has in the critical theory of the twentieth century and thus to stress the theoretical tradition of modern media theory. Furthermore, a juxtaposition of, and an investigation of the similarities between, the cyclography of things and the media ecology of literature can shed new light on the material dimension of literature.

The biography of the object

In the late 1920s, against the backdrop of the proletarian society LEF, avant-gardist Sergei Tret'iakov took a stance against what he perceived as the individualistic ideology and anthropocentrism of the novel. Tret'iakov revolted against the 'idealist' formula that 'man is the measure of all things' (2006, 58) perpetuated by the genre. His target was the classical Russian novel describing personal neuroses, emotions and experiences of human protagonists who consider themselves 'suns [. . .] around which characters, ideas, objects, and historical processes orbit submissively' (59). Tret'iakov wanted to oppose this 'Ptolemaic system of literature' (2006, 59) with the cultural-revolutionary, praxeological programme of *literatura fakta* (see Hansen-Löve 1978, 502–7; Dohrn 1987) or 'factography' (Fore 2006), and a method which he called the 'biography of the object': '[n]ot the individual person moving through the system of objects, but the object proceeding through the system of people – for literature this is the methodological device, that seems to us more progressive than those of classical belles lettres' (Tret'iakov 2006, 62).

He describes the process of the becoming of material artefacts as 'fact'. The biography of objects, then, is a literary technique that should make 'facts' representable: 'The compositional structure of the biography of objects is a conveyer belt along which a unit of raw material is moved and transformed into a useful product through human effort. [. . .] People approach the object at the cross-section of the conveyer belt. Every segment introduces a new group of people' (Tret'iakov 2006, 61).

Experimental biography

Another formalist branch of *literatura fakta* from the 1920s, represented by Viktor Shklovsky, rejects the social and economic pragmatism and realism inherent in Tret'iakov's project and proposes a different technique of destabilizing conventions of biographical writing. Shklovsky's fictional memoir entitled *Third Factory* (Shklovsky 1988; 2016) from 1927 is a piece of literature which constantly constructs itself self-referentially as a product of processing pre- and co-existent literary and non-literary material or 'facts' (Dohrn 1987, 68).

In this formalist variant, 'fact' stands for the dynamics, but not the one inherent in production cycles outside of the realm of art, which is the case with Tret'iakov, but for the processuality and materiality of literary craftsmanship. The fictionalized memoire *Third Factory* is engaged in renewing and dynamizing the habituated formal techniques of autobiographical writing through experiments with the narrative voice. Shklovsky deconstructs the figure of the conventional autobiographical protagonist by using multiple narrative voice masks, oscillating between his different literary personalities.

There are also voices of literary sources, which are obviously intended to be read as floating in processes of constant intertextual transformation or recycling, and there are also vocal masks narrating from the point of view of an object entangled in the flow of manufacturing. All of these voices tell analogous life histories turning out to be stories of processing and constant modulation, stories of putting in form or shaping and moulding in accordance with norms, which afflict humans as well as things, and literary material. 'We've been stamped with different forms, but we all have the same voice under pressure.' (Shklovsky 2016, 161).

Novels of circulation

Although the Russian Formalists' experiments were directed against the dominant forms of the bourgeois novel and thus were avant-garde, they were not without historical precursors. In the second half of the eighteenth century, the cyclography of things was a literary fashion. Above all, in England there was a surge of so-called 'it-narratives' or 'novels of circulation' (see Link 1980; Blackwell 2007; Blackwell et al. 2012; Lupton 2012). The narrative structure of these texts is similar to the assembly line of narration recommended by Tret'iakov, only that here the circulating-metamorphosing objects take the role of the narrators of their own life histories, talk for themselves and serve as focalizers, thus representing the emerging capitalist society. Coins and banknotes, pieces of paper, dresses, and a wide range of utensils, carriages and other vehicles narrate not seldomly in the first-person about the production cycles of transformation they are involved in and about their circulation as commodities, means of transportation or objects in an emerging commercial society (see Flint 1998).

As Francis Doherty (1992) has shown, even the advertisers of quack remedies readily joined the literary fashion by letting their product – the so-called 'anodyne necklace', a sort of charm necklace relieving all sorts of pain – speak for itself in the manner of literary novels of circulation. This 'anodyne necklace' seems to be a predecessor of a dancing coffee bean, evil bacteria in a toilet bowl or a machine presenting itself with 'I am Mercedes', which are populating our TV screens.

'Merry tale' and sermon

Even earlier, in the Early Modern period, the cyclography of things was primarily a comic device. From the beginning of the seventeenth century onwards, German literature features versed moral sermons containing humorous speeches of plants, first-person narrations of the various operational stages of the production of canvas, paper and even beer, as experienced first-hand (see Tharaeus 1619). Early Modern pastors and moralists used the comical cyclography of things in sermons to tone down the severity of the underlying critique of the moral decline among the believers and to add to their educational and entertainment value (see Bolte 1897).

Deriving from the tradition of the antique metamorphosis kept alive by the popular translations of Apuleius, the cyclographical device is also employed in the Early Modern comical tale by Hans Sachs featuring a horse skin and guilder narrating their life cycles (see Sachs 1870). Another example is Grimmelshausen's novel *Simplicissimus*, in which toilet paper – called Schermesser – tells its tale (Grimmelshausen 1996; see also Steiner 2010; Dallett 1976; Zeman 2015a). In the following section, I want to use this passage in Grimmelshausen and analyze it in the context of the cyclographical literary media theory proposed here. The life story of this peculiar speaking object draws attention to a whole range of unperceivable cycles in which the cultural segment of literature is entangled through its materiality.

Cycles of literature

Piece of paper: Natural cycles, reproduction cycles of transformations

In the so-called 'Schermesser Episode', the protagonist Simplicius heads to a place 'which some people call a bureau' to 'relieve' himself of a 'burden' (Grimmelshausen 1986, 239). After finishing his business, he reaches for a piece of toilet paper and is just about to 'execute it, for it and its comrades had been condemned and held prisoner for that purpose' (Grimmelshausen 1986, 239) when suddenly and unexpectedly the toilet paper speaks up in order to avert this embarrassing destiny by delivering its autobiographical account. Its life story develops as a retrospective narrative about continuous changes of form, places and owners that the loquacious object went through in its 'life'.

The future toilet paper starts its life cycle as a hemp seed. Harvested, sold and planted, it then has to 'rot and die away in the stink of horse, pig, cow and other kinds of dung' (Grimmelshausen 1986, 240) in order to be born again out of itself as a hemp stalk. As such, it gets into textile production and experiences a long chain of processes, which the narrator refers to as 'harrowing torture'. Together with its congeners it is taken to a big pit, weighted with stones, drowned and heated, a thousand times crushed, beaten up, stamped, squeezed, swung and rubbed, countless times stored, packed, sold and transported until it is turned into a yarn from which sewing female hands finally make a fine Dutch cloth and eventually a shirt.

The social life of this constantly form-changing object consists of short-term interactions with profit-seeking farmers, workers and merchants and a longer physical contact with a chambermaid, who wears the shirt and eventually throws it away. In the form of a rag, the future toilet paper finds its way into a paper mill, where it is recycled into a fine piece of writing paper. As a paper-sheet in a journal belonging to a merchant, it provides its surface for fraudulent accounting inscriptions of its owner and once again changes its form and function to become packing paper, before it is finally condemned to its sanitary function in the toilet.

Simplicius's critique of the paper's narrative reads as follows: 'Because [. . .] your growth and propagation received its origin, descent and nourishment from the richness of the earth, which has to be maintained by means of the excretion of animals and because you are used to such crude material and are an uncouth fellow to talk of such things anyway, it is only right that you return to the origin to which your owner has condemned you' (Grimmelshausen 1986, 243). Consequently, he executes the judgement.

In what follows, I want to read this anecdote in the light of late twentieth-century criticism. In his thoughts on Marx published in 1983, Jürgen Link makes an argument for analyzing the totality of 'society' and 'nature' as consisting of a whole range of structurally coupled reproduction cycles, which are linked with each other to varying degrees but which operate independently of one another (Link 1983, 24–6). Marx, for example, recognized that 'natural systems, such as the nutrient cycle, had their own metabolism, which operated independently of and in relation to human society, allowing for their regeneration and/or continuance' (Clark and York 2008). The toilet paper's life story in Grimmelshausen's novel draws attention to a relatively self-sufficient operating cycle of natural reproduction (hemp seed – hemp stalk – hemp seed) as well as to the cyclical metabolic interaction between humans and the earth – in Marx's words: 'the return to the soil of its constituent elements consumed by man in the form of food and clothing' (Marx 2011, 293, my translation, MZ; see Link 1983, 27) (excrements – hemp stalk – shirt – paper – excrement). Besides these natural cycles Link (1983, 26) calls 'primary', Grimmelshausen's object narrative reveals a series of socio-economic cycles, for example the cycle of capital. The toilet paper frequently speaks about monetary investments, which are transformed via production into raw material (hemp) and commodities (cloth, shirt, paper) sold for money, whereby the last movement closes the cycle, which starts once again with the new investment.

By and large, the life story of 'Schermesser' is a media-ecological one, uncovering the interchange between early capitalism, society and nature, stressing the natural cycles as fundamental and primary to all the others. This it-narrative also makes clear that the realms we call art and literature will always stay coupled with natural cycles. The couplings constantly cross the threshold between immaterial content and material form – in other words, these links highlight the ways in which literature becomes manifest in corporeal or physical form. In most cases those entities are paper and printed book.

A book: Cycles of production/distribution/mediation

Robert Darnton maintains that every printed book passes through roughly the same life cycle, a process he names 'communication circuit' (Darnton 1982, 67). It runs 'from the author to the publisher, the printer, the shipper, the bookseller and the reader' (Darnton 1982, 67). According to this model, the cycle begins and ends with the reader, because, as Darnton argues, the 'reader influences the author before and after the act of composition. Authors are readers themselves' (Darnton 1982, 67).

An alternative concept proposed by Thomas R. Adams and Nicolas Barker shifts the focus away from groups of people involved in the process of production and dissemination of printed books. Instead, they organize their model in accordance with a hypothetical perspective of the bibliographical object or its life cycle, respectively, progressing through phases of publishing, manufacture, distribution, reception and survival. According to Adams and Barker, the reason for the cycle of the book is the text: 'its transmission depends on its ability to set off new cycles' (1993, 15).

A short story written in the fashion of English it-narratives entitled 'Autobiography of a Book' ('Selbstbiographie eines Buches'), published 1829 by the Viennese author and journalist Franz Gräffer, fictionalizes such a cyclical book history as theorized by Adams and Barker (Gräffer 1829). It contains the autobiography of a book speaking for itself and in the times of industrial book-production also for the masses of identical comrades. The artefact named 'Große enzyklopädische Buchlese' undergoes substantially less transformation-phases than Grimmelshausen's toilet paper, yet the torments caused by the torturing machines the object meticulously describes are experienced as much more gruesome:

> Soon after, I found myself in a room that looked like a murderer's den. Here I met a lot of relatives, but in which condition? I saw some drowned in a sea of liquid glue, others stretched out on torture-like machines and pierced with sharp tools; still others had scorching burn marks imprinted on them; in particular, I pitied one of my relatives of very handsome stature, having whole long strips cut from his body with a round iron. [. . .] But I had hardly begun to tremble when one of these cannibals grabbed me with bare arms, threw me onto the anatomical table, and tore me apart limb by limb. [. . .] The barbarian seized me, placed me on an anvil, and beat me mercilessly with a large iron hammer. I hardly noticed from these murderous blows that this murderer was also harnessing me into one of the many torture machines, until incessant pinpricks brought me back to my senses. (Gräffer 1829, 14; my translation, MZ)

The fictional distribution phase is narrated as a transmission of the book through space and time with intermediary instances such as the auction house, transport package and an antiquarian bookshop. Paratextual references to the 'enzyklopädische Buchlese' pile up and communicatively mobilize the product - while people talk positively and negatively about it - and the book experiences the ups and downs of the reception, passing from hand to hand, as it wears out materially. In the end, the book shares the fate of Grimmelshausen's toilet paper.

Processing: Media cycles

The links between it-narratives and the cyclology/media ecology of literature can be further clarified when read with and through the Formalists' materialist conception of literature and culture. According to Victor Shklovsky, authors are entangled in the recycling processes. He writes about his own practice:

> I start work with reading [. . .]. I use differently coloured bookmarks or those of different width. It would be good to mark down the page number for the case these bookmarks fall out, which, however, I omit. Then I review the bookmarks and make notes. A stenotypist, the same that is writing this article now, types the excerpts, marking down the pages. I hang these paper slips on the walls of my room. It is very important to capture a quote, turn it around and connect it with the others. The excerpts stay on the wall for a long time. I group them, order them next to each other and then very concisely formulate connecting transitions. (qtd. in Dohrn 1987, 68; my translation, MZ)

Authors, who read their source material, take it apart and dissolve it into quotes, process them, and finally store them in their own product, are, according to Hartmut Winkler, involved in 'microcycles' of media 'processing' in relation to their product and the medium (Winkler 2015, 151). Winkler refers mainly to the computer and the simple case that the author – while writing a book on the computer – always processes single elements of the manuscript or, in Shklovsky's words, 'ruins of the future work' (qtd. in Dohrn 1987, 68; my translation, MZ) – then saves and thus stores the temporary result (a version of the text), only to again dissolve this interim snapshot in the next stage of processing. Winkler shows how these microcycles of processing – which repeat themselves time and again and in which the product fluctuates between 'liquid' and 'solid' aggregate states – these 'small loops' are embedded in 'large loops' (Winkler 2015, 151; my translation, MZ), that is, 'macrocycles' (221) of processing. The media theorist Winkler models these macrocycles in reference to a concept of transcriptivity by Jäger/Jarke as an interaction between the author and material archive: an author extracts an instance of source material from the archive (a prescript). It is then processed microcyclically – modified and temporarily stored in many stages – until a new product (transcript) is formed, which, in turn, enters the archive where it is stored and 'frozen' – awaiting a new intervention in the form of the next re-edit.

Analogous procedures are described on two levels: first, as an *écriture-lecture* process developing between the author and his/her media product, and, second, as a productive interaction between an author and the archive. This second level is a common subject matter within literary studies, for instance, in theories of intertextuality or Moritz Baßler's (2005) New

Historicist concept of circulation. Unlike the latter's model, Winkler's model focuses mainly on the dynamic quality of the material.

Referring to the content of Grimmelshausen's 'Schermesser Episode', Joseph B. Dallett notes: 'Now, the disparate sources, largely withheld by the author, have no advocate,' but still 'these sources [may be] considered analogous to the processed hemp stalks. Grimmelhausen has, so to speak, separated and combined them again in such a way that they can only be discerned with a thorough critical analysis' (1976, 28, my translation, MZ). Media theory helps in specifying the analogies Dallett is referring to on a deeper level, in the realm of literary production, that is, within the praxeo-material 'spinal cord' of intertextual-semantic recycling that is both part of and constitutes its media ecology. While Winkler sees macrocycles of processing as coupled with overarching discourse chains, he leaves open the question of transition between macrocycles of media processing and the large-scale time spans constituting media history.

The wig: Self-parodistic metamorphosis

An attempt to bridge the gap between literary recycling and the long trajectories of literary history can be found in yet another work of German literature: the it-narrative and novel of circulation *Die Staatsperücke*, written by Ignaz von Born and published anonymously in 1773 (von Born 1774). The narrator of the satirical tale is a wig, which is found in the upholstery of a sofa, telling its life story to an admirer of literary salons. The wig is a paradoxical creature, a sign constantly switching its referent, designating by turns a corporeal wig, a rhetorical device of prosopopoeia and a fashionable wig. 'You are familiar with the goat, whom Aesop, La Fontaine and fortunate fabulist have heard speaking, I am their descendant' (von Born 1774, 30; my translation, MZ). The personalized hybrid creature makes a case for individualism in the autobiographies of things as it spins the yarn of its personal story of origin. It goes back to ancient pastoral poetry until it reaches the head of a monarch of the imaginary Kingdom of Schetura, standing metaphorically for England, who commissions the compilation of the wig from the hair of the many. Consequently, the hair of the poor, the beggars, the miserable and many others is collected and woven into a complex web which 'Penelope with all her patience would not be able to dissolve in ten days' (von Born 1774, 16; my translation, MZ). The wig tells how, at some point, it falls out of fashion and – constantly changing its owners – socially descends from head to head until a new fashion catapults it onto the heads of the councilmen. Subsequently, it provides its services to jurists, magistrates and actors. Finally, the fading of the fashion condemns the wig to its transformation into upholstery material, and thus it comes into the possession of the recipient of the story, who has meanwhile fallen asleep, bored by the conventional it-narrative. Dropping the wig on the candle he sacrifices it to fire and to good taste: 'Ein Brandopfer dem guten Geschmacke' (von Born 1774, 28).

Born's metafictional and autoreflexive social and literary satire is of particular interest here, because it narrates the story of literature as a history of fashions and parodies in the manner of fashionable English it-narratives. But what are literary fashions in the first place?

Fashion cycles

I propose to define literary fashions as excessive transcriptivity.[2] The concept of transcriptivity stems from the operational theory of media that has been developed by the German philologists and media theorists Ludwig Jäger, Matthias Jarke, Ralf Klamma and Marc Spaniol (2008; see also Jäger 2002). In the broadest sense of the word, transcriptivity stands for the 're-writing of discourse artifacts within or across media' (Klamma, Spaniol, and Jarke 2005). In the case of a fashion, a multitude of producers are busy transcribing, recounting and generating derivatives of arbitrary source material. A fashion can be identified as the temporary accumulation of similarities. This can mean similar contents, forms and also similar devices. Heuristically, fashions can be categorized as cyclical, reappearing with similarities, repetitions (with and without variance) and agglomerations, piling up in the stream of discourses, and these accumulations regularly occur again once a fashion resurfaces.

In the case of a thematic literary fashion in the postmodern or contemporary period, a piling up of text-mobilizing microformats takes place, which repetitively multiplies references to a literary text and turns it into a discursive and a media event. The term 'text-mobilizing microformats' stands for a heterogeneous set of small medial forms and formats enabling texts to circulate in the process of communication (Zeman 2014, 345). These include all those liminal devices Gérard Genette calls paratexts, as well as other oral, written, visual and digital material which play a part in the promotion of a text in the broadest sense of the word (see Genette 1989; von Merveldt 2012). Clustering of text-mobilizing microformats, such as reviews in the press, interviews and other attention-grabbing frames and formats in mass media, which all quote, repeat, and name the author, title, stereotypical typographic elements and suchlike, can be said to drive a literary fashion by referring beyond the literary text to its media ecology.

In a short time span, the events constituting the reception of this text are repeated and merge into subsequent literary texts and other-medium transcripts or translations, whereby a series of similar text and media products emerge. Storefronts of bookstores have stacks of books on display, using similar book-covers and title illustrations and so on, that is, materially signifying their affiliation to their respective fashion wave. The fashion is carried on by further objects, for example, by spin-offs – consumer goods, fan objects and clothing, products for daily use – which extend beyond the realm of literary fiction into the real world of daily life. Symbols and signs such as country-of-origin labels (South American 'boom'), names (Werther, Yorick), labels, logos and brands (Harry Potter), by means of (identical) repetition, also play a role in the proliferation of a fashion. All kinds of different forms of practical enactments of a literary fashion also appear. Using different practices and formats – like fan fiction and conventions – fans are involved in rewriting and extending as well as in restaging and performing popular fictions in reality. All these and many other players – publishers, critics, book retailers and so on – are part of temporary 'communities of practice' (Bowker and Star 1999, 16), which are also a factor in determining the 'life cycle' of a literary fashion.

The fading away of a literary fashion can also be defined according to criteria of accumulation and repetition. Processes of 'unfashioning' (going out of fashion) manifest themselves through the clustering of texts and/or media-products parodying transcripts of the 'epigones', exposing and displacing the imitated, formulaic model through variant repetition, and work towards a shift in the original receptive valuation of fashion, in the direction of its devaluation. The fading away of a fashion also manifests itself through accumulation of paratexts proclaiming the exit of a fashion by declaring it 'out', 'passé', 'over', 'old-fashioned', 'outdated' – in short, going out of fashion is a discursive event or an event in mediation.

In addition, the accumulations in the string of events following the originator of a former fashion become rarer, and a cumulation of text-mobilizing microformats ensues, acting towards the stabilization of a competing fashion in the synchronous system of literature. I propose to call this movement consisting of mutually and dialectically related processes of structuring and de-structuring through excessive respectively vanishing repetition 'fashion cycles'. According to Winkler, repetitions which 'do not result in the production of identity but in pre-defined variation', that is, 'in the creation of something new that cannot be predicted in advance' (Winkler 2004, 173) can be described as 'recursive loops' (Schäfer 2010, 31). A useful model for describing fashions is the concept of 'automatisms' understood as processes that run independently of a central direction and largely elude the predictability and the control of its participants.[3]

The fashion in 'Wertheriads', for example – texts, objects and practices modelled on Goethe's epistolary novel *The Sorrows of Young Werther* – arose through the complex interplay of various actors who composed *Werther* reviews and imitations independently of each other, wore *Werther*-style clothing or manufactured Werther porcelain cups. Neither Goethe nor any other instance was in a position to predict or control this fashion. Historical fashions such as 'Wertheriads', 'Sterne-isms', '*Ossianomania*' and suchlike can only be partially reconstructed. The problem is that the link, that is, the discursive connection between objects, texts, practices and suchlike from a faded fashion-cycle is in most cases lost and no longer kept in cultural and discursive archives. Thematic fashions can be reconstructed only if links between content-related objects, texts, practices in the archive are preserved by historiographical, journalistic or some other narratives.[4]

There are, however, also fashions which can be called structurally formative, because they have hardened into more stable structures, identified by literature historians as genres or subgenres. In the case of structurally formative fads – like it-narratives or novels of circulation in the second half of the eighteenth century – imitation practices concentrate around formal narrative patterns. If we follow Franco Moretti (2005) and his digital method, some genres continue to occur throughout history in a series of discrete waves, and those waves I propose to be nothing else than recurrent cycles of formative fashions.

Tracking cyclography

Recently, a new thing-cyclographic variant has become fashionable. Instead of letting an old and used book collect dust or throwing it away, one can label it, tag it with an ID-number and leave it in a public space, so it can be found by other readers. The website *bookcrossing.com* makes it possible to track the subsequent travels of an ex-captive of one's own bookshelf passing from hand to hand and to virtually participate in the recycling of its contents in acts of reading through other internet users. Since a team of programmers inspired by a project of tracking a one-dollar bill on the internet started *bookcrossing.com*, the practice of releasing bibliographical objects into the wild is steadily gaining popularity. The practice of releasing, hunting and tracking books, implanting the principles of a message in a bottle and GPS-gaming in the sphere of literature consumption has become a global movement, boosted both by the current sustainability trend and an anti-trend characterized by blatant opposition to concentration and monopolization processes on the late-capitalist book market. Bookcrossing is interesting not only as a form of social recycling and a new form of web-medial and literary-social 'as-sociation' (Parr 2000) of readers and consumers, but also as a mode of literature consumption itself generating fictional narratives. That is to say, the bookcrossing community imputes circulating books with agency and a voice, and projects these objects into the role of focalizers of adventures they experience during circulation. The labels featuring sentences like 'Howdy. Holla. Guten Tag. I am a special book. You see, I am travelling the world making new friends' simulate the voice of an object and the ability to speak up out of the processes of its circulation. The old literary cyclography of things celebrates its comeback as a new tracking technology.

Cycles of literary history

By way of conclusion, I would like to summarize the previous investigations by applying this media-ecological conception of the cyclography of literary objects to the concept of literary history itself. 'In the occidental countries,' Jürgen Link writes, 'one is from childhood onwards constantly fed with evolutionary trajectories: series of images depicting evolutionary progress, an upwards movement from crawlers to brisk quadrupeds, then to primates gradually more and more uprightly walking and finally to homo sapiens. [. . .] Evolutionary trajectories are constructed for all sorts of specialized discursive practices,' Link argues, 'there are evolutionary trajectories of art, of economy, of history, of fashions, etc' (2015, 9; my translation, MZ). Sometimes these evolutionary trajectories represent forward and backward movements, constructing cycles of progress and decline. Link suggests naming arcs and cycles construed on the base of the evolution of certain types – for example, types of animals, vehicles, or types of artistic styles – 'cycles in the third degree' (2015, 9). Because we are dealing with a technique of producing, organizing, constructing and representing knowledge of history, we can describe these trajectories as epistemic.

There are many cultural techniques of complexity reduction within a literary system, and still only one of them has made it to become a leading principle of writing and teaching literary history: canons. A canon-guided literary historiography is based on a historicist narration linked to the notion of history progressing through consistent epochs, periods or phases (see Link 1998). Inherent in this kind of literary historiography is the notion of progress or development, and, of course, there are evolutionary trajectories representing literature as progressing through distinctive epochs, which – following Link's typology – could be named 'third-order trajectories of literature'.

The arcs and cycles of literary history are constructed by the cultural technique of writing and – on a semantic level – by what Link calls 'sem-synthesis'. By this he means 'that the underlining scheme of the historicist principle (in the case of German literature progressing through 'Aufklärung', 'Empfindsamkeit', 'Sturm und Drang', 'Klassik', 'Romantik', 'Realismus' [. . .]) is construed as a motion of semantic units or semes' (Link 1998, 386). Consequently, German literary history can be constructed, for example, as a movement from 'Sturm und Drang' via 'Klassik' up to 'Romantik,' or as an oscillation between semantic attributions 'objective' versus 'subjective', leading from an 'objective' style of writing ascribed to the epoch of 'Aufklärung' to an extremely 'subjective' style allegedly typical of 'Sturm und Drang' to an again more 'objective' writing, which would then be seen as characteristic of 'Klassik' and then again back to 'radical subjective' writing ascribed to the epoch of 'Romantik' (Link 1998). Another example Link finds in literary historiography is a movement from the rationalism of the 'Aufklärung' to the irrationalism of the 'Sturm und Drang' and once again to more rational 'Klassik' and then again to the allegedly radical irrationalism of the 'Romantik' period. Yet another common design applying semantic units 'open form' – 'closed form' – 'open form' – 'closed form' follows the same principle (Link 1998).

Crucial for this trajectory is the discursive link between the historicist structure and concrete texts and authors. Following the aesthetics of originality, that is, the principles of individuality, subjectivity and innovation, the mainstream literary historiography operates almost exclusively with the categories of author and work, and selects from among a multitude those who represent a particular literary period to be accepted as objectively canonical. It is then, in Link's words, 'a matter of plausible preparation (that means interpretation) of concrete texts in such a way, that the interpretation through the chain of abstract descriptions leads to exactly those kinds of sem-complexes which can be coupled with the sems of the historicistic base-line' (Link 1998, 386; my translation, MZ). Because fundamental semantic units (for example, 'subjective' vs. 'objective', 'open' vs. 'closed', 'rational' vs. 'irrational') reoccur in different combinations, a kind of wave-like movement emerges with semantically related wave-crests – a structure, which Link identifies as the basis for historicist canon formation processes (Link 1998, 387).

Besides third-degree trajectories there are also those Link terms 'second-degree trajectories' (Link 2015, 9). These second-degree cycles are constituted of finished, completed, reified products – cultural objects or artefacts – which belong to the same type. In the realm of historicizing literature, the second-degree cycles can be identified in the work of Franco Moretti, extracting cycles of literary genres on the basis of quantitative analysis of series of works belonging to the same type (genres). Moretti argues:

> Event, cycle, *longue durée:* three time frames which have fared very unevenly in literary studies. Most critics are perfectly at ease with the first one, the circumscribed domain of the event and of the individual case; most theorists are at home at the opposite end of the temporal spectrum, in the very long span of nearly unchanging structures. But the middle level has remained somehow unexplored by literary historians; and it's not even that we don't work within that time frame, it's that we haven't yet fully understood its specificity: the fact, I mean, that cycles constitute *temporary structures within the historical flow*. [. . .] the short span is all flow and no structure, the *longue durée* all structure and no flow, and cycles are the – unstable – border country between them. Structures, because they introduce repetition in history, and hence regularity, order, pattern; and temporary, because they're short (ten, twenty, fifty years, this depends on the theory). (Moretti 2005, 14)

As Rolf Parr rightly points out (Parr 2013) and as the contemporary German literary- and media-theoretical investigations of the cyclography of literature have shown, such a research is by no means *terra incognita* as Moretti claims. And it seems that the 'flow' can be revealed only if we focus on processes and generative cycles of literature and literary history as a dynamic media ecology. Generative cycles should be analysed on the level of material production and reproduction of literature and on the level of literary form and structure building, as well as on the level of literary semantics and application of literary semantics into the processes of subject-formation on the recipient side.

Notes

1 This paper is a revised and extended version of my German paper 'Zyklographie der Literatur. Materialistische Variante' (Zeman 2015b). On the concept of 'cyclography of things', see also my 'Literatur und Zyklographie der Dinge. *Bookcrossings* in *simplicianischer* Manier' (Zeman 2015a).

2 On literary fashions, see Zeman 2012; Zeman 2014.

3 On the concept, see various publications of the Research Training Group 'Automatisms' at Paderborn University, for example, Bublitz et al. (2010).

4 My thanks go to Matthias Beilein, to whom I owe these and following insights.

References

Adams, Thomas R., and Nicolas Barker. 'A New Model for the Study of the Book.' *A Potencie of Life: Books in Society: The Clarke Lectures, 1967–1987*. Ed. Nicolas Barker. London: British Library, 1993. 5–43.

Baßler, Moritz. *Die kulturpoetische Funktion und das Archiv: Eine literaturwissenschaftliche Text-Kontext-Theorie*. Tübingen: Francke, 2005.

Blackwell, Mark, Ed. *The Secret Life of Things: Animals, Objects, and It-Narratives in Eighteenth-Century England*. Lewisburg: Bucknell University Press, 2007.

Blackwell, Mark, et al., Eds. *British It-Narratives, 1750–1830*. vol. 4. London: Pickering & Chatto, 2012.

Bolte, Johannes. 'Introduction.' *Klage der Gerste und des Flachses*. By Andreas Tharäus. Ed. Johannes Bolte. Berlin: Verlag des Vereins für die Geschichte Berlins, 1897. 35–68.

Born, Ignaz von. *Die Staatsperücke. Eine Satyre*. Amberg, 1774.

Bowker, Geoffrey C., and Susan Leigh Star. *Sorting Things Out: Classification and Its Consequences*. Cambridge, MA: MIT Press, 1999.

Bublitz, Hannelore, et al., Eds. *Automatismen*. München: Fink, 2010.

Clark, Brett, and Richard York. 'Rifts and Shifts: Getting to the Root of Environmental Crises.' *Monthly Review: An Independent Socialist Magazine* 60.6 (2008). <https://monthlyreview.org/2008/11/01/rifts-and-shifts-getting-to-the-root-of-environmental-crises/> 24 September 2021.

Dallett, Joseph B. 'Auf dem Weg zu den Ursprüngen: Eine Quellenuntersuchung zu Grimmelshausens Schermesser-Episode.' *Carleton Germanic Papers* 4 (1976): 1–36.

Darnton, Robert. 'What Is the History of Books?' *Daedalus* 111.3 (1982): 65–83.

Doherty, Francis. *A Study in Eighteenth-Century Advertising Methods: The Anodyne Necklace*. Lewiston: Edward Mellen Press, 1992.

Dohrn, Verena. *Die Literaturfabrik: Die frühe autobiographische Prosa V.B. Šklovskijs: Ein Versuch zur Bewältigung der Krise der Avantgarde*. München: Otto Sagner, 1987.

Flint, Christopher. 'Speaking Objects: The Circulation of Stories in Eighteenth-Century Prose Fiction.' *PMLA* 113.2 (1998): 212–26.

Fore, Devin. 'Introduction.' *October* 118 (2006): 3–10.

Genette, Gérard. *Paratexte. Das Buch vom Beiwerk des Buches*. Frankfurt a.M.: Campus, 1989.

Gräffer, Franz. 'Selbstbiographie eines Buches.' *Momus. Nämlich: iocose Geschichtchen, humoristische Erzählungen, phantastische Scenereien und Schwänke, lyrische Seifenblasen und sonstige Allotria*. Wien, 1829. 12–16.

Grimmelshausen, Hans Jacob Christoph von. *An Unbridged Translation of Simplicius Simplicissimus*. Trans. Monte Adair. Lanham: University Press of America, 1986.

Grimmelshausen, Hans Jacob Christoph von. *Der abenteuerliche Simplicissimus Teutsch*. Stuttgart: Reclam, 1996.

Hansen-Löve, Aage A. *Der russische Formalismus: Methodologische Rekonstruktion seiner Entwicklung aus dem Prinzip der Verfremdung*. Wien: Verlag der Österreichischen Akademie der Wissenschaften, 1978.

Jäger, Ludwig. 'Transkriptivität: Zur medialen Logik der kulturellen Semantik.' *Transkribieren: Medien/Lektüre*. Eds. Ludwig Jäger and Georg Stanitzek. München: Fink, 2002. 19–41.

Jäger, Ludwig, Matthias Jarke, Ralf Klamma and Marc Spaniol. 'Transkriptivität: Operative Medientheorien als Grundlage von Informationssystemen für die Kulturwissenschaften.' *Informatik Spektrum* 31.1 (2008): 21–9.

Klamma, Ralf, Marc Spaniol and Matthias Jarke. 'MECCA: Hypermedia Capturing of Collaborative Scientific Discourses about Movies.' *Informing Science Journal* 8 (2005): 3–38.

Link, Jürgen. 'Marx denkt zyklologisch: Mit Überlegungen über den Status von Ökologie und "Fortschritt" im Marxismus.' *kultuRRevolution. Zeitschrift für angewandte Diskurstheorie* 4 (1983): 23–7.

Link, Jürgen. 'Diskursives Ereignis, Zyklologie, Kairologie: Überlegungen nach Foucault.' *Spuren* 34/35 (1990): 78–85.

Link, Jürgen. 'Hölderlin – oder eine Kanonisierung ohne Ort?' *Kanon – Macht – Kultur: Theoretische, historische und soziale Aspekte ästhetischer Kanonbildung*. Ed. Renate von Heydebrand. Stuttgart: J. B. Metzler, 1998. 383–95.

Link, Jürgen. 'Thesen zu Zyklologie und Evolution.' *kultuRRevolution. Zeitschrift für angewandte Diskurtheorie* 68 (2015): 9–12.

Link, Viktor. *Die Tradition der außermenschlichen Erzählperspektive in der englischen und amerikanischen Literatur*. Heidelberg: Winter, 1980.

Lupton, Christina. *Knowing Books: The Consciousness of Mediation in Eighteenth-Century Britain*. Philadelphia, PA: University of Pennsylvania Press, 2012.

Marx, Karl. *Das Kapital: Kritik der politischen Ökonomie. Im Zusammenhang ausgewählt und eingeleitet von Benedikt Kautsky*. Stuttgart: Alfred Kröner, 2011.

Merveldt, Nikola von. 'Textmobilisierung: Überlegungen zur Transferleistung von Paratexten am Beispiel von Joachim Heinrich Campe.' *Die Bienenfremder Literaturen: Der literarische Transfer zwischen Großbritannien, Frankreich und dem deutschsprachigen Raum im Zeitalter der Weltliteratur (1770–1850)*. Eds. Norbert Bachleitner and Murray G. Hall. Wiesbaden: Harrassowitz, 2012. 103–24.

Moretti, Franco. *Graphs, Maps, Trees: Abstract Models for a Literary History*. London: Verso, 2005.

Parr, Rolf. *Interdiskursive As-Sociation: Studien und Texte zur Sozialgeschichte der Literatur*. Tübingen: De Gruyter, 2000.

Parr, Rolf. 'Sind Mode(n) und Modezyklen Formen von Wiederholung? Einige unsystematische Überlegungen aus Perspektive der Forschung zu "Wiederholen" und "Zyklologie".' Conference Paper presented at the workshop 'Moden, Trends, Hypes' at Paderborn University in 2013, unpublished manuscript.

Sachs, Hans. 'Schwanck: Der ellend klagent roßhaut.' *Hans Sachs*. Vol. 5. Eds. Adelbert von Keller and Edmund Götze. Stuttgart: Literarischer Verein, 1870. 146–53.

Schäfer, Jörgen. 'Reassembling the Literary: Toward a Theoretical Framework for Literary Communication in Computer-Based Media.' *Beyond the Screen: Transformations of Literary Structures, Interfaces and Genres*. Eds. Jörgen Schäfer and Peter Gendolla. Bielefeld: Transcript, 2010. 25–70.

Shklovsky, Viktor. *Dritte Fabrik*. Frankfurt a. M.: Suhrkamp, 1988.

Shklovsky, Viktor. 'The Third Factory.' *Viktor Shklovsky. A Reader*. Ed. and trans. Alexandra Berlina. New York: Bloomsbury, 2016. 161–9.

Steiner, Uwe C. 'The Problem of Garbage and Resurrection of Things.' *Trash Culture: Objects and Obsolescence in Cultural Perspective*. Ed. Gillian Pye. Oxford: Peter Lang, 2010. 129–46.

Tharaeus, Andreas. 'Eine erbermliche Klage Der lieben Fravv Gerste, vnd ihres Brudern Herrn Flachs [. . .].' *Amphitheatrum Sapientiae Socraticae Ioco-Seriae* [. . .]. Ed. Caspar Dornau. Hannover: Aubrii & Schleichius, 1619. 222–32.

Tischleder, Bärbel. *The Literary Life of Things: Case Studies in American Fiction*. Frankfurt a.M.: Campus, 2014.

Tret'iakov, Sergej. *Die Arbeit des Schriftstellers. Aufsätze-Reportagen-Porträts*. Trans. Karla Hielscher and ed. Heiner Boehncke. Hamburg: Rowohlt, 1972.

Tret'iakov, Sergej. 'Biography of the Object.' *October* 118 (2006): 57–62.

Winkler, Hartmut. *Diskursökonomie: Versuch über die innere Ökonomie der Medien*. Frankfurt a.M.: Suhrkamp, 2004.

Winkler, Hartmut. *Prozessieren: Die dritte, vernachlässigte Medienfunktion*. München: Fink, 2015.

Zeman, Mirna. 'Literarische Moden. Ein Bestimmungsversuch.' *Doing Contemporary Literature: Praktiken, Wertungen, Automatismen*. Eds. Maik Bierwirth, Anja K. Johannsen and Mirna Zeman. München: Fink, 2012. 111–31.

Zeman, Mirna. 'Häufungen des Kleinen. Zur Struktur von Hypes.' *Kulturen des Kleinen: Mikroformate in Literatur, Medien und Kunst*. Eds. Sabiene Autsch, Claudia Öhlschläger, and Leonie Süwolto. München: Fink, 2014. 335–52.

Zeman, Mirna. 'Literatur und Zyklographie der Dinge: *Bookcrossings* in *simplicianischer* Manier.' *Entsorgungsprobleme: Müll in der Literatur* (= Beiheft der *Zeitschrift für deutsche Philologie)*. Eds. David Christopher Assmann, Eva Geulen and Norbert Eke. Berlin: Schöningh, 2015a. 151–73.

Zeman, Mirna. 'Zyklographie der Literatur: Materialistische Variante.' *kulturRRevolution. Zeitschrift für angewandte Diskurtheorie* 68 (2015b): 32–9.

6

Flipping, flicking, turning

Cultural practices of reading in B. S. Johnson, Alan Ayckbourn and Mark Z. Danielewski

Sabine Zubarik

Introduction

Texts printed on paper in commercial formats (like books, magazines and newspapers) share a certain material feature: through the stitching and the cover, the pages are bound together into one coherent medium. The conventional activities of operating the pages are usually subsumed under the category of reading and not estimated *per se* as an important cultural technique independent from the semantic processing of the text on the pages. Yet, even at a very early age, children are made familiar with the cultural practice of handling a book and turning the pages long before they learn how to semantically approach it. Toddler toy books – small booklets made of plastic, textile fabrics or wood, either in the style of an exercise book, centrally tied or as an accordion book – seem to serve as evidence that more importance should be attached to the very haptic approach to the book as a medium and indeed to the act of page-turning as such.

If turning and flipping the pages were important only in the context of semantic reading, it would make little sense to give a book or an accordion leaflet in plastic or textile material with no letters to infants at a stage of their development where they cannot even identify pictures, nor follow a narrative sequence. Obviously, it is not done to teach the babies at that age how to read or connect the images to a story; instead, what the babies are supposed to learn is how to handle an item that is made of pages. The children have to learn how to handle individual pages that are bound together, creating a unit, and thus they figure out that in order to retain the unity of the book, they should not rip out the pages. Gradually, they will learn to control their fingers in a way that enables them to move one page after the other, back and forth, and with time they will understand how to hold and handle a book in such a manner that will later enable them to read it.

I want to argue that we acquire the cultural techniques of handling and operating the material medium of the book and its pages independently of the practices that are needed to semantically process its content through reading, although the activities themselves eventually merge into one coherent activity. Thus, the very act of reading establishes a form of media ecology that combines different activities that are originally separate. Hence, it is my aim in this chapter to analyse the activity of turning the pages of a book, of flipping and flicking through them, as a cultural technique in its own right. This has important consequences for our understanding of the concept of reading, as it presupposes that reading a book with bound paper sheets is an activity fundamentally different from reading a text on another medium, say an e-book reader or a computer screen. The material medium of the book with its very own properties requires cultural techniques that differ categorically from those attached to other media.

These properties become evident once books become self-reflexive and metamedial in the sense that they question and thus highlight their material format. In this chapter I argue that the works I analyse, which all experiment with the materiality of their pages – B. S. Johnson, *The Unfortunates* (1969), Alan Ayckbourn, *Intimate Exchanges* (1982) and Mark Z. Danielewski, *Only Revolutions* (2006) – transcend the limits of the traditional book and thus draw attention to their very materiality.

B. S. Johnson: *The Unfortunates* (1969)

The British author B. S. Johnson published his novel *The Unfortunates* (1969) as a collection of loose papers and single leaflets without bookbinding. If you order the book online or happen to find it in an antiquarian bookshop, you receive a beautiful box with a hinged lid, which at first looks like a book cover, and opens like one, too.[1]

The first leaflet operates like the first pages in a book. It contains the conventional paratext that reveals the information about the novel that readers are used to finding at the very beginning: author, title, publishing house, year and place of publication and so on. This is followed, in modern editions at least, by an introduction by Jonathan Coe added to the 1999 edition.

Readers will furthermore find a note on the inner side of the cover lid that gives them the following advice:

> Note
>
> This novel has twenty-seven sections, temporarily held together by a removable wrapper.
>
> Apart from the first and the last sections (which are marked as such) the other twenty-five sections are intended to be read in random order.
>
> If readers prefer not to accept the random order in which they receive the novel, then they may re-arrange the sections into any other random order before reading. (Johnson 2007, cover, inside)

When the Hungarian edition was published, it was issued – for economic reasons – as a regular paperback with bound pages. Johnson added a special introduction to the translation, proposing to the Hungarian readers a way to make up for the defective form:

> Another device has occurred to me which goes some little way towards achieving an effect similar to that of the English edition. Each of the twenty-five sections in between those marked *First* and *Last* has a symbol printed on at its head. And on the last page, all the symbols so used are printed again, but together. The really interested Hungarian reader is invited to remove the last page [. . .] and to cut up and therefore separate the twenty-five symbols. (2007, xii)

Johnson then explains how the readers receive their very own order by mixing the twenty-five symbols in a receptacle and laying them out in a row. He continues:

> What all Hungarian readers cannot help but miss is the physical feel, disintegrative, frail, of this novel in its original format; the tangible metaphor for the random way the mind works, as I have said. (2007, xii)

We will have to come back to the last sentence about the 'random way the mind works'. But let me first digress into a more personal account of my own reading experience: Admittedly, I belong to those readers who did not trust the advice fully or did not want to destroy the given order yet. Both aversions keep the readers from embracing the task of shuffling the pages. The advice did not say you must disrupt the order, only that you can, and therefore reading the pages in the order they come in the box is a legitimate option as well. The social-cultural conditioning of me as a reader as someone who is supposed to both respect the material intactness of bound books and fear the losing of torn pages created an anxiety that once I had shuffled the leaflets, I would not be able to restore the 'original order' (if we might call it that) which the box came with. Furthermore, there are no page numbers for the full opus, but only for the leaflets (where one would actually not need them, as in a text with merely six pages one hardly gets lost). The single page units and the leaflets have imprinted a symbol, instead, a mixture of geometric and floral designs, all different in principle, but some very similar in practice. I was so paranoid about destroying the given order – being incredulous that this order could be random, indeed – that before I was able to start my reading, I had to draw the sequence of the signs of the units in the manner they followed each other in the box. The arbitrariness was then tamed by my creation of a linear sequence, and in the absence of a numeric order throughout the novel, the floral signs, though by their paradigmatic design ill-equipped for this purpose, had to serve as substitutes for page numbers and function as markers of the sequence. Only then I dared to begin with the actual reading. The insight gained from this digression from the prescribed reading practice is this: One might deal extensively with experimental, a-chronological and fragmentary literature and deeply appreciate the disruption of textual hierarchy and linearity on a theoretical level, and still feel a strong attachment to the idea of a fixed and therefore proper order of a published text and a low tolerance for the eccentric emphasis on the materiality of the book as medium in one's own reading practice.

After my first – confused – reading of the entire book, I was still not willing to shuffle the pages and leaflets, but reflected on the question how one could order the parts, form groups and shift them in different ways. Once more I drew the signs on a piece of paper, this time not in their order of appearance but according to the timeline of the narrated events. Some of the events could be located easily with an exact date or even daytime, others floated around in a vague timelessness, a cloud of temporal possibilities. At this point one might want to look deeper into the content(s) of the novel in order to find answers to the question of why the events are presented in this form (or rather the lack thereof). What is actually narrated? Is there a coherent narrative at all that connects the singular bits and pieces given in the leaflets, or are there only loose episodes? Who is the narrator, or are there even several? How many alternative lives and lifetimes are included in this story?

This novel is about Tony Tillinghast, the narrator's best friend, who became sick and died of cancer in his early years of marriage and academic success. The first-person narrator recalls situations, events and happenings in the course of the years they had together from their freshman year until Tony's death. There is a departure time set for the narration, that is, a present or a 'now', the launching point from which the narrator's memory departs and to which he returns back, just to set out to return to the past again. This time of 'now' is a Saturday in London where the narrator has to attend a football match as a journalist in order to write a report about it. Randomly, he remembers details of meetings with Tony and tries to locate them properly on the timeline. Often, he does not succeed, and thus the readers also fail to establish an accurate line of events in the act of reading and re-tracing this friendship.

In the last sentence of the preface of the Hungarian edition quoted earlier, Johnson gives a reason why this book cannot but have a loose and changeable order: he spoke about 'the physical feel, disintegrative, frail, of this novel in its original format; the tangible metaphor for the random way the mind works' (2007, xii). The unfolding memories of Tony came, as most memories do, in a non-structured, non-linear way, and they were interrupted at random by the task of watching the match and taking notes. As Jonathan Coe in his introductory notes points out:

> It was this randomness, this lack of structure in the way we remember things and receive impressions, that Johnson wanted to record with absolute fidelity. But randomness, he realized, is 'directly in conflict with the technological fact of the bound book: for the bound book imposes an order, a fixed page order, on the material'. His solution, as always, was simple and radical: the pages of *The Unfortunates* should not be bound at all. (2007, ix)

Further down he adds: 'Disintegration and frailty: these are the themes of *The Unfortunates*, and its tone is one of restless, enquiring melancholy' (2007, xii).

Iris Hermann (2002), in an article on psychoanalytic methods as procedures of aesthetic production, writes on the analogy of the psychoanalytical work as one that constantly flicks pages. Memory, she states, is not a linear movement but is constructed by the backward movement of the rereading of events passed. To remember is to dig deeply into the sediments stored a long time ago. Memory, according to Hermann, is never complete, never undamaged, and memory is only apparent in fragments, as a described and overwritten one (see 2002, 200–1).[2]

In *The Unfortunates*, Johnson seems to persistently refrain from pretending that memories – albeit memories of a chronological passage of time, like the ongoing friendship with Tony – can ever be captured in a coherent narration. At the same time, however, he exhibits the tendency of the human brain to still try to do so. As much as the narrator fails in his attempts to find coherence, the author succeeds in a realistic depiction of how memories escape relatability. With his decision to publish the novel in the format of loose pages and leaflets, Johnson manages to avoid conventions of writing which means constructing a linear narration; but for this he has to use another artificial, highly formal construct of medial fragmentation. With his choice of writing in this way,

Johnson criticizes, denies as well as confirms that the process of narrating is always done as an act of constructing.[3]

Alan Ayckbourn: *Intimate Exchanges* (1982)

My next example engages the cultural practices of turning pages and flipping through books in a different way. Unlike Johnson's novel, it does propose order – just of such complexity that it exceeds our common capacity of capturing simultaneous information in the attempt of coherent reading. Alan Ayckbourn's British theatre play *Intimate Exchanges* from 1982 is not one play but many; in fact, the author calls it 'a related series of plays' (Ayckbourn 1985, first page of each main story line). It consists of eight major stories and sixteen possible endings. Six of the eight stories were also made into a film – in fact, two films – in 1993 by the French director Alain Resnais, under the title *Smoking/No Smoking*.

Intimate Exchanges follows the logic of the so-called forking-path technique:[4] one original situation with which the book starts – the decision of one character, Celia Teasdale, to smoke a cigarette or not – diverges into two possibilities, meaning two versions of a second chapter, each of which again splits up into two further possible ongoings, and so on – until there are eight main stories and sixteen endings (Figure 6.1). Each fork is caused by a decision, albeit small or banal, that one of the characters has to make. The biographies of the main characters differ immensely in the various parallel paths, so that a minor change of routine (like smoking), after a long line of binary choices, can lead to important events in the end, like divorce or even death.

Ayckbourn's strategy is very technical and consistent: The first bifurcation shows the happenings five seconds later after Celia's decision to smoke or not. The next split of scenes is situated after five days, then after five weeks and finally after five years. The nodal point, a binary decision that causes the two splitting options, is always posed at the end of one scene. A line is drawn on the page where the unilinear scene ends. The first option is introduced with the words 'EITHER he says', followed by a short dialogue and the information on which page this line will continue and how the next scene is called – as each episode has its own title. Then there is another line on the page and the second option starts with the words 'OR he says', again followed by the short alternative dialogue and the logistic instructions where to go on. Readers who have dealt with Julio Cortázar's novel *Rayuela* (*Hopscotch* in English), or other forking-path narrations, as for example, Svend Åge Madsen's *Days with Diam*, will be familiar with the techniques of jumping back and forth in the book and re-aligning the chapters.

The audience's awareness of the simultaneity of parallel versions is one of the main goals the author follows, as we can deduce from his introductory stage direction:

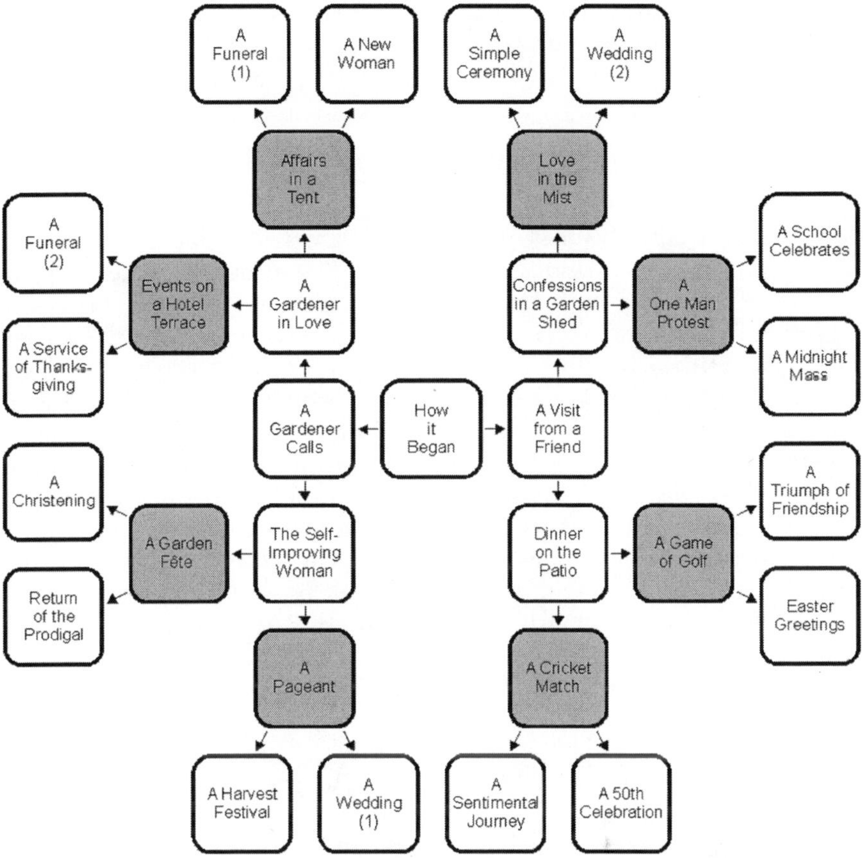

FIGURE 6.1 *Structure of scenes in the written play* Intimate Exchanges *(eight main stories). Courtesy of GDallimore and accessed on https://commons.wikimedia.org/wiki/File:Intimate_Exchanges_structure3.png.*

> it's possible to do just one version but far less theatrically exciting. If, for some unavoidable reason, a decision is taken to mount only one alternative, [. . .] I would be grateful if the audience could be informed of my original preferences. This would serve (a) to explain why the plays are so idiosyncratically constructed and (b) to let people know what they've missed. (Ayckbourn 1985, author's note)

In this chapter with its emphasis on leaves and pages and the cultural techniques connected with them, however, the focus will be on the script as a written and printed medium and not on the staging of the plays.

Following Ayckbourn's forking storylines, the readers can, just like in Johnson's *The Unfortunates*, go through the two volumes chronologically without ever revisiting former pages. But it is highly improbable that one has the determination to do so. In order to connect the branches of each story with their narrative roots and to remember where in the bifurcating tree they are located and which parallel branch is the one *not* read, the reader repeatedly has to go back at least to the table of contents (the drawing), but, more probable, even to the nodal points of splitting. To understand one chosen version, one has to keep in mind the other branch that one momentarily does *not* read. Ayckbourn explicitly invites the readers to return to previous junctions, as he introduces a heterodiegetic directing voice after each episode that announces the either-or-option: 'EITHER he/she says' – 'OR he/she says'. This voice reminds the readers constantly of the operating game and their task in it to flip through the text. Interestingly, this practice of flipping through pages back and forth in order to find connecting episodes, does not trespass the boundaries of either volume, as each of the two volumes has its completely independent branch. Only the first scene (before Celia's decision to smoke or not) is repeated identically; after that, the volumes do not interfere nor appear to be repetitive. This is consistent not only in terms of the lines of the narrative choices – one volume following all possibilities after smoking, the other after not smoking – but also in terms of mediality. The layout of the collection of the sixteen endings does not suggest disrespecting the limits of the book format. *Intimate Exchanges* is not designed as a net, a rhizome or a web of hypertext and links; it is clearly the figure of the forking tree that is at work here; this means that, unlike in a net, the branches do not connect backwards with a former nodal point, as a new branch only produces further forkings but does not grow back into an older branch, whereas the connection points of a web do not know this hierarchy of 'older' and 'newer'.[5] Also, if you cut off a full branch, the other branch is not injured, there is no problem of disentangling the whole structure, because the forkings do not criss-cross. In consequence, the one side of the story-'tree' of *Intimate Exchanges* can exist without being in touch with the other, meaning you do not need both volumes for enjoying one of them.

Mark Z. Danielewski: *Only Revolutions* (2006)

Mark Z. Danielewski is a US-American author known for his highly experimental fictional works which challenge the format and the medium of the book. In his first novel *House of Leaves*, published in 2000, leaves, papers, notes and the never-ending layers of editing turn into a labyrinthine project of remediation. Even though one could dwell extensively on *House of Leaves* in the context of this chapter,[6] I want to concentrate, instead, on the author's second novel from 2006, *Only Revolutions*. Here, Danielewski accentuates the practice of turning and revolving pages, as the novel can be read from four angles, starting either from each side or from the top or from the bottom, upside down (Figure 6.2). The author suggests changing direction every eight pages (which is the length of each chapter). The last page of one storyline is the first of the other; in addition, there are mutually related marginal columns and manifold intratextual references. The main text consists of 360 pages, each one containing two times ninety words (the marginalia not counted), and there are ninety chapters altogether (forty-five from each side). Just by these numbers, one can detect a reference to the 360 degrees of a full circle, the 180 degrees of the two turning directions the reader has to follow, and the 90 degrees of the right angles of the shape of a book. The book's title is programmatic: re-volutions, *revolvere*, turning around, turning back (Bunia 2013); readers are kept occupied with turning the book, which, in turn, highlights its materiality and mediality.[7]

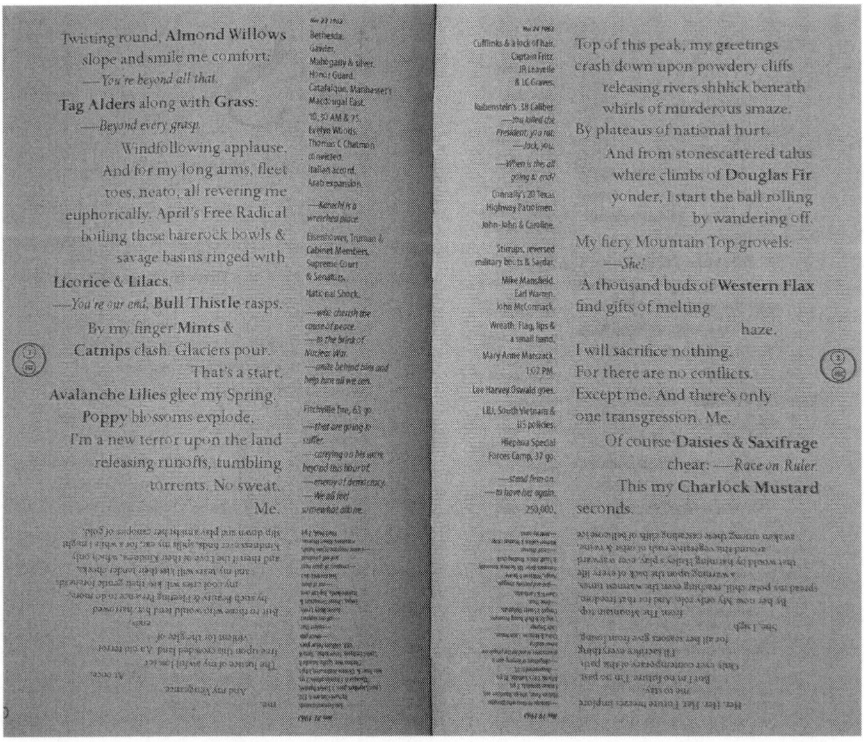

FIGURE 6.2 *A double page from* Only Revolutions *by Mark Z. Danielewski, copyright © 2006 by Mark Z. Danielewski. Used by permission of Pantheon Books, an imprint of the Knopf Doubleday Publishing Group, a division of Penguin Random House LLC. All rights reserved.*

Further optical and typographical peculiarities heighten the semantic complexity: all round-shaped characters like o, O and 0 are emphasized by colour, brown in the case of the story told by the female narrator (called Hailey) from one side, green in the case of the male narrator (called Sam) from the other side. The font size changes as well; it continuously becomes smaller towards the middle of the book. Quotes are in italics, animal names in Sam's storyline and botanical names in Hailey's are bold (both are abundant). The capital initials of every chapter lead to the infinite repetition of the names of the protagonists: HAILEYANDSAM – The letters 'US' are always capitalized, therefore every 'us' signifies at the same time the US-A, and as it is not distinguishable for the readers if the personal pronoun or the name of the country is meant, both meanings collapse into each other. There are numerous neologisms and puns reminiscent of James Joyce: 'al' as a syllable is always spelled with two *ll*; the word *al(l)one* therefore also contains *all-one*, suggesting all kinds of linguistic interpretations – such as we are all alone, all alone people are one, all being one means being alone, and so on – a perpetual play on the dichotomic words *alone*/*one* and *all*, implying the oxymoron of all people being alone and therefore not being alone.

Furthermore, there are the marginalia – the so-called *Chronomosaics* – which contain extracts from the world's history with places, dates, hours, quotes and numbers of deaths (like '226 go'). One can definitely say that *Only Revolutions* is in every sense overstructured – which simultaneously allows for strenuous and rewarding readings of the novel, as it is at the same time barely readable in a meaningful way and immensely rich in meaning.

Again, one might ask: Is there a plot, a narrative time span, a fictional world, and are these accessible to the readers? Hailey and Sam are a couple, both sixteen years old, living in the USA. They go through stages of their relationship from the first meeting until the death of the other one (in both narrations, the partner dies, once Sam, once Hailey). The narrated events mirror one another, in the relative position of the other narrative line. Both narrations are chronological in themselves, go forward in time, but are at the same time timeless, as the dates are separated by 100 years: Hailey begins her report on 22 November 1963, Sam on 22 November 1863 – and the protagonists do not get older. (These chronological inconsistencies are not further explained in the novel; readers are left in the dark how the protagonists can live a century apart and still be a couple.)

Only Revolutions confronts both its readers and critics with exceptional challenges. Scholars, for instance, have the task of citing the work correctly; giving the page number is not enough: Is it Sam's or Hailey's part, is it the main text or the marginalia? Bunia, for example, invents typographical abbreviations, writes S or H before the page number, and a superscript D behind it for the marginal texts. In the novel itself the page number is given in the middle of the outer margin of the page, in a coloured circle that, again, contains two little circles in brown and green with the corresponding page numbers for Hailey and Sam. It is a fact, though, that for scholars, accurate quoting, that is, referencing all signifiers correctly (with font, colour and layout) is practically impossible. If one wants to refer to *Only Revolutions* in an effective and applicable manner, one is either forced to simplify and reduce – if not ignore – visual and formal elements of the novel, or extensively describe them as in an ekphrasis.

Needless to say, *Only Revolutions* is a genuine product of script. If '*Graphic Novel*' as a genre-specific term was not occupied already, it would well fit here in its literal sense. We could say, instead, that it is a *Typo-Graphic Novel*. Jacques Derrida, in his article 'This is not an oral footnote' (1991), analysed the 'unspeakability' of genuinely written proceedings like annotations, and the same can be said about typography and textual architecture in general. *Only Revolutions* is not an oral story! All its aspects of heterogeneity and of polyphony are built on graphic dimensions of the printed page. *Only Revolutions* cannot be summarized, retold or performed, it can only be read – if reading is the correct term for this practice of visual perception. And one must flip through its pages. In Danielewski's case, the cultural technique of turning the page is not a necessary and rather mindless activity in order to read but is already a crucial part of the semantic reading itself, because the fact that one has to go back and forth in the chapters and therefore connect different parts of the text in a continuous act of patching pieces of information together generates meaning and nourishes the work of interpretation. Such a reading is very different from what we are conventionally used to doing, as it pays attention to the materiality of the book and the text *on* the pages; however, by overindulgence in the activity, one cannot fully read a semantically coherent text *and* immerse in it.

Conclusion

The three presented literary works engage in the practice and cultural technique of page-turning in strikingly different manners, but all three put an emphasis on the activity itself and mark the readers' option to use, abuse or deny it. In the case of Johnson's novel, the materiality of the leaves is more than evident. The reader is confronted with it before any semantic reading can begin. Johnson's choice of format and the open order makes clear that every reading is an act of assembling textual material at the same time, and, according to where the pages are situated in the individual row, creates a very different reading experience. Ayckbourn's plays operate on a similar basis: no flicking, no reading! Moving back and forth in the book is inevitable; choosing pages and reading paths is a necessity, not an option. In Danielewski's novel, finally, the double-sidedness of the book and the partition on each page reminds readers constantly of the mirrored text *not* read – meaning the 'twin' narration of the second protagonist, starting at the other end of the book and running straight through the halves of all pages. For a full semantic understanding, the reader has to have his/her finger on the other side and make the effort of turning the book regularly (after no more than eight pages at least, if not more often). It turns the practice of reading into a slow, physically tiring and difficult process that demands concentration and obliges the readers to deal with the book as an object rather than as a medium that contains a text.

Interestingly, contemporary works of fiction – such as the novels of Mark Z. Danielewski or B. S. Johnson – use aspects of digital text-processing on the level of structure, for example, infinite linking, open beginnings and endings, polyperspectivity and multiple authorship. They achieve this, though, on the level of mediality, exactly by exploring traditional elements associated with the materiality of the book, like page formatting, page numbers, orders of chapters and the fact that printed texts have – through fixed binding – definite and defined beginnings and endings, and therefore they require the technique of turning pages back and forth. Although structurally mirroring techniques of digital media (like hypertext and links), these texts reinforce the significance and potential of the very core techniques of paper-print media – a fact that renders them highly interesting in the context of a theoretical discussion on mediality, materiality and cultural techniques of contemporary literature. The virtual simultaneity of text as versions, comments, paratexts and so on that is hidden behind the screen in digital literature – as the web itself is not visible in its entirety – becomes exhibited in the print novel, where one cannot escape the material density and weight of the entire book. The simultaneity of storylines is realized and thus made visible in the material form, whereas in digital texts this dimension usually remains hidden from the readers, as they have no manual grip on the aforementioned haptic qualities and therefore cannot quite grasp them.

I do not believe the anxiety, uttered repeatedly during the first years of digital media – that with the rise of new technology print literature loses its power and its formal potential – was justified. I think the contrary is the case: The potential of digital literature comes fully into its own by the remediation into printed books. In turn, the intrinsic potential of the printed book is rendered visible by the existing digital possibilities. This is the real strength of texts on paper and a fruitful use of remediation, because it reflects on the materiality of the medium per se without being limited by its traditional usage. A page that denies its limits and transgresses its proper form is emphasizing even more that it *is* a page, and at the same time it dispenses with its rigorous definition. This is subversive as well as conservative. It conserves the format of the book, its very own material mediality, and it subverts the once defined and automatized pragmatics.

Another look into the contemporary toddler's toy box, with which this chapter began, shows a development towards the digital even at this young age: the baby books that we declared important for the acquisition of skills needed for dealing with objects made out of pages are now often accompanied and sometimes even substituted by items like simplified plastic imitations of smartphones and tablet computers. As necessary as it might be to teach young children the cultural techniques of scrolling and clicking, which they need to master ever sooner for operating tablets, phones, and personal computers, it is also highly reductive for their later understanding of reading and writing texts if none of the pleasures and possibilities of handling actual material pages enters their early activities.

Notes

1 For a first impression, see <https://biblioklept.org/2021/06/02/b-s-johnsons-the-unfortunates-book-in-a-box-acquired-2-june-2021/>. Accessed 30 September 2020.

2 In the German original: 'Die Erinnerung ist unter den nachgebenden Schichten nie vollständig, nie unversehrt, sie ist immer nur als beschriebene und überschriebene in Bruchstücken sichtbar' (Hermann 2002, 200–1).

3 B. S. Johnson had his predecessors and his successors: the French author Mark Saporta published a book in a box in 1962, called *Composition no. 1*, which was also translated into English and newly edited in 2011. The German author Francis Nenik followed the idea of Saporta and Johnson in 2012, with his novel *XO*, which can be read as a digital text as well as on paper, the printed text is sold in loose-leave form without pagination. The Georgian author Aka Morchiladze created another work of loose booklets with *Santa Esperanza* in 2004. It is a collection of sixteen leaflets (exercise books) in a felt sleeve, all about a fictive island, its history, geography and the stories of its people. Morchiladze, similar to Johnson, invites the reader to shuffle the units – but in an even more sophisticated way. He designed a full card game (fictitious as well, and part of the invented island's tradition), and the leaflets function like cards with different symbols and functions in rows of 8, 4 and 2. A similar idea, with lesser fragments, was realized by the Danish writer Svend Åge Madsen already in 1967 with *Tilføjelser* (additions), a collection of five exercise books in a box, titled 'Om sorg', 'Om lidt', 'Om tale', 'Om sig' and 'Om ikke' (about grief, about little, about speech, about self, about not).

4 The term '*forking path narration*' goes back to a short story by Jorge Luis Borges: 'El jardín de los senderos que se bifurcan' Borges (1944), in English translation 'The Garden of Forking Paths', in which the protagonist talks about a novel that contains all possible versions of a story in a paradigmatic outline. It was later coined by scholars to describe any kind of narrative (text as well as film or computer games) that splits up from one nodal scene into several proceeding options; repeating this operation, it renders the structure of a branching tree to the piece. See Meifert-Menhard (2013, especially 187–196); McHale (1989), especially 107–111; for film studies, cf. Bordwell 2002,

Bordwell 2014 and Schenk 2013. Two well-known examples are the films *Lola rennt* (BRD 1998, Tom Tykwer) and *Sliding Doors* (USA 1998, Peter Howitt); the first elaborates on three different outcomes, shown in consecutive order, of how a problem can be solved, the second alternates in short segments two bifurcating journeys through life after an initial scene with a decisive split. The novel from the Danish author Svend Åge Madsen, *Days with Diam* (Madsen (1994), takes Borges' suggestion seriously and realizes a 'many worlds' story', see Zubarik (2016)).

5 For a fundamental discussion on the differences between a rhizomatic and a branching system, see Deleuze and Guattari (1977).

6 I have discussed *House of Leaves* previously on another occasion: see Zubarik (2014).

7 I follow Bunia's main argumentation here and use some of his observations.

References

Ayckbourn, Alan. *Intimate Exchanges*. Vol. I and II. London: Samuel French, 1985.

Bordwell, David. 'Film Futures'. *SubStance* 31.1 (2002): 88–104.

Bordwell, David. 'What-if Movies: Forking Paths in the Drawing Room.' <http://www.davidbordwell.net/blog/2014/11/23/what-if-movies-forking-paths-in-the-drawing-room/> Accessed 30 September 2020.

Borges, Jorge Luis. *Ficciones*. Buenos Aires: Emecé, 1944.

Bunia, Remigius. 'Was vom Sichtbaren bleibt, ist Semantik. Über *Only Revolutions* von Mark Z. Danielewski.' *Den Rahmen sprengen. Anmerkungspraktiken in Literatur, Kunst und Film*. Eds. Bernhard Metz and Sabine Zubarik. Berlin: Kadmos, 2013. 406–27.

Coe, Jonathan. 'Introduction.' Brian Stanley Johnson. *The Unfortunates*. London: New Directions, 2007. v–xv.

Cortázar, Julio. *Rayuela*. Madrid: Cátedra, 1934.

Danielewski, Mark Z. *House of Leaves*. New York: Random House, 2000.

Danielewski, Mark Z. *Only Revolutions*. New York: Random House, 2006.

Deleuze, Gilles, and Felix Guattari. *Rhizom*. Trans. Dagmar Berger. Berlin: Merve, 1977.

Derrida, Jacques. 'This is Not an Oral Footnote.' *Annotation and Its Texts*. Ed. Stephen A. Barney. New York: Oxford University Press, 1991. 192–205.

Hermann, Iris. 'Aufblättern, Entblättern, Abblättern, Durchblättern. Psychoanalytische Verfahrensweisen betrachtet als Prozeduren der ästhetischen Produktion.' *Literatur als Blätterwerk. Perspektiven nichtlinearer Lektüre*. Eds. Jürgen Gunia and Iris Hermann. St. Ingbert: Röhrig, 2002. 183–203.

Johnson, Brian Stanley. *The Unfortunates*. London: New Directions, 2007.

Lola rennt. Dir. Tom Tykwer. X-Filme Creative Pool, 1998.

Madsen, Svend Åge. *Tilføjelser*. Kopenhagen: Gyldendal, 1967.

Madsen, Svend Åge. *Days with Diam – Or: Life at Night*. Norwich: Norvik, 1994.

McHale, Brian. *Postmodernist Fiction*. London/New York: Routledge, 1989.

Meifert-Menhard, Felicitas. *Playing the Text, Performing the Future: Future Narratives in Print and Digiture (Narrating Futures 2)*. Berlin and Boston: De Gruyter, 2013.
Morchiladze, Aka. *Santa Esperanza*. Zürich: Pendo, 2004.
Nenik, Francis. *XO*. Leipzig: ed.cetera, 2012.
Saporta, Marc. *Composition No. 1*. London: Visual Editions, 2011.
Schenk, Sabine. *Running and Clicking: Future Narrative in Film. (Narrating Futures 3)*. Berlin/Boston: De Gruyter, 2013.
Sliding Doors. Dir. Peter Howitt. Miramax, 1998.
Smoking/No Smoking. Dir. Alain Resnais. Studios 91 Arpajon, 1993.
Zubarik, Sabine. 'Figurale (Un)Möglichkeiten im Roman: Mark Z. Danielewskis *House of Leaves*.' *Fontes Litterarum*. Eds. Markus Polzer and Philipp Vanscheidt. Hildesheim: Georg Olms, 2014. 289–311.
Zubarik, Sabine. 'The Ethics of Time: Stasis and Dilation in Thomas Lehr's *42* and Svend Age Madsen's *Days with Diam*.' *Critical Time in Modern German Literature and Culture*. Ed. Dirk Göttsche. Frankfurt a.M.: Peter Lang, 2016. 271–84.

7

Craftsmen versus dandies

Designing the scene of reading through aestheticism and Arts & Crafts

Balazs Keresztes

Theory: Craft and design

Looking back at the tendencies that dominated the philosophical and theoretical landscape in the last century, one can claim that cultural studies at the turn of the millennium identified *language* as well as its conceptual companion, the *text*, as the main protagonists of the academic discourse. As a result, the main research object of cultural studies, that is, culture itself, was considered to be something textual in nature. Culture was primarily seen as a network of 'discursive signs and referents', accessible therefore mostly through a 'semiotic and structuralist' inquiry (see Krämer and Bredekamp 2013, 20–1). In other words, the main activity of the humanities, that is, the professional dealing with cultural artefacts, was identified as the extraction of meaning from beyond the surface (Gumbrecht 2003, 25).

According to a tendency that started in the 1980s, labelled 'material turn' or 'practical turn', the analytic gaze has now shifted from 'how to do things *with words*' to 'how to do *things with things*', or even just '*how to deal with things*'. This change in the academic fashion brought about interest in the non-semiotic, which nevertheless conditions meaning-production but demands an approach that is non-interpretive.[1] It is topical, we could argue, for the current academic discussion in the humanities to develop concepts that are suitable to describe acts, encounters and possible relations with the material world, in which both the non-interpretative approach and the material features and affordances of the examined object are taken into consideration. The concepts that this chapter proposes against this background are *craft* and *design*.

In his now classic 1991 article, Rüdiger Campe invoked and disentangled the various strands of meaning the word 'writing' held in the oeuvre of Roland Barthes.[2] As Campe clarified, the concept of writing and its subsequent inauguration to and apotheosis within the semiotic and post-structuralist discourse was rooted in its power to abolish the boundary between poetic and critical texts (namely, literature and criticism), as well as in its mediatory status which enables a specific text to be seen as a trace of writing which acts independently of a writing subject (see Campe 1991, 759).

Similarly, the evident potential of the terms 'craft' and 'design' is that they are able to negotiate transmissions between institutional subsystems, such as art and everyday life. Craft fulfils the same forms and functions in cooking, sewing and carpentry as in painting, writing and playing a musical instrument, for example. The proper adjustment to the material affordances as well as 'making things well' (Sennet 2008, 8) is not the prerogative of any field of expertise alone. Simultaneously, it is extremely difficult to differentiate in terms of design between artistic or everyday products. Both concepts, the one describing a corporeal engagement with a specific material, and the other denoting the layout of a given surface, seem to play a supplementary role: 'whereas craft is a supplemental of making, [design] is a supplemental of form' (Adamson 2007, 12), to quote Glenn Adamson's pertinent formulation.

Campe further developed his theory by placing writing itself into a network of non-scriptural actants, such as gestures, writing tools, and linguistic elements, laying the basis, one could argue, of a unique formation of actor-network theory. In this model, the various literary documents are conceived of as traces of unique constellations of these actants, latently exhibiting former *scenes of writing*. However, Campe remained within the radius of language; dismissing the 'evident framing of the scene' (1991, 761) to emphasize the 'lingual-gestural connection' (1991, 760), his formulation could not cover those acts that had not influenced the textual aspect of a given document. More recent contributions to this conceptual development have proposed a more 'object-oriented' approach, expanding the scope of inquiry to the non-scriptural elements as well (see Benne 2015, 45–153; 600–13). Simultaneously, the scene of writing was complemented with scenes of reading and objecthood (Benne 2015, 45–153; 600–13), as well as of editing (see Wirth 2004, 156–174), respectively.

This chapter relies on the theory of these scenes in a twofold manner. First, it uses them as sites of operation where the concepts of craft and design can unfold their potential: the scene of objecthood exhibits specific objects as the traces of craft and design practices. By concentrating on individual constellations of craft and design scenes, the terms could obtain their function through a 'test mode' operation. Second, this chapter uses the scenes structurally, in so far as it concentrates on two cases to unfold its argument. The first, a literary example, exhibits a scene where the practices of decoration are enacted, the second deals with a more concrete media event.

Context: Craftsmen and dandies

To anchor this theoretical (and experimental) investigation historically, these scenes are selected from the Victorian period, which not only witnessed a renaissance of the practices of decoration, but during which the concepts of craft and design emerged in the first place (see Adamson 2013).[3]

With the industrial means of production (of both literary documents and fabricated objects) growing and expanding rapidly, a divergent media process developed for which the individuality of a given object was fundamental. This individuality was to be obtained through the various practices of decoration, which affected fields from interior design to clothing of the human body. Not incidentally, this mediatory reorganization initiated one of the greatest periods in book design. Against the grain of the dominant form of serial publishing in periodicals as well as the emergence of technological media that defined the discourse network of 1900 (see Kittler 1990), the decorated book as an artefact exhibited its material properties openly. This meant that reading a decorated book relied as much on the readers' awareness of visual and tactile features of design as on their skills in decoding semiotic structures.

This cultural-mediatory context serves as a background for a comparison between the leading ideological positions concerning decoration: aestheticism and the Arts & Crafts movement. By analysing two scenes of reading (one from each movement), in which the actor-network relations concerning the handling of a decorated book are displayed, this chapter has a twofold aim: first, to reveal how the practices of decoration and literature are intertwined through craft and design, and second, to deconstruct the ideological opposition between the two movements by identifying their common origin in the realm of practice.

The scene of design: Huysmans|Wilde

6 April 1895, London, Cadogan Hotel. Oscar Wilde is arrested and taken into custody by the Scotland Yard 'on a charge of committing indecent acts'

(Hyde 1973, 153). Although this arrest and the subsequent trial had a strictly biographical aspect, books were involved in the incident as well. The fact that Wilde left the hotel with a yellow book in his hands got serious media attention. This yellow tome was misperceived as a volume of the decadent periodical *The Yellow Book*, which, as a consequence of its (albeit incorrect) association with Wilde, was no longer able to proceed with its publication. The yellow book in question turned out to be just a French decadent novel,[4] but its identity, both in the context of Wilde's biography and of the late Victorian literary scene, retained a highly mystified aura.[5] As it was not identified properly, the yellow book mobilized and intertwined fictional and factual references. Not only was it (mis)identified as the periodical, but it was also linked to the mysterious novel bound in yellow paper that was read and reread by the title character of *The Picture of Dorian Gray*. It also invoked Wilde's novel itself as it entered into a judicial discourse when the trial's cross-examiner forced Wilde to identify the fictional yellow book as Joris-Karl Huysmans's *À rebours* (1884), in order to morally discredit *Dorian Gray* and, ultimately, its author.

In this chapter, the connection between the two novels will not be retraced on the beaten tracks of literary historiography, however. Through a media-analytical gaze, these works – as confirmed masterpieces of the aestheticist|decadent canon – will be treated as documents that latently exhibit various practices of decoration, as well as the aestheticist|decadent ideology concerning these practices, which are exemplified by dandyism, interior design and reading performances.

Huysmans's *À rebours*, which served as a key source of inspiration for Wilde's novel in question, is often labelled as the breviary of decadence (see Cevasco 2001). It features only one character, the reclusive Jean Floressas Des Esseintes, who – for the entire novel – does not leave his villa situated on the outskirts of Paris. He spends his time decorating his eccentric home, where he collects exotic plants, jewels and artworks, samples peculiar perfumes and liquors and experiments with bookbinding and interior design.

Design becomes the novel's central motif as well as its poetic strategy on various levels. First, all of the protagonist's activities are motivated by the redesign of his material environment, as he adds an 'artistic stamp' or 'rare touch' to the objects he deals with (Huysmans 2009, 93). To acquire greater sensual pleasures, Des Esseintes mobilizes all the instruments of psychophysical stimulation: artificial lighting, air-conditioning and ambient noise. Design is identified with the addition of a substance which has no distinguishing characteristics in itself, and its presence is noticeable only on the object it adorns. This mediatory aspect is illustrated in the novel by lighting, tone, atmosphere, make-up or by the 'blends of alcohols and spirits', which are able to substitute for the real scent of a flower, as they 'usurp the very *personality* of the model, endowing it with that *elusive something*, that *extra quality*, that heady bouquet, *that rare touch*, which is the *stamp* of a work of art' (Huysmans 2009, 93; emphasis added, BK). Instead of the dualisms between real|fake or natural|artificial, what makes Huysmans's poetics of design interesting is the way the additional qualities alter the given object by bringing out its essential 'personality' (Huysmans 2009, 93). Here, Huysmans evokes Baudelaire's reflections on the art of cosmetics or *maquillage*. Baudelaire argues that the cultural practice of *maquillage* is based on the following principle: '*Nothing* embellishes *something*' (Baudelaire 1995, 31). Consequently, cosmetics are not there to turn ugly faces beautiful, since 'artifice cannot lend charm to ugliness and can only serve beauty'. In this way, the cultural practice of *maquillage* works as a 'seasoning' (*condiment*) (Baudelaire 1995, 30) or 'pedestal' (*piédestal*) (Baudelaire 1995, 36) for a beautiful face. Both terms evoke Jacques Derrida's concept of *supplementarity*, which is expressed in his theories about the frame or *parergon* (see Derrida 1987), as well as in his writings about *translation as seasoning* (see Derrida 2001, 195–200). Although framing and seasoning as design techniques are considered external elements or secondary qualities, they provide the conditions of possibility for something to be present or perceived in a particular space (see Böhme 1993, 121). Design as such makes it possible for something to be itself, to obtain its individuality.

This poetics of design gains relevance in at least three ways in Huysmans's novel: as a reflection on the individual personality of the decadent dandy; as a media-strategy behind the stimulating atmospheres in his interiors; and as a way the book and the act of reading is incorporated into and modelled by these media ecologies. Although one of the driving motives of Des Esseintes's eccentricity is to 'draw attention to himself [*se singulariser*]' through his refined taste and personality, this act of individuation is unveiled as a result of various design practices. While Baudelaire argued that dandyism 'does not even consist, as many thoughtless people seem to believe, in an immoderate taste for the toilet and material elegance', because '[f]or the perfect dandy these things are no more than symbols of his aristocratic superiority of mind' (Baudelaire 1995, 27), *Á rebours* seems to lean towards a more Carlyleian stance on this matter. Thomas Carlyle, in his satirical novel *Sartor Resartus*, which itself places the 'philosophy of clothes' (2008, 5–6) at the centre of its argument, provides a definition of dandies. A dandy is, as Carlyle writes,

> a Clothes-wearing Man, a Man whose trade, office and existence consists in the wearing of Clothes. Every faculty of his soul, spirit, purse and person is heroically consecrated to this one object, the wearing of Clothes wisely and well: so that as others dress to live, he lives to dress. (Carlyle 2008, 207)

While Baudelaire presents an argument that moves within the paradigm of expression, dematerializing clothes and exposing them as pure symbols of a hidden, interior soul, Carlyle – though satirically – deconstructs this personality and presents it as something which is enacted in the process of 'wearing' these material objects. If it is true that charisma, 'like a theatrical role', is something which is to be 'performed' (Horn 2011, 11), then the essence of dandyism is not to be found in mere objects alone, nor is it just a manifestation of some immaterial personality. As Barbey d'Aurevilly writes: 'It is not a suit of clothes walking about by itself! On the contrary, it is *the particular way of wearing these clothes* which constitutes Dandyism' (d'Aurevilly 1897, 18 – emphasis added). This performance-oriented description of dandyism is also present in Huysmans's novel. The very eccentricity, which enables him to set himself apart from society, is expressed in decorative performative acts which are related to the design of his environment in which he presents himself:

> And then, during that period when Des Esseintes had felt the need to draw attention to himself [il jugeait nécessaire de se singulariser], he had devised sumptuous, peculiar schemes of decoration [. . .] he had a high-ceilinged room prepared for the reception of his tradesmen; they would enter and seat themselves side by side in church stalls, and then he would climb up into an imposing pulpit and preach to them on dandyism [sur le sermon du dandysme], exhorting his bootmakers and tailors to comply in the most scrupulous manner with his briefs on the cut of his garments, and threatening them with pecuniary excommunication if they did not follow to the letter the instructions contained in his monitories and his bulls. (Huysmans 2009, 11)

His eccentricity is also manifested in his attire:

> He acquired a reputation for eccentricity, to which he gave the crowning touch by dressing in suits of white velvet and gold-embroidered waistcoats, with, in place of a cravat, a bunch of Parma violets set low in the open neck of the shirt. (Huysmans 2009, 11)

Although both segments are extremely hyperbolic, they present the enactment of the eccentric personality in relation to the material attributes of design. *Á rebours* does not state that personality is *expressed* symbolically in clothing, or that personality is something which is just a mere sum of the pieces of attire; it suggests that it comes into being at the meeting point of performance, dress and environment.

This self-identification of dandies is relevant because it sheds light on the similar performative logic of design operating in the interior spaces of *Á rebours*. One of the most famous passages in the novel is the description of Des Esseintes's eccentric dining room:

> [It] resembled a ship's cabin with its vaulted ceiling, its semicircular beams, its bulkheads and floorboards of pitch-pine, its tiny casement cut into the panelling like a porthole. Like those Japanese boxes which fit one inside the other, this room was inserted into another larger room, the actual dining-room built by the architect.
>
> The latter had two windows; one was now invisible, concealed by the bulkhead [. . .]; the other, directly opposite the porthole in the panelling, was visible but no longer served as a real window; in fact, a large aquarium filled all the space between the porthole and the genuine window, housed in the actual wall.
>
> Sometimes of an afternoon, when Des Esseintes happened to be up and about, he would set in operation the various pipes and ducts that permitted the aquarium to be emptied and refilled with clean water, and then pour in some drops of coloured essences, thus creating for himself, at his own pleasure, the various shades displayed by real rivers. [. . .] He would then imagine he was between-decks in a brig, and would watch with great interest as marvellous mechanical fish, driven by clockwork, swam past the porthole window and became entangled in imitation seaweed; or, while inhaling the smell of tar which had been pumped into the room before he came in, he would examine some coloured engravings hanging on the walls. (Huysmans 2009, 17–18)

Des Esseintes's dining room exploits both usages of the word 'cabin', as it formally simulates the cabin of a ship and simultaneously functions as a cabinet of curiosities. The randomly scattered nautical objects, such as 'chronometers and compasses, sextants and dividers, binoculars and maps' (Huysmans 2009, 17–18), and the media-effects of artificial lighting and air-conditioning both serve as design elements for a maritime illusion: 'In this manner, without ever leaving his home, he was able to enjoy the rapidly succeeding, indeed almost simultaneous, sensations of a long voyage' (Huysmans 2009, 18). Through the focalization of the narration, this illusion is assigned to the product of the human imagination and intellect:

> Besides, he considered travel to be pointless, believing that the imagination could easily compensate for the vulgar reality of actual experience. [. . .] By applying this devious kind of sophistry, this adroit duplicity, to the world of the intellect, there is no doubt that you can enjoy, just as easily as in the physical world, imaginary pleasures in every respect similar to the real ones. (Huysmans 2009, 19)

The irony of the novel, however, lies in the conflict between the protagonist's aesthetic ideology and the material environments he constructs and inhabits. The reason most critics received the novel as a break from nineteenth-century realism – seeing it as one of the first psychological novels to concentrate on a single character's phenomenology – is that they overlooked this irony. Such an 'immaterial' reading of the novel neglects the media constructions that enable the 'imaginary' hallucinations in the first place. Des Esseintes's clear distinction between 'the world of the intellect' and the 'physical world', or between 'actual experience' and 'imaginary pleasures' (Huysmans 2009, 19), is possible only because he claims to be able to observe the world from the outside, that is, to experience it as something meaningful. But just as his personality could only be performed *with* (and not *through*) his clothes, his imagination is no less dependent on his material surroundings. The spatial installation as a whole functions as a stimulating mechanism; it excites his senses, thus revealing the protagonist – who was thought to be occupied only by his dreams and fantasies – as an eminently physical being whose imagination is technically conditioned and psychosomatically enhanced.

This structure repeats itself in the way the novel presents Des Esseintes's books and the way he handles them. It is common to link aestheticism|decadence to a form of commodity fetishism, and in a first reading, the richly decorated volumes in Des Esseintes's possession seem to reinforce this approach. Books are part of his interior ('[a]s to furniture, [. . .] the only luxuries he intended to have in this room were rare books and flowers' (Huysmans 2009, 15)) and are interlinked with this interior through their material surface, as his walls are bound in the same 'heavy smooth Morocco leather' (Huysmans 2009, 14) as his books. Specific literary works function as part of the spatial installation and vice versa, such as in the case of the only book exhibited in his dining cabin, 'bound in sealskin, *The Adventures of Arthur Gordon Pym*, printed specially for him on pure linen-laid paper, selected by hand, bearing a seagull as its watermark' (Huysmans 2009, 18).

In scenes like this, the above-mentioned poetics of design, which were exemplified in connection with dandyism and interiors, is now associated with the act of reading itself. Although the materiality of the book, in the discourse network of Romanticism, served as hindrance to the imagination, *Á rebours* presents it as a key factor contributing to the scene of reading. Just as the personality or charisma of a dandy is enacted in relation to his clothes, or a hallucinatory atmosphere is conditioned by the sensuous stimuli of the media-technological environment, the decadent scene of reading is conditioned by the design techniques of the book as an object. As the materiality of the book obtains agency, the physical interaction between the book and the body of the decadent reader is emphasized: after taking a richly ornamented volume containing Baudelaire's poems, and '[c]aressing it with reverent fingers and rereading certain pieces', he finds them to be 'in this simple but incomparable format [*cadre*] [. . .] more than usually profound' (Huysmans 2009, 117).

Essential to the decadent scene of reading is the non-interpretative relation towards the book as an object in and of itself. Instead of turning these design elements into meaningful signs or symbols, that is, consigning them to the 'world of the intellect', these scenes allude to the atmospheric potential of design:

> [H]e had devised sumptuous, peculiar schemes of decoration, dividing his salon into a series of variously carpeted alcoves, which could be related by subtle analogies, by indeterminate correlations of tone, either cheerful or gloomy, delicate or flamboyant, to the character of the Latin and French works he loved. He would then settle himself in that alcove whose furnishings seemed to him to correspond most closely to the essential nature of the work which the whim of the moment induced him to read. (Huysmans 2009, 11)

Given that the atmospheric effect is conditioned by the material environment and the book as an object and given that these are actants interlinked through design on several levels, the act of reading is exhibited as a corporeal activity, where the sensual experience (mood) is the result of a practical engagement with the book in a specific space. Although the book, after the dissemination of print, had been heralded as an eminently mobile object usable independent of its environment, the aestheticist|decadent reading scene reveals, by displaying the material reality connecting book and space, that there is always a latent atmospheric effect that comes into being at the meeting point of these two. The scene of reading can therefore be acted and re-enacted within different spaces holding different atmospheric potentials.

'Acting' and 're-enacting' will become the central terms used to describe the primal scene of aestheticist|decadent reading which occurs at the encounter of the two main canonical novels of decadence, *Á rebours* and *The Picture of Dorian Gray*. This interaction (and subsequent influence) is itself enacted, as both books are embedded in the practices of decoration. This is how Wilde describes the novel Dorian encounters:

> For years, Dorian Gray could not free himself from the influence of this book. Or perhaps it would be more accurate to say that he never sought to free himself from it. He procured from Paris no less than nine large-paper copies of the first edition, and had them bound in different colours, so that they might suit his various moods and the changing fancies of a nature over which he seemed, at times, to have almost entirely lost control. The hero, the wonderful young Parisian in whom the romantic and the scientific temperaments were so strangely blended, became to him a kind of prefiguring type of himself. And, indeed, the whole book seemed to him to contain the story of his own life, written before he had lived it. (Wilde 2007, 105)

By binding the various editions in different colours, Dorian re-enacts the design practices exhibited in *Á rebours*, redesigning *Á rebours* itself. Similar to the French novel, where the scenes of reading were conditioned by the material environment as well as the stimulating effects of the book artefact, and composed for an eminently sensual experience, Dorian continuously redesigns each scene of reading to generate new reading experiences. Just as Des Esseintes had to choose the proper room to stimulate a psychophysical hallucination, Dorian applies several formats (or one could say, exhibitionary frameworks, media ecologies) to a specific literary work.

Regarding the practical handling of the book, as well as the corporeal aspect of reading, there are two conclusions to be formulated. First, what *Á rebours* expresses inherently (veiled by the ironic conflict between the protagonist and the narrator) is addressed directly in Wilde's novel: if we also consider the material aspects of the book and not just its interpretable textual layer, then there is another dimension that we could call the *presence* of the book (see Gumbrecht 2003). This presence, which exists on a different level than the meaning of the text, influences this meaning fundamentally, as it is channelled through the various design techniques. The decadent scene of reading, which makes these design techniques overflow, aims at a purely sensual reading experience. While this was already expressed in the psychosomatic stimulations of Des Esseintes, Wilde connects it to the act of reading, too. For the decadents, reading, that is, reading while handling (or 'caressing' in the case of Des Esseintes) a book 'in exquisite raiment', brings about the experience of specific *moods*. These moods, which are fundamentally corporeal experiences (see Gumbrecht 2011, 11–13; 24), were the reason Des Esseintes constructed his installations in the first place: to experience the atmospheres of a long sea voyage or a monastery, or as Wilde writes, 'to *realize* in the nineteenth century all the passions and modes of thought that belonged to every century except his own, and to sum up, as it were, in himself the various *moods* through which the world-spirit had ever passed' (Wilde 2007, 104 – emphasis added, BK). Instead of interpreting the past, that is, instead of transforming it into knowledge in a semiotic manner, the practices of decoration enable the decadents to simulate it for a corporeal encounter. Just as Des Esseintes strove to stimulate his moods through the design of his environment, Dorian bound these books 'to suit his various moods and the changing fancies'.

Second, if the scene of reading is a network of various material actors, including environment, design and atmosphere, then the term 'influence' has to be interpreted differently. Dorian's account seems to suggest that the French novel's influence on him was hermeneutical in origin, as the French hero served as a 'prefiguring type of himself'. Similar to Lord Henry's influence on Dorian, the readers in this case are influenced by the 'voice' of the author, with whom they enter into a dialogue. But this Romantic model is undermined here. The 'voice' and 'author', central concepts of the Romantic discourse network, function only through the repression of the material reality of the book as an object as well as the physical reality of the reader's body. What happens here is clearly a different case: through the practices of decoration, the scene of reading is presented as a fundamentally physical activity, where reading itself turns into a scene of editing, or, rather, a *scene of design*. Instead of the influence manifested in the *Horizontverschmelzung* of two spirits or intellects, this influence is to be described by the term 're-enactment'. Just as Dorian Gray was influenced by 'putting into practice' Lord Henry's aphorisms (Wilde 2007, 43), and as the young dandies imitated Dorian's clothing, gestures and speech, Dorian can only see a 'prefiguring type of himself' in the French hero when he re-enacts the various practices (collecting jewels, experimenting with clothing, listening to exotic music) and redesigns the scene of reading itself.

One could say that Dorian personalizes the novel by assimilating it to his moods and fancies. But instead of the duality of this model, the scene of reading is presented through disseminated actants of material: what Dorian is able to do with the book depends on institutional systems and design techniques that underline the whole scene of reading in the first place, that is, the volumes are 'procured from Paris' (just as Huysmans's novel is imported into the text) and even the work of binding is outsourced.

Just as the personality of the dandy, this 'clothes wearing m[a]n' was exhibited as the intersection of various techniques of self-fashioning, such as dress, behaviour and gestures, the various 'literary works' are reverse-engineered into unique design scenes, intertwining binding, paper and decoration to form a specific media ecology.

The scene of craft: Chaucer|Morris

While the dandy Oscar Wilde spent his time in 1895 in the courtroom on account of these ill-omened yellow books, the leading figure of the Arts & Crafts Movement, William Morris, was preoccupied with another volume. After publishing more than fifty richly decorated, carefully edited books, the Kelmscott Press began to finalize the Chaucer edition, which is known today as the Kelmscott Chaucer.

The Kelmscott Chaucer is often positioned as the culminating achievement of the Gothic Revival. The book was adorned by Morris with lavish border ornamentation, contained eighty-seven woodcut drawings by Edward Burne-Jones and was printed on vellum with high-quality ink from Italy. Morris even had to design new typefaces for this new edition, as the former ones used in the Kelmscott Press (Golden, Troy) were too big for a two-column edition (see Peterson 1991, 240). Emblematic, this newly designed font was named after Morris's beloved author: Chaucer. Although the binding of the previous Kelmscott editions were considered less refined than the other aspects, such as type and border, in the case of the Kelmscott Chaucer an improvement in this area has taken place. It is telling that Oscar Wilde himself wrote a letter to Morris praising his achievements and suggesting that they should concentrate on the bindings as well. Regarding the binding, the Kelmscott Chaucer was available in two editions, bound either in full or half pigskin, all designed by Morris. The book was the culmination of both the Kelmscott Press and the lifelong collaboration between Morris and Burne-Jones. After its publication, Burne-Jones referred to it as a 'pocket-cathedral' (Peterson 1982, xvi). The cathedral is a telling comparison, indeed, as it was the central model for art in Morris's oeuvre. In the following we will see in what sense the Kelmscott Chaucer encapsulates the Arts & Crafts position within the late Victorian discourse of decoration.

Following the argument that John Ruskin presented in his three-volume architectural treatise, *The Stones of Venice*, especially in its chapter entitled 'The Nature of Gothic', gothic architecture functions as the ideal form of building in Morris's work. In some of his lectures, Morris made it clear that 'by modern art I do not mean the art of the Victorian era' (Morris 1914, 206). What he referred to as 'modern' was the Gothic, although he added that 'you may call it Gothic art if you will, little as the Goths dealt with it' (Morris 1914, 230).

This evaluation was not based on stylistic criteria, as Morris opposed the 'pedantic' (Morris 1914, 299) focus on style only. For Morris, regarding architecture only in terms of the abstract characteristics of style is a fundamentally flawed approach, as it is based only on derived and abstracted knowledge. In Morris's thought, this kind of approach was replaced by two other lines of inquiry: the first concentrated on the organization of the working process, the second on the affordability of building materials.

Even for Ruskin, the gothic cathedral stood for a mode of building in which the distinction between designer and workman remains undefinable. The construction of gothic cathedrals, a process that lasted hundreds of years, should not be seen as the work of a single architect or author,[6] but as the result of a working process that was essentially cooperative. Ruskin and Morris imagined the gothic building process, which operated within a guild structure, to be a preceding state of the division of labour. As Ruskin pointedly stated, 'it is not the labour which is divided; but the men' (Ruskin 1853, 165). Infused with the naivety of Victorian medievalism as well as proto-socialist thought, the building process of the gothic cathedral was imagined as a collaboration between equals: instead of one architect, the various guilds (specializing in stonemasonry, woodcarving, stained-glass, etc.) complemented each other to achieve a common goal. Apart from the social aspects of this ideology, it had one main systemic significance as well: it was based on the objection to the principle that 'one man's thoughts can be, or ought to be, executed by another man's hands' (Ruskin 1853, 169).

Morris went even further in the sense that he introduced a third element: the role of the building material. As style is seen as the abstracted quality that enables the transition from mind to hand (making imitation and restoration possible), Morris strove to reveal that the material lies behind the style itself: '[W]e are in a period when style is a desideratum which everybody is seeking for, and which very few people find; and it seems to me that nothing is more likely to lead to a really living style than the consideration, first of all, as a sine qua non, of the suitable use of material.' (1914, 391) For Morris, to abolish the distinction between designer and builder (i.e. mind and hand), the practical handling of the material, namely craft must be considered as well:

> In fact, I do not see how we are to have anything but perpetual imitation, eclectic imitation of this, that, and the other style in the past, unless we begin with considering what material lies about us, and how we are to use it, and the way to build it up in such a form as will really put us in the position of being architects, alive and practising to-day, and not merely architects handing over to a builder and to builder's men all the difficulties of the profession, and only keeping for ourselves that part of it which can be learnt in a mechanical and rule-of-thumb way. (1914, 391–2)

Simultaneously, Morris argues, the study of architecture should be based on the consideration of material as well. In a public lecture that was supposed to be about different styles, he decided to concentrate exclusively on stone, wood and brick, instead (1914, 392). Instead of a hermeneutics of 'reading architecture', Morris advocated an archaeology of building materials. This way, he was able to formulate an architectural history neither inflected by the concentration on authorship nor open to misinterpretation:

> You look in your *history-books* to see who built Westminster Abbey, who built St. Sophia at Constantinople, and they tell you Henry III., Justinian the Emperor. Did they? or, rather, men like you and me, handicraftsmen, who have left *no names* behind them, nothing *but their work*? (Morris, 1914, 7; emphasis added, BK)

This material approach is inherent in the way Morris dealt with books, or rather, this material approach is conditioned by the specific artefacts Morris dealt with. When referring to the 'ideal book', Morris usually had the medieval ornamented and illuminated manuscripts or gothic woodcut books in mind. These formats belonged to different media ecologies, and by eminently displaying their material reality, they encumbered a hermeneutic interpretation that was characteristic of the discourse network in Victorian Britain. The medieval manuscripts were the products of various scriptural and design practices: they were lavishly ornamented and illustrated, commented, the writing itself being continuously scratched off and rewritten, as the vellum and parchment itself as a surface was constantly reused. In a sense, these books shared features with the gothic cathedrals: they were the product of cooperative labour between illuminators and scribes, of whom most were illiterate. These anonymous craftsmen of the medieval manuscripts did not leave behind their names, but their work. And this work as a material remnant of the past not only communicates (least of all in the form of a single authorial voice) but also exists as a crafted and designed object. This object, in turn, requires an approach that does not try to ignore this fact through immaterializing acts of communication. Morris's 'object-oriented' reading practice is expressed in passages like the following:

> For a short period at the end of this and the beginning of the next century many copies of the Apocalypse were produced, illustrated copiously with pictures, which give us examples of serious Gothic design at its best, and seem to show us what wall-pictures of the period might have been in the North of Europe. (Morris 1982, 12)

By concentrating on the ornamental aspect of the book, Morris was able to reconstruct, or at least experience, the material reality of the medieval 'designed universe' (Baudrillard 1981, 201). Instead of hallucinating some Romantic authorial voice, the craftsman-reader encounters the ornamentation of medieval walls alluded to by the book ornamentation, thus demonstrating one of the classic theses of media theory: the medium is the message.

Even in the rare cases that Morris seems to evoke the reading routine of the Romantic discourse network, he undermines it with a materialist twist:

> The Clerk of Oxenford if he took up one of his 'Twentie bookes clad in black and red;' the fellow of the college, when with careful ceremony he took the volume from the chest of books which held the common stock of literature; the Scholar of the early Renaissance when he sold his best coat to buy the beworshipped classic new-printed by Vindelin or Jenson, each of these was dealing with a palpable work of art, a comely body fit for the *habitation* of the dead man who was speaking to them: the craftsman, scribe, limner, printer who had produced it had worked on it directly as an artist, not turned it out as a machine or a tradesman. (Morris 1982, 2; emphasis added, BK)

Although an authorial voice seems to be heard here, this author, this 'dead man', is not revived through some prosopopoeia provided by the reader's voice. This dead man is kept alive by the 'craftsman, scribe, limner and printer', who had produced a 'palpable work of art' in which he not only rests as a corpse but which he also *inhabits*. The crafted and designed materiality of the book is what provides the conditions for the author to speak at all. Life is provided by its 'natural environment', that is, the presentational mechanism of its original medium, the 'palpable object', which must be handled 'with careful ceremony'.

The Kelmscott Chaucer reflects the practices of decoration that Morris had come to know thoroughly as both a medievalist and an archaeologist, as well as a practitioner of the decorative arts. To reread Chaucer in the 1890s meant that a fitting 'comely body' must be produced for his work in order to provide a 'habitation' for the dead author. As a craftsman, Morris understood that in order to reread a medieval work from the manuscript network it is necessary to re-enact the specific scenes of reading in which it was originally embedded. This was not a nostalgic imitation of styles, though; rather, it meant that if a book were to be 'architecturally good' (Morris 1982, 67), it must consider the 'suitable material' as well as the re-enactment of the cooperative working system.

The Kelmscott Chaucer became a monument for the Arts & Crafts scene of reading: its creation incorporated the revival of various techniques, such as hand-printing, gothic typeface and rich floral ornamentation, as well as suitable materials such as full pigskin, quality vellum and ink. It was a result of the joint work of Morris, who designed the border ornaments, the typefaces and the layout, of Burne-Jones as illustrator and several other craftsmen. If there is a voice to be heard while reading the Kelmscott edition, it is certainly that of Chaucer, but it can be heard only because of the collaboration of these craftsmen. At the same time, this book serves as an example of serious Arts & Crafts design at its best.

Media ecology of craft and design

The examples of Huysmans and Wilde, on the one hand, and Morris, on the other hand, have demonstrated how the practices of craft and design are deployed as essential aspects of the scene of reading in the Victorian period. As a result, in both aestheticism and Arts & Crafts, the scene of reading can only be conceived of as a scene of objecthood. Despite the ideological differences between the two movements, which were expressed in manifestos that occupied text-oriented scholarship, their craft and design practices, latently exhibited even in their literary and artistic legacy, are able to bridge these differences.

In both scenes described previously, the book as a designed and decorated material object serves as a scene where the various forms of craft and design intersect, and which is in itself embedded in a wider scene of design. Reading these books, that is, engaging with the past they represent, requires a fundamentally practical and physical gesture from the reader. This gesture goes beyond the revivification of the author through a semiotic interpretation: it is the necessary corporeal re-enactment of the former media ecology through the practices of craft and design.

Since these 'eccentric' examples of reading are exhibited by the most prominent representatives of aestheticism and Arts & Crafts from the late nineteenth century, one could easily argue that their media-consciousness is no less prevalent than ours at the turn of the millennium. The interest in media ecology, namely the interest in the media, practices and cultural techniques underlying our most mundane gestures (i.e. reading), emerged only after these started to alter rapidly. In this sense, we, the media theorists of literature, have much to learn from these craftsmen and dandies who seem to resemble much more than they differ from each other.

Notes

1 See also the chapter by Sabine Zubarik in this volume.

2 For an assessment of Roland Barthes's role in the theoretical development of a media ecology of literature, see Christoph Reinfandt in this volume.

3 This term originates in the title of Nicholas Frankel's forthcoming book, *The Discourse of Decoration: Design and Visual Mediation in Victorian Britain.*

4 Its title was *Aphrodite* and it had been written by Pierre Louys, a friend of Wilde (see Hyde 1973, 154).

5 The fact that French decadent novels used to be bound in yellow paper made the colour yellow be associated with decadence as such. *The Yellow Book* itself adjusted its media profile to this fashion.

6 Except, of course, for Goethe, who, by praising Erwin von Steinbach, the 'Baumeister' of the Strasbourg Cathedral as a creative genius, retrofitted the concept of the Romantic author into the Middle Ages.

References

Adamson, Glenn. *Thinking Through Craft*. London: Berg, 2007.

Adamson, Glenn. *The Invention of Craft*. London: Bloomsbury, 2013.

Baudelaire, Charles. *The Painter of Modern Life and Other Essays*. Ed. Jonathan Mayne. London and New York: Phaidon, 1995.

Baudrillard, Jean: 'Design and Environment.' *For a Critique of the Political Economy of the Sign*. Trans. and ed. Charles Levin. St. Louis, MO: Telos, 1981. 185–203.

Benne, Christian. *Die Erfindung des Manuskripts*. Frankfurt a.M.: Suhrkamp, 2015.

Böhme, Gernot. 'Atmosphere as the Fundamental Concept of a New Aesthetics.' *Thesis Eleven* 36 (1993): 113–26.

Campe, Rüdiger. 'Die Schreibszene: Schreiben.' *Paradoxien, Dissonanzen, Zusammenbrüche: Situationen offener Epistemologie*. Eds. Hans Ulrich Gumbrecht and K. Ludwig Pfeiffer. Frankfurt a.M.: Suhrkamp, 1991. 759–72.

Carlyle, Thomas. *Sartor Resartus*. Eds. Kerry McSweeney and Peter Sabor. Oxford: Oxford University Press, 2008.
Cevasco, G. A. *The Breviary of Decadence: J.-K. Huysmans's À Rebours and English Literature*. New York: AMS Press, 2001.
d'Aurevilly, Barbey. *Of Dandyism and of George Bummel*. Trans. Douglas Ainslie. Boston, MA: Copeland & Day, 1897.
Derrida, Jacques. *The Truth in Painting*. Trans. Geoff Bennington and Ian McLeod. Chicago, IL: Chicago University Press, 1987.
Derrida, Jacques. 'What Is a "Relevant" Translation?' Trans. Lawrence Venuti. *Critical Inquiry* 27.2 (2001): 195–200.
Gumbrecht, Hans Ulrich. *The Production of Presence: What Meaning Cannot Convey*. Stanford, CA: Stanford University Press, 2003.
Gumbrecht, Hans Ulrich. *Stimmungen lesen*. München: Hanser, 2011.
Horn, Eva. 'Introduction.' *New German Critique* 38.3 (2011): 1–16.
Huysmans, Joris-Karl. *Against Nature*. Trans. Margaret Mauldon. Oxford and New York: Oxford University Press, 2009.
Hyde, Harford Montgomery. *The Trials of Oscar Wilde*. New York: Dover, 1973.
Kittler, Friedrich. *Discourse Networks 1800/1900*. Trans. Michael Metteer. Stanford, CA: Stanford University Press, 1990.
Krämer, Sybille, and Horst Bredekemp. 'Culture, Technology, Cultural Techniques: Moving Beyond Text.' *Theory, Culture, Society* 30.6 (2013): 20–9.
Morris, William. *The Collected Works. Vol. 22: Hopes and Fears for Art*. Ed. May Morris. London: Longmans, 1914.
Morris, William. *The Ideal Book: Lectures on the Arts of the Book*. Ed. William S. Peterson. London and Berkeley: California University Press, 1982.
Peterson, William S. 'Introduction.' William Morris. *The Ideal Book: Lectures on the Arts of the Book*. Ed. William S. Peterson. London and Berkeley: California University Press, 1982. xi–xxxviii.
Peterson, William S. *The Kelmscott Press: A History of William Morris's Typographical Adventure*. Oxford: Clarendon, 1991.
Ruskin, John. *The Stones of Venice. Vol. 2. The Nature of Gothic*. Chicago and New York: Belford & Clarke, 1853.
Sennett, Richard. *The Craftsman*. New Haven, CT: Yale University Press, 2008.
Wilde, Oscar. *The Picture of Dorian Gray*. Ed. Michael Patrick Gillespie. New York and London: Norton, 2007.
Wirth, Uwe. 'Die Schreib-Szene als Editions-Szene: Handschrift und Buchdruck in Jean Pauls Leben Fibels.' *'Mir ekelt vor diesem tintenklecksenden Säkulum:' Schreibszenen im Zeitalter der Manuskripte*. Ed. Martin Stingelin. München: Fink, 2004. 156–74.

PART III

Digital | Spaces | Platforms

The third section addresses the most recent development that currently leads to a fundamental paradigm shift in the media ecology of literature: digitization. While the contributions to Parts I and II examined semiotic and processual negotiations of theoretical aspects of the media ecology of literature as well as the aesthetic and praxeological dimensions of the materiality of literature in historical perspective, the digital revolution has changed the materiality of the literary medium as such. This revolution has had an enormous impact not only on the form of literature, but also on the modes of its production, distribution and reception. Together, the three chapters assembled here propose a re-negotiation of literature in the wake of the digitization of all forms of mediation. Earlier media-ecological entanglements that centred around, for instance, print and paper, are now being subsumed and redefined by virtual ones: the computer, the internet of things and video games, to name but a few.

The section opens with Zita Farkas's chapter 'Remediations of canonized literary texts in the digital space', which examines the transformations classic texts undergo when adapted to a digital medium in order to unfold the characteristics of the newly created literary digital texts and to analyze the similarities and differences of these textualities. By investigating the transformations of canonized literary texts into digitalized multimedia textualities within the contemporary literary media ecology, the chapter reflects upon how the new medium affects several important literary concepts such as the reading process, authorship and reception. The chapter highlights the different application strategies by presenting two iPad apps: the *iPoe* Collection by Play Creatividad is a selection of Edgar Allan Poe's stories combining text with soundtrack and images that operates as a transmedia narrative. *The Waste Land* by Faber Touch Press, however, is an iPad app that works as a paratextual hypertext, as T. S. Eliot's poem is surrounded by a web of interactive features including Fiona Shaw's performance, readings and the original manuscript as well as a selection of photographs and images related to the poem.

In 'Reading listening interfaces', Birgitte Stougaard Pedersen focuses on the transformation of cultural practices connected to the technological changes and their impact on the concept of literature and the book as a medium. What happens to our conceptions of reading when the technological and medial shapes of the book change? As a result of a general mediatization of our everyday practices, reading seems to be reshaped as a multimodal, sensory and aesthetic practice. It is for this reason that her chapter addresses the need to reconfigure the concept of reading in terms of interactive and intersensory axes including both listening and new kinds of tactility and visuality – a new media ecology of contemporary literature manifesting itself by means of digital platforms like smartphones, iPads or Kindles.

The section concludes with an analysis of 'Reading player one' by Sebastian Domsch. The chapter asks for the ways that games – in general and in the form of video games – relate to and have an influence on literature. After looking at playfulness within the field of literature in general, it focuses on the newly emerging genre of the 'gamic novel', and discusses two examples, Ernest Cline's *Ready Player One* (2011) and Cory Doctorow's *For the Win* (2010). Domsch claims that literature is inherently playful, firstly because both games and literature are self-referential in the sense that they are not primarily about something else but about themselves, and secondly because players of a game understand and accept the rules of the game in a way that is analogous to the way that readers of fiction understand and accept fictional propositions. Literature explored the possibilities of that inherent playfulness to an increasing degree from the Enlightenment through romanticism all the way into postmodernism. The most recent development in the convergence of games and literature is a group of novels that take video games not only as their central topic, but also as a structural frame and as a guiding metaphor. These novels are about specific video games, yet but they are also about how games and game-like virtual environments structure our own ways of sense-making, and about the (geek) culture that goes along with games.

8

Remediations of canonized literary texts in the digital space

From paratextuality to hypermedia[1]

Zita Farkas

This 'tangled web of medial ecology'

Within the area of Digital Humanities, the attention attributed to literature focuses either on the new possibilities offered by cyberspace to disseminate canonized texts or on the analysis and interpretations of electronic and 'ergodic literature' (Aarseth 1996),[2] that is, on texts such as hypertext and cybertext written and composed for and by the digital environment. The internet with its vast space stores the reproductions of the majority of canonized literary works, thus offering a wide variety of resources. According to Stephanie Browner et al. (2000), it generates and sustains a 'sense of canonicity [. . .] so exploded' (171), that it can no longer be encompassed by any physical library or archive. It also facilitates interdisciplinary approaches to literature as the materials necessary for such a research trajectory, 'that could once be only laboriously and expensively assembled' (Browner et al. 2000), are readily available through internet sites. George P. Landow (1997), an advocate of cyberspace, considers computer technology to have a beneficial effect upon the 'old-fashioned job of traditional scholarly editing [. . .] at a time when the very notion of such single, unitary, univocal texts may be changing or disappearing' (24). Furthermore, as demonstrated by Peter L. Shillingsburg in his thorough examination of an electronic infrastructure of textual scholarship, 'electronic editions are now the only practical medium for major projects' (2006, 82). Due to their technological systems, electronic versions are 'open-ended' and offer users 'the practical power to select the text or texts most appropriate for their own work' (2006, 82). The assembly of digital and non-digital virtually establishes, in the words of N. Katherine Hayles, a 'tangled web of medial ecology' (2002, 33). Thus, the theory of media ecology provides the wider framework for the following analysis of the electronic infrastructure of literature in the twenty-first century in this chapter.

All these digital activities – the storage of canonical texts in cyberspace, the enhancing of interdisciplinary literature research through hyperlinks and the performance of electronic textual scholarship – have as their primary material the printed text that is simply reproduced on the screens of digital devices. Transported to a new medium, the printed text, a product of print technology, is subjected to a remediation as it is incorporated into the digital environment. Thus, the web constituting literature's media ecology fundamentally changes. The materiality of the printed text is dissolved in the digital space, appearing as an image on the screen, a reproduction of the original. As indicated by Jay David Bolter and Richard Grusin, the integration of old technologies into new media is at the core of cultural productions:

> No medium today, and certainly no single media event, seems to do its cultural work in isolation from other media, any more than it works in isolation from other social and economic forces. What is new about new media comes from the particular ways in which they refashion older media and the ways in which older media refashion themselves to answer challenges of new media. (1999, 15)

The medium of literature and literary performance as a cultural event are thus transformed and remodelled by the amalgam of old (printing) and new media. However, in some cases, this refashioning of printed texts exceeds their simple reproduction on screens, their mere re-creation in a different medium. Many literary applications for tablets, for example, consist of adaptations of canonical literary texts such as T. S Eliot's *The Waste Land* or Mary Shelley's *Frankenstein* to new media. These literary texts, originally produced with the use of ink and paper and then disseminated for centuries with the help of printing technology, are refashioned as digital texts.

Elaborating on the metaphor of 'refashioning', we can observe that the fabric, the texture of the old material, influences the design of the new garment as its materiality affects the types of stitching and sewing that can be performed. Excited by the new medium of storytelling, Janet H. Murray

(1997) specifies that cyberspace opens up new possibilities for narratives. The kaleidoscopic structure generated by computers has 'the ability to present simultaneous actions in multiple ways' (157). While in a novel 'simultaneous actions are presented consecutively' (157) due to the linearity of the printed text, '[o]n the computer we can lay out all the simultaneous actions in one grid and then allow the interactor to navigate among them' (157). Murray's differentiation between the applicable narrative trajectories for novels and on computer screens illustrates that the materiality of these products prescribes and requires distinct stitching. However, what happens when the novel (the once printed text) is transposed onto the computer screen and is refashioned to operate as a digital text? How does this change in medium alter the textuality of literary works? Literary applications of canonized works offer the possibility to investigate these questions by examining the different ways printed literary works are refashioned to appear on the screens of tablets. Their analyses show the interconnections between the two mediums and demonstrate their effects upon each other.

Literary criticism and analysis of electronic literature focuses on works that have been produced for and by digital technology. The discussion revolving around the operations produced by the digital media such as hypertexts, cybertexts and ergodic texts induces a media-specific analysis as it 'pays attention to the material apparatus producing the literary work as physical artefact' (Hayles 2002, 29). Literary interpretations deciphering the meaning of the digital text generally become entangled with the text's technology, as its meaning is bound to hyperlinks, navigation and interface(s) created by the software. N. Katherine Hayles (2002) considers that this heightened interest in the 'inscription technologies' of the electronic texts has altered the field of literary criticism '[l]ulled into somnolence by five hundred years of print' (29) as 'digital media have given us an opportunity we have not had for the last several hundred years: the chance to see print with new eyes' (33). Thus, the attention paid to the 'inscription technologies' of electronic literature started to shape the trends of literary criticism as it has heightened our perception towards the materiality of the literary work – be that on screen or on paper.

The continuous comparison of the two mediums ensnared them into a binary opposition, highlighting 'what difference the materiality of the medium makes' (Hayles 2002, 30). However, their connection goes beyond a mere opposition as they have been moulding each other by borrowing literary structures and techniques, provided their mediums can reproduce and integrate them. For example, the first generation of hypertexts[3] highly resembled print literature because, Hayles argues, 'they operated by replacing one screen of text with another, much as a book goes from one page to another' (2002, 37). The second generation, due to advances in computer hardware and software, worked with navigation systems that allowed not only to turn the pages on screen, that is, to move from one lexia[4] to another, but also to navigate between image and text, and 'the text and the computer producing it' (39). This advancement[5] in computer technology can be construed as a step towards a wider gap between print and electronic literature. While digital hypertext shifted away from printed texts, some novels in print started playing with digital hypertextual elements/icons. John Barth's *Coming Soon!!!* and Don DeLillo's *Underworld*, for example, incorporate electronic hypertextual elements by using 'visual indicators of hypertextual links' (30). While both mediums have their own specificities, in this 'tangled web of medial ecology' (33), the changes induced by machines writing electronic literature effect new works in printed literature, whereas the styles of the printed medium still reverberate in electronic texts.

From book to book-app, from page to touchscreen

The interferences between the two mediums, digital and print literature, not only influence the stylistic structure of literary texts but also affect the format and the materiality of the book. The book, primarily the physical manifestation of printed texts, has undergone major changes in the digital space by turning into e-books and book apps. E-books are merely reproductions of printed texts on the screen, as they do not change the text of the 'original' book. The enclosed documents of e-books, similar to printed texts, consist of words flowing continuously from one page to another. The difference lies in the materiality of the e-book as the words flicker on the screens of laptops, tablets or e-readers instead of paper. Book apps of classical literature, on the other hand, not only change the form of the book, but also transform its textuality in the process of adaptation of the literary work to the digital medium. As they make their transition from print to interactive media through multiple sensory and semiotic channels, the medium-specificity of these types of book apps plays an important role in their adaptation. Since, as Linda Hutcheon argues, 'it is when adaptations make the move across modes of engagement and thus across media [. . .] that they find themselves most enmeshed in the intricacies of the medium-specificity debates' (2006, 35).

Major publishers such as Cambridge University Press, Faber & Faber and Random House Group ventured, in order to keep up with the market's pressure and the shift towards digital reading, into the field of digital publishing by establishing affiliations with app developers or created their own digital publication departments. Random House Group, for instance, recreated Anthony Burgess's most famous novel, *A Clockwork Orange*, as an app (2013). This edition presents the text of the novel embedded into an array of additional materials that create a fully tagged network of texts, video and audio resources. The reader can delve into the world of the novel by listening to the author and Burgess experts discussing and commenting on every aspect of the book. One can also use it as an audiobook by activating Tom Hollander's synchronized reading of the text. Furthermore, the app incorporates the novel's textual scholarship as it presents not only 'the restored edition of the text, freshly edited and introduced by Andrew Biswell, Anthony Burgess's biographer' but also 'the previously unpublished full original 1961 typescript, replete with annotations, illustrations and musical scores' (Anon. n.y., n.p.).

Comparable to the structure of the *A Clockwork Orange* app, Penguin Books digitalized yet another iconic novel, Jack Kerouac's *On the Road* (2013). The reader can navigate among a myriad of different materials connected to the novel from family photographs of the author, audio clips, documentary footage, reviews or a detailed biography of Kerouac's life to an interactive map of the trips described in the book. The app also includes several components that reveal the editorial work shaping this novel. Encompassing reproductions of the first draft with corrections made by the author and his editors, editorial documents from the archives of the novel's publisher and the comparison of the first draft and the final text displaying the changes, the differences between the two texts engage the reader with the textual scholarship of this literary work.

In 2012, Cambridge University Press launched its *Explore Shakespeare* interactive app series 'bringing *Romeo and Juliet* and *Macbeth* to life on iPad', (n.p.) followed by the *Twelfth Night* and *A Midsummer's Night Dream* in 2013. The *Sonnets* (2015) were moulded into an app by Touchpress in collaboration with Faber & Faber. Their partnership led to the publication of the following literary works as book apps: Seamus Heaney's *Five Fables* (2014), Iain Pears's *Arcadia* (2015) and Michael Morpurgo's *War Horse* (2014). Their most successful app, however, was T. S Eliot's *The Waste Land* (2015). This app, a prospering investment for the publisher as it started to make profits after only six weeks of its launch, demonstrated that there is a market for book apps. Stuart Dredge (2011) in his review of the app for *The Guardian* considered that '*The Waste Land* and other apps have proved that book apps can be innovative, but proving also that they can be profitable will draw attention throughout the industry' (n. p.). Moreover, this example also indicates most importantly that the difficulty of a text does not hinder the transformation of a literary work into an engaging and entertaining app.

In an attempt to adapt another important piece of twentieth-century modernist literature, Robert Berry, a graphic artist, transformed two episodes, 'Telemachus' and 'Calypso' from James Joyce's *Ulysses* into a digital comic adaptation. *Ulysses 'Seen'* (2011), as the titles suggest, visualizes Joyce's first and fourth episodes by turning them into graphic stories. A combination of images and text, each page/lexia has links to 'Reader's Guide', where one can find further information on each scene, and to a discussion forum where readers can leave their remarks and interact with each other. The app is the inaugural project of Throwaway Horse, a 'company devoted to fostering understanding of public domain literary masterworks by joining the visual aid of the graphic novel with the explicatory aid of the internet' (Anon. 2016). Adhering to the concept, the company also created *The Waste Land 'Seen'* app (2012), in which Martin Rowson envisions the poem as a film noir murder mystery graphic novel. Similar to *Ulysses 'Seen'*, there is a second layer behind the main text to be opened by tapping on the screen. The signpost icon 'Behind the Seen Reader' activates an array of visual materials, literary allusions and historical resources compiled by the scholar Mike Barsanti. Readers can also engage in in-app discussions with each other or with the authors themselves. While Touchpress and Faber & Faber's *The Waste Land* app leaves the original text intact, the *The Waste Land 'Seen'* app dismantles the source text and transforms it into a completely new literary work fashioned in the garments of another genre, a murder mystery graphic novel in film noir style. Similar liberties are taken by Ryan North who turns Shakespeare's famous tragedy *Hamlet* into an entertaining gamebook. The user of the app *To Be or Not to Be* (2015) creates her/his version of the story by enacting one of the characters, Ophelia, Hamlet or Hamlet Sr.

The major common characteristic of the following set of book apps is their genre – they belong to popular culture ranging from gothic to detective fiction. Edgar Allan Poe's gruesome characters, Mary Shelley's monster, Bram Stoker's vampire and Arthur Conan Doyle's detective have all come alive on the touchscreen. The iPoe Macabre collection, consisting of three apps, was created by Play Creatividad. This interactive and illustrated Edgar Allan Poe collection is part of a larger project, the iClassics by the same company. Besides Poe's horror stories, Play Creatividad has also developed the digital adaptations of Charles Dickens's ghost stories, *iDickens*, and H. P. Lovecraft's bizarre science fiction, *iLovecraft*. All these book apps recreate the scary and ghoulish world of these literary fictions by combining the main text with eerie music, neo-gothic drawings and animation. These elements aim to enhance the sensations of horror and fear in the reader. The interactive components of the apps further heighten this reading experience. For example, in one of the stories from the first iPoe app, *The Tell-Tale Heart*, bloody fingerprints appear by tapping on the screen or the reader can splash blood around the page by dismembering an anatomical sketch of a human body with several swipes across the screen.

In the case of Dave Morris's *Frankenstein* app (2012), the reconstruction of a dismembered body constitutes the driving mechanism of the app's structure as the sewing together of the monster's body is turned into the metaphor of reading. The readers create their own version of *Frankenstein* as they stitch together the textual body of Mary Shelley's novel. The app's opening sentence, 'I begin the creation of a human being', which is also the first moment of the reader's immersion into the text, aligns the forming of 'a human being' with the production of the novel through the process of reading. Several pieces of texts headed by a single sentence appear on the screen and the readers have to choose one to open and connect it to the main text. The readers have to make these choices continuously throughout the whole reading process. Thus, each reading can create a new version of the novel the readers can then compare to the original text, as the uncut version is also included in the app's extra section. The app also uses visual material, reproductions of 'painstakingly-detailed pictures of dissections and cross-sections of the human body' (Morris 2012, n.p.) from anatomical books from the sixteenth to the nineteenth centuries to enhance a sense of macabre beauty. These drawings, however, function only as a background to the text, since the interactive feature of this app, unlike the one used in the iPoe apps, focuses primarily on the interconnectivity between reader and text, and not on the playful tactile engagement of visual materials.

Interactive storytelling is also the key feature of several book apps based on Arthur Conan Doyle's *Sherlock Holmes* series and Bram Stoker's *Dracula*.[6] *Dracula: The Official Stoker Family Edition* (2010) published by PadWorx Digital Media – similarly to *Dracula's Guest: An Interactive Classic* (2013) published by dCipollo Designs – is an interactive book-app version of the classic vampire story combining the text of the novel with a whole range of other media functions: images, animations, music and film. *Sherlock Holmes for the iPad* by Gutenbergz presents five short stories, mixing the texts with music and artwork. *Sherlock: Interactive Adventure* by HAAB recreates only one story, 'The Adventure of the Red-Headed League'. Besides, it includes new components such as the search mode or 3-D-animated plot-based scenes. The search mode activated by zooming in on drawings identifies the readers with the famous detective. In this mode the users occupy the position of the main character as they search for clues and evidence to be stored in the collection section where one can view them again from all angles and read additional information about them. The 3-D feature also adds to the interactivity of this book-app as the pictures above the text can be rotated creating the illusion that one is walking around a room or walking down a street. Furthermore, it can multiply the points of view of the readers since they are able to shift from one character's position to another's with a full rotation.

Typology of book apps: Paratextuality and hypermedia

All the presented book apps share one major feature: they are all adaptations of canonized literary works. They repackage these writings into new digital book formats. This transformation, however, requires the conversion of the printed text to the structures of the digital medium. Thus, an analysis of the different types of these book apps focusing on the treatment of the printed text illustrates how the digital shapes the medium of printed literature. The examination of distinct digital features of these book apps aims 'to explore how media specific possibilities and constraints shape the text' (Hayles 2002, 31).

Based on this shaping of the text, these book apps can be divided into two major groups. Book apps such as *A Clockwork Orange*, *On the Road*, the *Explore Shakespeare* collection and *The Waste Land* by Touchpress build an extensive paratextual web around the primary text whereas book apps such as the *iClassics* collection by Play Creatividad, *Dracula: The Official Stoker Family Edition* (2010) or *Sherlock: Interactive Adventure* by HAAB, transform the original text into a hypermedia narrative. The first type of book-app reproduces the original text, embedded in a network of cultural and historical information, while the second type of book-app infuses the adapted literary work with music, pictures or, for purposes of interactivity, animated drawings that can be activated by swiping the screen. Thus, the major difference between the two models of book apps lies in their dissimilar methods of integrating the original text into the app. However, a more in-depth analysis of the functionalities of the text in these book apps is required to unravel the remediation of print, of canonized texts within the digital. Hence, I will examine the specific technologies and material structures of one book-app from each group, *The Waste Land* app and the *iPoe* app, more closely in order to observe the role of the printed text and whether in this process of digitalization print is reproduced or transformed into digital narrative texts. What kind of digital and print dialectic drives these book apps?

The diversity of digital narratives generated by the prolific and rapid technological changes within the digital sphere created a very abundant terminology within the field of digital literary criticism. Electronic or ergodic literary works can be classified as hypertexts, hypermedia narratives (Ensslin 2007), cybertexts (Aarseth 1996) or kinetic digital narratives (Eskelinen 2012). Each definition presents complex literary theoretical issues. For example, Espen Aarseth (1996) defines cybertext as 'the wide range (or perspective) of possible textualities seen as a typology of machines' (24). He develops a textual typology that, according to Markku Eskelinen (2012), 'made the crucial move away from media essentialism to functional differences among the wide variety of literary media' (20). Cybertextuality is assigned as based on the functionalities of the text, the text operating as a machine, and not on the basis that it was made by and for a digital machine. However, Ennslin's (2007) inclusion of the term in her diachronic presentation of 'hypertextal developments' (19) designates the term to machine-generated texts. In comparison to first-generation hypertexts and second-generation hypermedia, third-generation cybertexts are 'text machines' that are 'literally "writing themselves" rather than presenting themselves as an existing textual product' (22). In her analysis of several cybertexts, Ensslin highlights as cybertextual feature the inability of the reader/user to control the text. The electronic work contains built-in programmes that diminish interactivity by expropriating the power of the reader over the reading process. For example, Jacques Servin's BEAST has a programme that 'determines the speed at which lexias will be imposed on each other' and 'exposes [the readers] to continuously transforming, interacting semiotic systems' (Ensslin 2007, 108). The text, indeed, behaves as a machine.

The distinctions presented by Ensslin between these three types of hypertexts offer a framework to consider the digital characteristics of book apps. While the cybertext's main aspect is its 'machine' feature, the first-generation hypertext is defined by its network of links – how one lexia is linked to another. Hypermedia predominantly refers to the integration of other semiotic systems into the scripted text. These can be visual elements such as photographs, drawings, animation or performances, and audio elements such as music, different noises or the audio recording of the text. Since hypertext also contains various semiotic systems, the distinction lies in the method of integration and interactions among these elements.

While hypertextuality and hypermedia are related to both groups of book apps, none of them behave like cybertexts. The readers are in full control over the reading process. However, uncontrollable elements surface occasionally in hypermedia book apps. For example, *The Oval Portrait* included in the first volume of the iPoe collection opens with a lexia that consists of text imposed on a full-page still drawing. Though the text does not suggest that the story takes place during the wintertime, the small white dots falling down on the screen imply otherwise. This snowing is generated automatically and cannot be stopped. Besides its intractability, this small visual addition expands the opening of the story by adding information that is not within the text. It does not simply mirror or reproduce the meaning of the text, but it enriches it as the readers will automatically associate winter with the short story even though this is not within the writing.

These kinds of automatic media additions to the text, however, are very rare as the adaptations are dominated by drawings used as a visual background to the text or as a means of highlighting certain parts. Some of the drawings can be activated by swiping the touchscreen. These interactive components contribute to a reading experience that engages various senses. Reading becomes a multisensory process during which the reader has to negotiate visual with auditory and haptic effects. Auditory elements such as music or sound effects, similarly to drawings, function either as a backdrop setting establishing the general mood for the short story or as an intensifying component by reproducing particular noises. In case of *The Oval Portrait*, the reader can listen to a song throughout the whole story whereas the auditory parts of another short story included in the same iPoe app, *The Tell-Tale Heart*, consists of eerie music interrupted by sudden sound effects. The screen reflecting only the question 'Who's there?' is accompanied by a deep sigh and heavy breathing. The unbearably slow passing of time is intensified by the sound of a ticking wall clock. The page ending with the highlighted sentence 'but the noise steadily increased' is supplemented with a thumping sound as if the killed man were knocking on a wall. The story ends with the killer holding in his hand the victim's heart. On the last screen of this short story, the readers can see and hear an anatomic drawing of a beating heart.

Visual and auditory segments are also included in *The Waste Land* app that represents a model for paratextual book apps. In its menu the app lists the following sections: 'Poem, the full published text of The Waste Land (1922)'; 'Perspectives, commentary on the poem and on Eliot from a range of interesting people'; 'Manuscript, a facsimile of Eliot's original manuscript with handwritten edits by Ezra Pound'; 'Notes, annotations and references explaining the text of the poem'; 'Performance, a specially filmed performance of the entire poem by Fiona Shaw'; 'Readings, hear the poem spoken aloud by different voices including Eliot himself'; and 'Gallery, a selection of photographs and images related to the poem'. All this material supplements the readers with additional information about the poem. The collected interpretations and discussions of the poem and Eliot's work in the segment 'Perspectives' incite a particular reception, directing the reading of the text towards certain parts or specified issues. For example, in their respective interpretations, Seamus Heaney focuses on the end of 'The Fire Sermon' and 'Death by Water', and Fiona Shaw discusses the meaning of 'A Game of Chess', whereas Craig Raine, 'one of the world's leading experts on T.S. Eliot', analyses his favourite part, 'What the Thunder Said'. The various issues addressed in these interviews with academic and contemporary writers, such as 'Eliot and illness', 'Elliot's legacy', 'The original title of *The Waste Land*', 'Impact on audience', '*The Waste Land*'s lyrical qualities', 'Bob Dylan and Eliot', 'Is Eliot difficult?' or 'Why *The Waste Land* is unique' delineate the topics to be addressed when discussing this great modernist poem. The many literary and cultural allusions of the poem are presented to the reader in the 'Notes'-section. In order to enhance the close reading and the hypertextuality of the text, the caption of each note is linked to the part of the text it explains. These notes can be extended with readers' own thoughts and comments in 'My Notes'. Thus, the readers can add their own personal interpretation of the poem to the app.

The text of the poem is at the centre of the application as it is reproduced in each section except the gallery that consists only of visual materials. However, all the other links include the printed text of the poem. It is evident that the 'Poem', 'Manuscript', and 'Notes' sections would require the reproduction of the text. However, even the performative and auditory parts incorporate the text into their lexias. For example, while watching Fiona Shaw's performance, the screen is divided into two parts. In the top part, Shaw recites the poem in a desolate bleak room warmed by the roaring fire of an open fireplace. The lines uttered by Shaw are highlighted in the text in blue. The screen of 'Perspectives' is separated into four parts. In the upper part, there are three boxes. The interview is complemented by a short biography of the commentator and next to it on the right side, there is the selection of interviews to be opened with a tap on the screen. Underneath all these elements, the bottom part of the screen shows the text of the poem. The readings of the poem by various people such as T. S. Eliot (1933, 1947) himself, Alec Guinness, Ted Hughes, Jeremy Irons and Eileen Atkins, Viggo Mortensen and Fiona Shaw are also accompanied by the text. The text follows the recitations as the narrated lines change colour.

The text is always there, suggesting that the materiality of the poem, its printed medium, is fundamental to this book-app. However, besides the continuous reproduction of the written poem throughout the various sections of the app, the textuality of this literary work is accentuated by the addition of various manuscripts with edits. The book-app replicates not only the final product, the published version of the text, but it also presents the development of the text, the process of writing. Textual scholarship is a fundamental part of paratextual book apps that create a mini library centred around the canonized text. As maintained previously in this chapter, book apps such as Anthony Burgess's *Clockwork Orange*, Jack Kerouac's *On the Road*, William Shakespeare's *Sonnets*, and T. S. Eliot's *The Waste Land*, all value manuscripts since they occupy a large section of the app. Besides demonstrating the process of writing formed by edits, erasures and rewritings, these manuscripts also illustrate the varied formats of print. The facsimiles of the 1609 Quarto, the first published edition of the *Sonnets*; of Eliot's manuscript with handwritten edits by Ezra Pound or of Burgess's typescript from 1961, all present different versions of print. They exemplify that 'print is not a monolithic or universal term but a word designating many different types of media formats and literary practices' (Bolter and Grusin, 1999, xiii).

Conclusion

In this chapter I analysed the media ecology of canonical literary works with a particular focus on book apps. The methods of including the original text in the book apps defines the digital and print dialectic. This dialectic is constructed differently in the case of paratextual and hypermedia book apps. Whereas *The Waste Land* app reproduces the text without any modifications, apps such as iPoe adapt the text to the digital by mixing it with other semiotic systems such as 'graphics, digitized speech, audio files, pictographic and photographic images, animation and film' (Ensslin 2007, 21) in order to create a unified entertainment experience. This entertaining character of hypermedia book apps might be related to the genres of the canonized texts as most of these novels belong to genres that are recognized as popular culture such as detective, vampire, gothic and horror stories. Hutcheon (2006) considers that 'interactive storytelling', '[t]his carefully designed electronic staging is best for adapting certain kinds of narrative structures and therefore genres, namely those of thrillers, detective stories, and documentaries' (52). Thus, the distinct dialectic of print and digital is a reflection and reiteration of the hierarchy within a literary canon. Most of the works marked by the term 'high literature' such as *The Waste Land*, Shakespeare's plays and sonnets, Joyce's *Ulysses,* Burgess's *Clockwork Orange* or Kerouac's *On the Road* are adapted as paratextual book apps, whereas works belonging to popular culture such as *Dracula*, *Frankenstein* and *Sherlock Holmes* together with Charles Dickens's ghost stories, Edgar Allan Poe's and H. P. Lovecraft's horror stories receive the hypermedia treatment. However, there are transgressions. Ryan North envisions the tragedy *Hamlet* as an entertaining book game in which the players create their own version of Ophelia, the tormented Danish prince, or the ghost of the father. Difficult modernist literary works such as *Ulysses* and *The Waste Land* are transfigured into digital comic books by Robert Berry in *Ulysses 'Seen'* and by Martin Ronson in *The Waste Land 'Seen'*. These adaptations modify the materiality of the literary works by telling the stories through pictorial instead of textual narrative.

The remediation of canonized literary works within the digital space transposes the 'old' medium of print into a new medium. The analysis of book apps based on classical texts offers the possibility to examine the modalities of remediation. Since these literary works are the creations of print, the examination of their adaptations to the digital unfolds the dynamics between printed text and digital elements. An overview of the different types of adaptations showed that there are mainly two types of book apps: paratextual and hypermedia book apps. The difference between them lies in the ways they insert the text of the literary work into the digital medium. Paratextual book apps are constructed around the primary text that is reproduced intact and in various print formats. Textuality becomes the centre of these book apps, since textual scholarship is one of their key components. Hypermedia book apps, on the other hand, playfully mix text with visual, auditory and haptic elements transforming the reading process into a multisensory experience. Textuality is dispersed and sometimes even obstructed by a variety of semiotic systems.

Notes

1 A shortened hypertext version of this article was published in the e-journal *Alluvium* under the title 'Books and Digital Textuality' (2017).

2 On ergodic literature, see also Sebastian Domsch in this volume.

3 In the case of first-generation hypertexts, Hayles (2002) refers to Michael Joyce's *Afternoon, a story* created in Storyspace in 1987 and published by Eastgate Systems in 1999. Astrid Ensslin (2007) composes a more extensive list of first-generation hypertexts enumerating the following works besides Joyce's *Afternoon, A Story*: Stuart Moulthrop (1991) *Victory Garden*, Carolyn Guyer (1993) *Quibbling*, Jane Yellowlees Douglas (1994) *I Have Said Nothing*, Shelley Jackson (1995) *Patchwork Girl, or a Modern Monster*, Charles Deemer (1996) *The Last Song of Violeta Parra*, Geoff Ryman (1996) *253*, Bill Bly (1997) *We Descend* and Richard Holeton (2001) *Figurski at Findhorn on Acid*. However, Ensslin's categorization differs from Hayles's. While Hayles considers Jackson's *Patchwork Girl, or a Modern Monster* a second-generation hypertext, Ensslin includes it as first generation since in her terminology the second-generation operate as hypermedia texts. Still both base their categorization on the operational techniques these texts can perform, demonstrating again the importance of technological inscriptions for electronic literature.

4 Hayles (2002) defines lexia as 'one screen of text' (27).

5 Ironically, the rapid developments in computing technology pose the biggest threat to electronic literature as these advancements kill the programmes that operate the 'old' digital texts making it difficult to preserve those texts whose software becomes obsolete. To some extent this preservation issue also impacts the canonization of digital texts. It might be that electronic texts die even before having the chance to be included into a/the literary canon, a process that happens over a longer period of time.

6 These two popular literary texts are the source of many apps. However, most of these apps are game apps and not book apps. Game apps are inspired by the stories and the characters of the literary work but they do not reproduce or reshape the original text. For example, many Sherlock Holmes game apps such as *Detective Sherlock Holmes* (2015) by Crisp App or *Sherlock: the Network HD* (2015), the official apps based on the TV series, invite the user to play the famous detective or another character in the story. Throughout the game, the player has to solve different little puzzles in order to gather the clues that unmask the murderer.

References

Aarseth, Espen J. *Cybertexts: Perspectives on Ergodic Literature*. Cambridge, MA: Johns Hopkins University Press, 1996.

Anon. *Dracula: The Official Stoker Family Edition*. PadWorx Digital Media, 2010.

Anon. *Sherlock Holmes for the iPad*. Gutenberg, 2012.

Anon. *Dracula's Guest: An Interactive Classic*. dCipollo Designs, 2013.

Anon. *Sherlock: Interactive Adventure*. HAAB, 2015.

Anon. 'Robert Berry'. 2016. <http://www.stoneyroadpress.com/artists/robert-berry/>. Accessed 28 October 2021.

Anon. 'App Advice: *A Clockwork Orange*.' <https://appadvice.com/app/a-clockwork-orange/562227691>. Accessed 27 October 2021.

Berry, Robert. *Ulysses 'Seen'*. Throwaway Horse, 2011.

Bolter, Jay David, and Richard Grusin. *Remediation: Understanding New Media*. Cambridge, MA: MIT Press, 1999.

Browner, Stephanie, Stephen Pulsford and Richard Sears. *Literature and the Internet: A Guide for Students, Teachers, and Scholars*. London: Garland, 2000.

Burgess, Anthony. *A Clockwork Orange*. New York: Random House Group, 2013.

Dredge, Stuart. 'The Waste Land iPad Earns Back Its Costs in Six Weeks on the App Store.' *The Guardian*. 8 August 2011 <http://www.theguardian.com/technology/appsblog/2011/aug/08/ipad-the-waste-land-app>. Accessed 28 October 2021.

Eliot, T. S. *The Waste Land*. Touchpress, 2015.

Ensslin, Astrid. *Canonizing Hypertext: Explorations and Constructions*. London: Continuum, 2007.

Eskelinen, Markku. *Cybertext Poetics: The Critical Landscape of New Media Literary Theory*. London: Continuum, 2012.

Farkas, Zita. 'Book Apps and Digital Textuality.' *Alluvium* 6.2 (2017). <https://doi.org/10.7766/alluvium.v6.2.01>. Accessed 28 October 2021.

Hayles, N. Katherine. *Writing Machines*. Cambridge, MA: MIT Press, 2002.

Heaney, Seamus. *Five Fables*. Touchpress, 2014.

Hutcheon, Linda. *A Theory of Adaptation*. London: Routledge, 2006.

Kerouac, Jack. *On the Road*. London: Penguin, 2013.

Landow, George P. *Hypertext 2.0: The Convergence of Contemporary Critical Theory and Technology*. Baltimore, MD: Johns Hopkins University Press, 1997.

Morpurgo, Michael. *War Horse*. Touchpress, 2014.

Morris, Dave. *Frankenstein*. Inkle, 2012.

Murray, Janet H. *Hamlet on the Holodeck: The Future of Narrative in Cyberspace*. Cambridge, MA: MIT Press, 1997.

North, Ryan. *To Be or Not to Be: That Is The Adventure*. Tin Man Games, 2015.

Pears, Ian. *Arcadia*. Touchstone, 2015.

Ronson, Martin. *The Waste Land 'Seen'*. Throwaway Horse, 2012.

Shakespeare, William. *Sonnets*. Touchpress, 2015.

Shillingsburg, Peter L. *From Gutenberg to Google: Electronic Representations of Literary Texts*. Cambridge: Cambridge University Press, 2006.

9

Reading listening interfaces

Reconfiguring reading in the age of digital platforms

Birgitte Stougaard Pedersen

Introduction

Over the last decades developments in media and digitization have created new conditions for the book as a medium as well as for literature as an institution. These changes and the new interplay between literature and media have several consequences for the semantic, material, user and institutional levels. In turn, these shifts have created a need for new institutional and economic models and they call for new methods for analysing literature that are able to combine different research fields.

While the act of reading or discussions of reading interfaces seem crucial for the research field investigating mediatization (Hjarvard 2013), they are somewhat underexposed. What happens to our conceptions of reading when the technological and medial forms of the book change? Due to a general mediatization of everyday practices, reading seems to have been reshaped and become multimodal on new terms, changing the sensory and aesthetic aspect of reading practices. Consequently, this chapter addresses the need for reconfiguring the concept of reading (Stougaard Pedersen et al. 2021).

Consider first *The Fault in Our Stars* by John Green (2012), a best-selling young adult novel, which is available in a series of formats – printed book, e-book, audiobook and possibly a combination – each of which provides a different experience of the book. One can also choose to watch the 2014 film adaptation directed by Josh Boone. These different formats can be framed as instances of 'remediation' (defined as the representation of one medium, for example, the printed book, through another medium, for example, the audiobook), to use a term by Bolter and Grusin (1999). However, this chapter will argue that the act of remediation may not wholly cover the situation of the book in the contemporary publishing landscape, where different formats are published simultaneously. In Kittlerian terms, the different formats represent a transposition which, in fact, produces a new medial embeddedness. In *Discourse Networks 1800/1900*, Kittler writes on the matter of untranslatability and the transposition of media:

> A medium is a medium is a medium. Therefore it cannot be translated. To transfer messages from one medium to another always involves reshaping them to conform to new standards and materials. In a discourse network that requires an 'awareness of the abysses which divide the one order of sense experience from the other', transposition necessarily takes the place of translation. (1990, 265)

Thus, the different formats – e-book, audiobook, printed book – differ in various respects. They differ on a technological basis, on an aesthetic/sensory basis as well as on a sociological user-oriented basis, and the interplay between these three components creates specific reading situations. Together, they create a very specific media ecology. This chapter will reflect on these format-related differences.

The semiotic format – the reader as an active principle *of* the text

In classical textual analysis the concept of the reader represents an internal phenomenon reflected by the text itself. However, conceptions of reading and of the reader today may to a larger extent also need to reflect on the medium and the concrete use of the text. For instance, when we listen to a text, that is, read it with the ears instead of the eyes, the position of the reader *in* the text changes.

In *The Implied Reader* (1978), Wolfgang Iser, developing a theory of aesthetic response, examines what happens during the reading process. According to Iser, the reading process consists of a chain of events that depend both on the text and on the exercise of certain faculties of the reader:

> [Texts] not only draw the reader into the action, but also lead him to shade in the many outlines suggested by the given situations, so that these take on a reality of their own. But as the reader's imagination animates

> these 'outlines', they in turn will influence the effect of the written part of the text. Thus begins a whole dynamic process: the written text imposes certain limits on its unwritten implication in order [. . .], but at the same time these implications, worked out by the reader's imagination, set the given situation against a background which endows it with far greater significance than it might have seemed to possess on its own. (276)

Iser's concept of the reader to a large extent belongs to the text itself, as a structural implied reader position. In the case of *The Fault in Our Stars* these aspects could, for instance, deal with the following:

- The style of language: what type of implied reader is the novel addressing? Considering its hip, angry and funny tone, the implied author seems to appeal to a young audience.
- The theme: through the theme of the novel – children suffering from cancer – the reader is invited to engage in a strong emphatic relation. Although this could easily lead to a quite sentimental relation, such rhetoric is prevented by the text itself, which is both thematically and stylistically unsentimental. The narrator suffers from terminal cancer, but although her reflections on the disease play a major role in the novel, the main focus is on her love affair with Augustus (who also suffers from cancer) and their common fascination for the novel *Imperial Affliction* by the imaginary author Peter Van Houten. They both want to meet the author, and this wish plays a large part in bringing the young lovers together. The blanks of the novel or the questions that drive the plot forward concern, for instance, the conditions of the main characters: Will Hazel Grace live or die? Will Augustus Waters live or die? And will they ever meet the author of the novel that has helped shape the identity of Hazel? The novel in the novel is also about a girl suffering from cancer, thus creating a metareflective level.

Semiotic and material formats

When digital platforms such as smartphones or tablets change the way we deal with texts, not only the implicit reader, but also the position of the explicit reader shifts, and new reading interfaces emerge, reflecting the concrete technological and sensory reading situation and the new terms of reading: reading on a smartphone or tablet, we are able to switch between different reading interfaces, using various modalities, for instance, children's apps, newspapers (sound and print simultaneously), e-books (combined with an audiobook), different kinds of text formats, pictures or podcasts. Such a plurality of formats, emerging from the same technological media, creates new multimodal spaces of perception, which change the act of reading itself. Based on the idea that materiality and medium matter, pointing to concrete reading practices underlines the need for reconfiguring reading itself along new interactive and intersensory axes, including listening (audiobooks, apps) and new forms of interactivity, tactility and visuality (apps). The modal act of reading may affect the semiotic aspect of reading.

Different reading interfaces should be analysed as different concretizations, in both a technological and a modal sense, interfaces that will be positioned in between the concept of convergence and media sensitivity. Literature is available to us in a plurality of modalities. We have described this as the simultaneity of different formats, which no longer stem from or are adapted from the book as the primary medium, but are developed as parallel, yet distinct formats. This signals convergence. On the contrary, the formats become distinct in the sense that each – the printed, audiobook and app versions – offers different affordances. Each format creates a transmedial space of perception, yet these spaces are distinct on the sensory level:

- *Apps* are characterized by touchscreens, and the media utilize predefined multi-touch finger gestures like tapping, pressing and scrolling – which together convey an aesthetics of tactility.
- Listening to the *audiobook* version of *The Fault in Our Stars* read by Kate Rudd also reveals a series of different affordances: this is a sound recording of a book performed by a professional narrator, an actor; it could also have been read by the author. In addition, there are technical aspects to audiobooks, which must be taken into consideration in the analysis: how do we access the novel – through a mobile device, streaming or downloading? Eventually, the sensorial situation must also be considered: what do we do while reading? And how does the reading affect our experience of time and space (see Have and Stougaard Pedersen 2016)?

Reading activity – deep and surface

In the age of digital platforms, the centre of reading activity is shifting from unilateral perceptual reading shaped by the book as the agenda-setting medium towards new types of interactive reading, which involve more sensory dimensions and modes of reading: the tactile, the acoustic, the visual. This transformation calls for a reconfiguration of the concept of reading – understood as a basic cultural skill for the acquisition, dissemination and implementation of knowledge – a reconfiguration that is in tune with the dominant media development in the knowledge-based society and holds the potential for creating a new understanding of the relation between reading and the changing sensory dynamics of modern culture. This approach also begs the question whether a media ecology of literature should not take this specific reader-response theory into account. As a fundamental premise, we also need to reflect on the ongoing change in our general expectations concerning reading, possibly moving from a classical, *Bildung*-related conception of deep reading and surface reading as opposites towards a renegotiating of what we understand as deep and surface reading. Different sensory experiences lead to different processes of meaning creation, and our conceptions of deep and surface reading thus need to be considered from a media-ecological perspective. Deep reading an audiobook is not necessarily the same as deep reading a printed book. Deep reading may in itself be historically framed and changeable.

The multimodal sensitivity towards media specificity in reading interfaces, which I argue for in this chapter, also seems to strike back at the traditional act of reading a paper book. It seems that the multimodal aspect of contemporary reading practices makes us increasingly able to view the reading of a paper book in new ways; as it is no longer 'natural', but historically configured, it seems to represent a distinct situation. Furthermore, the debate about a reconfiguration of the act of reading also points to – and makes us aware of – the specific sensory and multimodal aspects of reading a paper book.

Technology and media from a material perspective

The debate about the interplay between technology, writing and reading is not new; it has, for instance, been considered in the critical discourses of media archaeology, focusing on 'analyzing the conditions of existence of media cultural objects, processes and phenomena', as stated by Jussi Parikka (2012, n.p.). Although this is based on German media theory, it also connects to a number of broader debates in cultural theory. Media archaeology appears to read old media and new media along parallel lines, creating an essentially non-linear theory practice, using media history to produce knowledge.

In the book *Reading Writing Interfaces* (2014), Lori Emerson, in continuation of the media archaeological position, examines how we can read and rewrite both historical and computing interfaces, framing the interface as an open-ended, cross-disciplinary term in computing. Here interface refers to the interaction between hardware and software components. Quoting Florian Kramer, Emerson states that these can be both human-to-hardware interfaces (keyboard, screen and mouse) and human-to-software interfaces (graphical user interface) (2014, x).

Seeing as Emerson appears interested in how interfaces limit and create certain creative possibilities, this may be productively applied to reading interfaces constituted by sound, tactility and interactivity. Furthermore, she appears to be critical towards the idea of interfaces as transparent, unable to call attention to themselves:

> When transparency not only transforms into that which is valued above all else but also becomes an overriding unquestioned necessity, it turns all computing devices into appliances for the consumption of content instead of multifunctional, generative devices for reading as well as writing or producing content. (xi)

Emerson thus accentuates two points which seem important to the present reading agenda: that the framing of the interface limits and creates certain creative possibilities, and that these possibilities ought to be highlighted and investigated, not hidden by the ideal of transparency. It may be useful to link this to the idea of literature available in different sensory formats. Emerson seems to be critical towards the idea of friction-free interfaces, and instead wishes to investigate the specific reading/writing interface, also in a historical context. Even though Emerson's interface studies describe the meeting between user and technology, her interest in the subject seems to be rooted in the affordances produced by technology and not in the specific use or experience, which has been the primary point of departure of the studies of the audiobook performed by Have and Stougaard Pedersen (see 2016).

Instead of building solely on a media archaeological position I prefer to push this agenda in the direction of postphenomenology, as suggested by Don Ihde: '*postphenomenology* is a modified phenomenology hybrid' (2009, 23). It is modified in the sense that Ihde, by combining a material/technological perspective with an experience-oriented perspective, is able to develop a pragmatic way of avoiding the problems of phenomenology as a subjectivist philosophy. Embodiment and active bodily perception are always linked to a materially based, dynamic understanding of a lifeworld. From his postphenomenological perspective Ihde seeks 'to probe and analyze the role of technologies in social, personal, and cultural life' (23).

Our work with the audiobook is built on this perspective, focusing on the interplay between a specific technology, a sensory-based experience and a concrete use. The combination of usage and technology reflected in the interface agenda is also central to discussions of the utopia of convergence culture, discussed in *Intermediality and Media Change*: 'The great utopia of convergence has been the assumption that various electronic communication technologies [. . .] will in the (not too distant) future merge in to a single entity' (Herkman, Hujanen, and Oinonen 2012, 1). Henry Jenkins points to the problematics of this fascination with media convergence when he advocates for a media technology divergence rather than a convergence:

> I will argue here against the idea that convergence can be understood primarily as a technological process – the bringing together of multiple media functions within the same gadgets and devices. Instead, I want to argue that convergence represents a shift in cultural logic, whereby consumers are encouraged to seek out new information and make connections between dispersed media content. (2006, 3)

Convergence culture and the ideal of the transparent interface seem intimately related to consumption. This becomes evident when we look at the sales promotion of the feature *Whispersync for Voice* (released 2014),[1] promising a friction-free experience. Kindle and Amazon have developed this hybrid feature as an addition to the e-book, making it possible to transfer between text and sound.

Imagine a scenario where a commuter is reading while travelling. Sitting in a bus or train she/he can choose to read either a printed book or an e-book on an electronic device. In both cases the sound environment becomes an audible background to the reading experience. While listening to an audiobook, however, the commuter's auditory attention frames the reading experience, and she/he is free to move around while reading (cycling, driving or walking). As a third option the commuter can start by reading the book on an electronic device and then switch to the audiobook when, for example, leaving the bus or train to walk the last part of his/her journey. This experience requires *Whispersync for Voice* (or a similar service), and naturally Amazon's marketing of the service emphasizes the seamless experience, enhancing the aspect of convergence or transparency of the reading interface.

The digitization of the book thus points to a media ecology that frames the activity of reading a book as a series of different experiences, emerging from a single platform, for instance, a smartphone or a tablet. *Whispersync for Voice* makes it possible to switch from one type of experience to another while reading, but I would argue that such a shift cannot possibly be considered seamless, as it changes the material condition of the act of reading. The media platform may offer a number of different media ecologies of a text through media convergence, but these ecologies are dependent on different sensorial modes and thus create distinct sensorial situations. These distinct situations are deliberately overlooked by Amazon's advertisement, instead addressing the omnivorous consumer. In continuation hereof, Don Katz states:

> We're moving toward a media-agnostic consumer who doesn't think of the difference between textual and visual and auditory experience [. . .]. It's the story, and it is there for you in the way you want it. (qtd. in Alter 2013, n.p.)

This prediction comes from the founder of Audible.com, a company selling and producing spoken audio entertainment, information and educational content on the internet, and it underlines the idea that the senses and different semiotic expressions are experiences which appear to be transparent and friction-free. From a consumer perspective Katz may be right that the user does not pay much attention to the specific sensory medium when experiencing a novel such as *The Fault in Our Stars*. Here he supports Jenkins' idea that the aspect of convergence seems closely linked to the idea of consumption, although Katz obviously does not take the same critical approach as Jenkins.

My counterargument here is that in analysing different formats of literature and concrete reading practices, whether paper books, apps or audiobooks, we need to consider the material conditions involved. The enunciation of a novel or poem, for that matter, changes when it is transposed from one medium to another (see Kittler), and to theoretically embrace the new conditions of literature we need to develop new materiality-sensible reading strategies (see Hayles 2004):

> The convergence of visual, textual, haptic and audio media output in the mobile digital technologies makes it possible for the readers to shift between formats in the middle of a story according to the situation. This possibility both supports *a flow* between different sensorial approaches to a concrete narrative, but the means of materiality also affects and changes the reading experiences [. . .] the transposition or convergence into computerised media actually changes the object itself. (Have and Stougaard Pedersen 2016, 148–9; emphasis added)

Reflecting on the technological friction of the reading interfaces, rather than striving for transparency, we need to develop a set of intermedial methods which can point to the reading situation as a specific, yet general event – for instance, listening to an audiobook while commuting or working in the garden. This critical agenda does not necessarily lead to a media-deterministic position, but can supply us with the instruments for conducting a proper investigation of different reading interfaces.

I would argue that an analysis of the audiobook version of John Green's novel must take into account the following, which will serve (only) as a draft for an analytical strategy. Focusing on the media specifically, the study of an audiobook should reflect on the technological conditions involved (Have and Stougaard Pedersen, 2020):

Address the *technology and distribution* that frame the listening experience:

- Storage medium (mp3, pc or cloud)
- Distribution medium (internet)

- Provider (library, book shop, streaming service)
- Media platform (computer, tablet, smartphone, speakers)

Describe and reflect on the *sensorial character* of the reading situation:

- Activity (walking, commuting, running, knitting, doing domestic work)
- Sensorial inputs (body movements, smells, light, wind, sound)
- Surroundings (domestic, rural, urban area, number of people)

Obviously, *the voice* is also important when trying to understand the distinct identity of an audiobook. The voice acts as the natural entry point and as a mediating factor between reader and text. It is a material medium creating material and rhetorical meaning. Describing the role of the voice in an audiobook, I would suggest using the concept of the performing narrator in order to distinguish it from the term 'narrator', in a narratological sense (see Have and Stougaard Pedersen 2016, 17). The audiobook can both be framed and understood as a transposition, transferring the text of the printed book to the sound of a voice. We can conceptualize the act of the performing narrator as an act of interpretation, linking the audiobook reading to the performance of a musical work based on a score.

In *Digital Audiobooks: New Media, Users, and Experiences* we propose the following five-step model for analysing the voice of the audiobook (Have and Stougaard Pedersen 2016, 87):

1. Recording and processing of the voice
2. The materiality of the voice
3. The rhetorical situation
4. The enunciation of the text
5. The ethnicity, age, nationality and gender of the performing voice

Let us now use the model in an analysis of the audiobook version of *The Fault in Our Stars*. The performing narrator is Kate Rudd, and the technological processing (1) of her voice is rather dry; it is recorded in a way that underlines the character of the actor's voice. The materiality of the voice (2) is characterized by a very distinct diction; we hear the performing narrator carefully pronounce each word. The tone of voice is rather light and nasal, and the tempo of reading is fast. It seems that the style of reading tries to accentuate the fresh language of the novel's characters.

The performing narrator dramatizes the content a great deal (3); the tone of voice varies considerably, changing between descriptive sections and sections of direct speech. The sections of direct speech can be very expressive, for example, exaggerating the outbursts of Hazel's mother. Considering the enunciation of the text (4), it may seem odd that a grown-up actor is the listener's point of contact with the sixteen-year-old protagonist. Some may find this problematic, but at the same time it may serve to support the grown-up identity of a teenage girl, who knows that she will not survive to see adulthood. Here the context of the voice (5), considering the gender, age and so on of the performing narrator, deals with similar aspects. This performing narrator is an actor, who is not well known to the greater public, and in this sense the voice in itself is not identifiable, as it would have been had it belonged to a well-known actor.

Other experiences and everyday dimensions can also be discussed when analysing an audiobook: how does the reading experience affect our sense of time and the relation between waste of time and quality time? Why and when do we read? How do we use and experience pauses in an everyday setting? In continuation hereof, it may also be relevant to discuss and reflect on distracted and deep reading.

On the one hand, these aspects of reading point towards multimodal meaning creation, a convergence of sensorial multitudes; on the other hand, this multitude is always experienced in the distinct situation. Thus, we need to address the reading situation as a singular event, which should be analysed as such. In this sense, the situation as a whole – the concrete book, its material condition and the concrete act of reading – interacts with the technological aspect of the reading experience (interactive app, audiobook, e-book, paper book).

Considering the reading situation from a perspective that highlights the material condition involved puts emphasis on distinction, not convergence – a distinctive analysis that reflects the media-specific character of reading. According to N. Katherine Hayles:

> Understanding literature as the interplay between form, content, and medium, media-specific analysis insists that texts must always be embodied to exist in the world. The materiality of those embodiments interacts dynamically with linguistic, rhetorical, and literary practices to create the effects we call literature. (2002, 31)

In this sense, the artefacts are multimodal, but we must address this multimodal experience as distinct events, a situation where more agents take part in creating meaning – as an interplay between technology, sensorial aspects and the surroundings – a postphenomenological position, in continuation of Ihde.

Conclusion

The current return of the oral, or of storytelling, seems to renegotiate the relations between modalities and stories on new conditions, not only as regards the audiobook, but also across media and platforms. Sound, multimodality, touch and motion configure a new phase in the mediatization of literature. This perspective on experiences based on different modalities highlights the need for an extended, yet precise and singular approach to reading as such, focusing on the multisensory aspects of the interfaces of the reading activity. However, working with the audiobook it has become clear that listening to audiobooks, especially historically, has been associated with children or conditions such as dyslexia or visual handicaps. Thus, the audiobook has been considered compensatory, and studies have focused mainly on its ability to overcome various kinds of insufficiencies (see Have and Stougaard Pedersen 2016). A similar agenda, struggling with the ideas of deep reading and surface reading, respectively, seems to characterize the studies of the activity of reading on a screen (Hayles 2012; Baron 2010).

Lutz Koepnick describes the intersensorial character of the audiobook experience as follows:

> To listen to audiobooks is to experience the ingestion of text as a kinaesthetic activity, one that at any moment may unsettle our perception of our bodies' boundaries or sensory extensions into the world. (2013, 235)

One of the main prospects of considering reading a multimodal practice is to challenge the historical notion of both listening and screen reading as compensatory, second-rate experiences, and alternatively conceptualize the contemporary use of audiobooks and e-books as a form of reading that can be considered a high-quality listening or haptic experience, hereby qualifying and conceptualizing the multimodal, yet media-specific aspects of a reading experience.

In continuation hereof it is important to highlight another aspect of both audiobook reading and screen reading: the fact that you can read with your ears in different ways, and that distracted ear reading can create a very intense *Stimmung* that is deep and based on different conditions than the classical '*Bildung*-related' form of deep reading, as a possibly primary hermeneutic or semiotic strategy. Concentration and contemplation may also be media-specific:

> To read between an audiobook's lines – to read an audiobook deeply – means to open your minds and senses to the productive interplay of ears, eyes, and bodily motions during the act of attending to the movements of a text. (Koepnick 2013, 236)

To deep-read an audiobook may mean to be immersed in the atmosphere of the book, created both by the voice of the performing narrator – the sounding aspects of language – and the narrative itself. Instead of simply accepting the idea of Amazon and Audible that the media-agnostic consumer wants only friction-free experiences, we need to insist on developing new reading skills and strategies that are sensitive both to the media and to the concrete situation.

Epilogue

One may rightly argue that using the concept of reading in analyses of audiobooks can seem non-productive. However, to claim that interaction with an app or listening to an audiobook is an act of *reading* is also to challenge the notion of reading as either an exclusive, high-absorbency practice, which monopolizes much of one's attention, or a non-exclusive, low-absorbency occupation – something one can do while engaged in other practices (see Have and Stougaard Pedersen 2016, 151). In this sense, the multimodal approach breaks with the critical normativity that clings to other forms of reading than visual 'deep reading', suggesting differentiated and media-sensitive modes of reading.

Note

1 An illustration can be found at https://www.amazon.com/gp/feature.html?ie=UTF8&docId=1000827761 (accessed 29 March 2022).

References

Alter, Alexandra. 'The New Explosion in Audio Books: How They Re-emerged as a Rare Bright Spot in the Publishing Business.' *The Wall Street Journal* 2013. <https://www.wsj.com/articles/the-new-explosion-in-audio-books-1375980039>. Accessed 12 October 2021.

Anon. 'When You Can't Read, Listen.' <https://www.amazon.com/gp/feature.html?ie=UTF8&docId=1000827761>. Accessed 13 December 2021.

Baron, Naomi. *Always On: Language in an Online and Mobile World*. Oxford: Oxford University Press, 2010.

Bolter, Jay David, and Richard Grusin. *Remediation: Understanding New Media*. Cambridge, MA: MIT Press, 1999.

Emerson, Lori. *Reading Writing Interfaces*. Minneapolis, MN: University of Minnesota Press, 2014.

Green, John. *The Fault in Our Stars*. London: Dutton, 2012.

Have, Iben, and Birgitte Stougaard Pedersen. *Digital Audiobooks: New Media, Users, and Experiences*. New York: Taylor & Francis, 2016.

Have, Iben, and Birgitte Stougaard Pedersen. 'Reading Audiobooks.' *Beyond Media Borders: Intermedial Relations among Multimodal Media*. Ed. Lars Elleström. London: Palgrave Macmillan, 2020. 197–216.

Hayles, N. Katerine. *Writing Machines*. Cambridge, MA: MIT Press, 2002.

Hayles, N. Katherine. 'Print Is Flat, Code Is Deep: The Importance of Media-Specific Analysis.' *Poetics Today* 25.1 (2004): 67–90.

Hayles, N. Katherine. *How We Think: Digital Media and Contemporary Technogenesis*. Chicago, IL: University of Chicago Press, 2012.

Herkman, Juha, Taisto Hujanen and Paavo Oinonen, Eds. *Intermediality and Media Change*. Tampere: Tampere University Press, 2012.

Hjarvard, Stig. *The Mediatization of Culture and Society*. London: Routledge, 2013.

Ihde, Don. *Postphenomenology and Technoscience. The Peking University Lectures*. New York: State University of New York Press, 2009.

Iser, Wolfgang. *The Implied Reader: Patterns of Communication in Prose Fiction from Bunyan to Beckett*. Baltimore: Johns Hopkins University Press, 1978.

Jenkins, Henry. *Convergence Culture*. New York: New York University Press, 2006.

Kittler, Friedrich. *Discourse Networks 1800/1900*. Trans. Michael Metteer. Stanford, CA: Stanford University Press, 1990.

Koepnick, Lutz. 'Reading on the Move.' *PMLA* 128.1 (2013): 232–7.

Parikka, Jussi. 'What Is Media Archaeology? – Out Now.' 2012. <http://jussiparikka.net/2012/05/08/what-is-media-archaeology-out-now/>. Accessed 8 May 2022.

Rubery, Matthew, Ed. *Audiobooks, Literature, and Sound Studies*. New York and London: Routledge, 2011.

Schulz, Winfried. 'Reconstructing Mediatization as an Analytical Concept.' *European Journal of Communication* 19.87 (2014): 87–101.

Stougaard Pedersen, Birgitte, et al. 'To Move, to Touch, to Listen – Multisensory Reading of Digital Interfaces.' *Poetics Today* 42.2 (2021): 281–300.

Whitten, Robin. 'Growth of the Audio Publishing Industry.' *Publishing Research Quarterly* 18.3 (2002): 3–10.

10

Reading player one

Interfaces between video games and literature

Sebastian Domsch

Introduction: Playing stories, reading games

Digital games enable players to inhabit narrative worlds and to 'play stories' (Domsch 2013). Although many games can be played successfully in a purely abstract way, that is, by taking into account nothing but the rule structure as a self-contained system referring to nothing outside of itself, one thing that almost inevitably happens when human beings play games is that they start to invest the elements of the games and the game's structure – and consequently their actions and decisions – with meaning that is not reducible to gameplay functions. They are starting to create a frame of reference for the game that is distinct from their own world yet whose understanding is modelled on ours. In other words, players mentally start to create a fictional world within which the game's actions happen.

It is by now widely accepted not only that video games can contain narratives, but also that these narratives can be complex and deep, and that games are well on their way to becoming one of the dominant storytelling media (Murray 1997; Jenkins 2004; Arsenault 2008). But this acknowledgement still contains an understanding of video games as antagonistic to reading and therefore to 'literature'. Yet even with the undeniable overwhelmingly visual nature of video games, a nature that relies on spectacle, verisimilitude and iconicity, gamers still often have to do a lot of reading. Some of it is part of the game's communication of its rules to the player, but most of it is concerned with the narrative content.

Video games are digital artefacts, and they are a metamedium in the sense that their underlying technology allows the non-reductive incorporation of all other major presentational media: spoken text, written text, all kinds of sounds and images, both still and moving. In some cases, games also imitate the materiality of the media they incorporate as well. Thus, players can encounter (virtual) tape recorders that they can use to play, pause and rewind a tape, and they can find a (virtual) book that they can pick up to turn the pages. Thus, gamers encounter texts in various (simulated) medial forms and contexts, and these texts fulfil different functions that are often related to the forms they imitate. The most obvious function in the context of this chapter is that of narrative. Text can provide narrative content in a video game in much the same way as it does in traditional literature, by providing a narrating voice and character dialogue (Domsch 2016 and Domsch 2017).

But straightforward narration is not the only function of text within games. Particularly the materiality of text can also provide it with an indexical function, pointing to the presence of the person who wrote it. The most common example of this would be the ubiquitous 'I was here' graffiti that one can find scrawled onto walls and carved into park benches – and that also exists in video games. This regularly happens in the context of environmental storytelling (see Cason 2000 and Domsch 2019). A special case of this can be found in the *Dark Souls* games, where players can leave written messages in the game that are visible to other players. These can take the form of hints or warnings about impending dangers, but also more index-oriented phrases such as 'I did it!'.

Often, players can find extended personal writing from characters within the game. These can be in the form of letters, diaries (both written and in audio form) or logs. In the case of many RPGs, such texts can provide clues for solving gameplay puzzles, but also narrative background for the characters and their worlds. In the relatively recent genre of the 'walking simulator', they can even become the central aspect of the game, as, for example, in *Dear Esther* (2012). In this game, the player is trying to find out more about the character Esther, which is done by roaming around the place where she lived and listening to a series of letters that can be found scattered throughout the gameworld.

At the border of narrative and gameplay information are the in-game databases or encyclopaedias that players can unlock in the course of the game. Often by simply playing, players gather information on elements of the gameworld, such as enemies, weapons, places and buildings. This information is then stored in a central place that is accessible to the player via a menu, and that imitates other medial forms. Thus, in the detective game *L. A. Noire*, the player character writes down everything in a notebook that is rendered visually on the screen. The *Civilization* strategy games have a 'Civilopedia' as a constant feature. It displays information about units, resources, civilizations, leaders, techs, civics, governments, Great People, buildings, improvements, wonders, promotions and game concepts. Historical information about each item is provided in a 'Historical Context' section. The various *Assassin's Creed* games have extensive 'Databases' that contain both information exclusive to the game's narrative world (such as fictional characters) and factual information on history and architecture.

Library of Blabber (2015) is a fascinating experimental game that is nothing but an (infinite) library. It is based on Jorge Luis Borges' short story 'The Library of Babel', in which he imagines an endless library of adjacent hexagonal rooms with books that contain all possible permutations of the twenty-five basic characters, and that must consequently contain every book that it is possible to write. The game is a direct adaptation of this concept, creating just such an endless collection of rooms filled with books that are randomly generated, and which the player can take out and leaf through, searching for meaning hidden in the noise.

As these brief examples show, textuality and its medial conditions, albeit in a simulated form, does play a (functional) role in many games. It has seeped in from the real world, of which they are after all a simulation. Depending on their ambition and their target audiences, games can be 'bookish' and even 'literary' in that they evoke similar ways of being received and understood. Games, at least some of them, are not only played but, instead, part of the process of using them can now also entail thinking about 'what they mean', thus employing a cultural technique that is usually associated with literature. With video games, the gamic has become meaningful in a new way (besides the general meaningfulness of play and games for human development and culture), a way that is similar to literature's model-building relationship to the actual world. They have therefore connected in some ways to the literary media network. Of course, traditional literature, in the form of published novels or stories, has not been unaffected by that development. The main focus of this chapter therefore is on asking for the ways that games – in general and in the form of video games – relate to and have an influence on literature. After looking at the place of playfulness within the field of literature in general, it will focus on the newly emerging genre of the 'gamic novel', focusing briefly on two examples, Ernest Cline's *Ready Player One* (2011) and Cory Doctorow's *For the Win* (2010).

Playful reading

Literature is inherently playful. There are two main reasons for this. The first is the general notion that what distinguishes literary texts from others is that the former do not have to have a purpose that is outside of themselves, or, as Terry Eagleton writes: 'Literature, then, we might say, is "non-pragmatic" discourse: unlike biology textbooks and notes to the milkman it serves no immediate practical purpose [. . .], we mean by literature a kind of self-referential language, a language which talks about itself' (2008, 7). This is comparable to the idea that games are characterized by their lack of consequence in the real world. Games in that sense are also self-referential, because they are not primarily about something else, but about themselves. Of course, they *can* be about something else (a game of soccer can lead to better health for the players, or make them rich), just like literature can serve a pragmatic function (think of agitprop literature), but one can argue that such functions are precisely where they stop being 'just' or 'pure' games, or literature.

The second reason is the notion that players of a game understand and accept the rules of the game in a way that is analogous to the way that readers of fiction understand and accept fictional propositions. In the latter case, this is usually referred to as the 'fiction contract'. For a limited time, readers of fiction agree to playact as if they were someone who believes that the fictional facts are factual. This has become so automatized that we do not even notice it anymore, but if we look back at the early development of fictional narrative, we can recognize the 'games' that authors like Daniel Defoe or Jonathan Swift played with their audiences, when they camouflaged *Robinson Crusoe* or *Gulliver's Travels*, respectively, as factual texts. These texts also introduced the feature of the fictional editor, a feature that became ever more playful, for example in Henry Mackenzie's *The Man of Feeling* (1771) or Maria Edgeworth's *Castle Rackrent* (1800). Even more explicitly game-like examples can be found in the literary 'hoaxes' that go at least from Swift's highly elaborate practical joke on the almanac maker John Partridge in 1708 through Orson Welles's radio adaptation of *War of the Worlds* to the Blair Witch project.

What readers of fictional literature implicitly acknowledge is also the manufactured nature of what they are encountering. Of course, every text is written by someone, was made in a specific way and does not *just* exist. But the default paradigm for texts outside of literature is that their own form is primarily determined by their referent. They look like they do because in this way they best reflect what they are about. This attitude, which is expressed, for example, in the ideal of scientific objectivity, can also be found in art, most prominently in the neoclassical notion that art should be a 'mirror to nature'. And yet, most investigations into the nature of literature agree that its essence lies in those aspects that go beyond the referent, where the signifiers are not in laborious duty bound to the signified, but enter into an undetermined play. If a literary text *is* duty bound, it is less to the referent and more to the recipient. Everything in the text is there because it was *made*, and as recipients we cannot but get the impression that it was made for us.

This means, for example, that the act of comprehension assumes the form of a challenge made by the writer specifically for the reader, or, in other words, a game. This is what we mean when we say that literature 'is difficult', because we imply that literature is *made* difficult. The prominent use of figurative meaning throughout literary history is an indication that this has been a feature of literature from the beginning. Romanticism then emphasized the role of both artistic creation and ambiguity, a development that led all the way to the extreme and demanding ambiguity of modernism and the explicitly playful ambiguity of postmodernism. We can therefore understand the activity of interpreting what is not being said directly as a game, with differing difficulty levels.

Even more game-like are instances where recipients are asked to piece together (incomplete) information. In this case, the omission of text or information that is necessary for full comprehension is a clear indication that the reader is asked to step outside of a purely passive position and become (more) active. An early example of this are epistolary novels that are, in fact, not so much narrative in the normal sense as simulations of a particular media ecology (handwritten letters that are exchanged between two or more participants, and that are sometimes delayed, or amended or get lost). Readers get an insight by being able to read (some of) the letters, but they are asked to fill in the gaps and to cognitively construct the full narrative.

The romantic fragment is a further step on this way, though it is also an indication that the 'game of literature' does not always have clear or obtainable win-states. Readers of a romantic fragment are clearly expected to imagine the missing parts of the text, while knowing full well that these absences are as fictional and fabricated as the present text. In addition, they are gradually becoming aware that the task is ultimately an impossible one. Just like Samuel Taylor Coleridge, we will never be able to 'find' the lost parts of 'Kubla Khan' and, indeed, that very impossibility is one of the things that the poem is actually about.

Ever since romantic aesthetics put the effort to express the inexpressible at the centre of their attention, recipients have been given a much more active, if sometimes frustrating, role. The act of reading increasingly became an explicit performance of meaning-generation,[1] first as an embodiment of the longing for transcendental truth (Romanticism), then as an exercise in the futility of objective truth and observation (Modernism) and finally as the recognition that meaning-generation had always been a constructive activity (postmodernism). This final realization, that all meaning is 'made up', in the sense that it is constructed in much the same way as is fictional truth, also finally brought the aspect of playfulness all the way to the foreground. If all meaning is a play of signifiers, playing becomes the most serious of activities, and literature becomes a playground because that is now understood as the best model of reality (or rather, our way of constructing the notion of reality). And, indeed, postmodern literature is characterized throughout by an ostentatiously playful spirit that extends from form to content. As Kuehl writes about postmodern authors, '[g]ames help them to construct their heterocosms or substitute worlds, and other aspects of play-linguistic experimentation, typographic/graphic/cinematic innovations, multiple genres/styles and parody/satire make these worlds vivid' (Kuehl 1986, 176). And Minemma claims that '[a]lmost anything in postmodern culture can be described in terms of play; even culture itself is described in terms of play' (1998, 21).

Frequently, play and games are being thematized, as in Don DeLillo's *Underworld* (1997) and Robert Coover's *The Universal Baseball Association, Inc., J. Henry Waugh, Prop.* (1968), a novel that already foreshadows the immersive nature of simulated gaming environments that would be explored further by authors of gamic fiction. But even more pervasive are playful attitudes towards form and genre. In addition, postmodernism took interpretative ambiguity to its extreme and made the inability to 'win' the game of interpretation a central feature.

Many of the examples so far can be said to be of a 'playful nature', to employ or evoke structures that are related to games and to play. They heighten the cognitive effort demanded of the reader in the 'game of interpretation' and in imagining missing parts of the narrative, but they usually do not demand any real activity from the recipient other than turning the pages. In contrast, Espen Aarseth coined the term 'ergodic literature' for such cases that go further, where 'nontrivial effort is required to allow the reader to traverse the text' (1997, 1). In these cases, recipients need to actively 'do things', activities like choices or recombinations, and these activities are usually guided by rule structures, just like they are in games.

While Aarseth's second term for such texts, 'cybertexts', seems to suggest digitality, he makes clear that ergodic literature can also exist within a more traditional materiality. In fact, the first example that he gives is that of the *I Ching*, or *Book of Changes*, an oracular book of recombination that emerged close to the Western Chou dynasty (1122–770 BCE). More recent examples can be found in postmodern literature, such as Marc Saporta's *Composition No. 1, Roman* (1963) or B. S. Johnson's *The Unfortunates* (1969).[2] Both are books with unbound leaves that can be freely arranged by the recipient, while Raymond Queneau's 'sonnet machine' *Cent mille milliards de poèmes* is a bound book, but with leaves cut in such a way that readers can recombine the lines of the represented poems. This '[s]huffling activity tolerates, indeed encourages, an openly playful engagement with the text' (Meifert-Menhard 2013, 67).

More limited in the quantity of options, but also more focused on their significance are so-called forking-paths narratives, that is, narratives that bifurcate at one or several points into multiple possible plot lines and leave the decision of which one to pursue to the reader. This form has its precursor in textual features such as the footnote, which could also be understood as a bifurcation and therefore a non-unilinear development of the text. Of course, footnotes are usually not part of the narrative content of a text, and they mostly are just short digressions that return the reader immediately back to the main text, but literary texts like Alexander Pope's *The Dunciad* (1728–1743), Vladimir Nabokov's *Pale Fire* (1962) and Mark Z. Danielewski's *House of Leaves* (2000) have artfully turned their texts into literary games through the use of footnotes (Zubarik 2014).

The idea of narrative bifurcation was famously evoked by Argentinian writer Jorge Luis Borges in his short story 'The Garden of Forking Paths', a text that is now understood as a spiritual ancestor of hypertext fiction. But before digital media made the linking of text into a basic principle of its organization, a printed version emerged that is basically the blueprint for all forms of non-unilinear or 'interactive' fictions: the Choose-Your-Own-Adventure books that were a brief hype in the 1980s and that clearly straddle the border between novel and game. Starting with what is now a 'classic', Edward Packard's *The Cave of Time* in 1979, the books claimed to give the development of the story into the hand of the reader, who becomes a player, is being addressed as 'you' and instructed to make choices at important moments in the story (or rather, stories). The different continuations could be found on different pages within the book, and the chunks of texts were distributed in a non-chronological order so that players could not guess how a choice would impact the development of the story.

The existence of such 'nodes'[3] in the text heighten the ludic quality of the narrative either by directly granting the user agency (as in a CYOA book or a combinatorial book like B. S. Johnson's *The Unfortunates*) or at least by forcing the user to make differential evaluations of multiple continuations (as in sequentially arranged multiple endings). Though originally developed in the print medium, the technical restrictions of that medium meant that their implementation always necessitated compromises (such as increased difficulty in producing the books, or a more cumbersome navigation of the text by the recipients). It is, therefore, hardly surprising that this form of playful narrativity jumped ship at the first opportunity (the high time of the CYOA books is also the first phase of the computerized 'text adventure') and made use of digital media. And while literary hypertext fiction, after promising beginnings in the 1990s (with texts like Shelley Jackson's *Patchwork Girl* (1995) or Stuart Moulthrop's *Hegirascope* (1995/1997)) never took off, video games quickly did.

The gamic novel

For a while, then, it might have seemed as if literature had ceded the territory of the playful and game-like to video games in order to get back to 'serious business'. Besides the exodus of game formats into the digital, the first years of the twenty-first century also saw a widespread rejection of the postmodernist type of playfulness and a return to a more realist paradigm (Domsch 2008, 10). Video games featured only very rarely in this period, but this has been rapidly changing in more recent years, as games have become more widespread and a whole video game culture has emerged.

The most recent development in the convergence of games and literature is therefore a group of novels that take video games as their central topic, but also as a structural frame and as a guiding metaphor. These novels are about specific video games (often fictionalized, near-future versions of popular contemporary examples), but they are also about how games and game-like virtual environments structure our own society and our own ways of sense-making, and about the (geek) culture that goes along with games. In addition, they also often function like games, or employ game-like features. Examples include Dennis L. McKiernan's *Caverns of Socrates* (1995), Douglas Coupland's *Microserfs: A Novel* (1995) and *JPod* (2006), Jonny Nexus's *Game Night* (2007), Charles Stross's *Halting State* (2007), Walter Jon William's *This is Not a Game: A Novel* (2009), Cory Doctorow's *For the Win* (2010), Ben Croshaw's *Mogworld* (2010), Diane Duane's *Omnitopia Dawn* (2010), Ken MacLeod's *The Restoration Game* (2010), Ernest Cline's *Ready Player One* (2011) and Neal Stephenson's *REAMDE* (2011).

Setting the mood for this newer generation of what are sometimes called 'gamic novels' was a group of novels that created their own genre, cyberpunk, at the end of the twentieth century, most importantly William Gibson's *Neuromancer* (1984), Orson Scott Card's *Ender's Game* (1985) and Neal Stephenson's *Snow Crash* (1992). Cyberpunk is an important precursor to the gamic novel because it created the nexus of tone, setting and technologico-social interface that influenced, first, the development of games themselves, and then, of the gamic novel. Most importantly, cyberpunk imagined the porousness of virtual worlds and reality. This theme is developed further into the interlocking nature of play and work in novels like *For the Win* or *Ready Player One*, books that take place as much within the virtual gameworlds as within the fictional real world. And it is further explored in books like Terry Miles' *Rabbits* (2021) that thematize alternate reality games, a game form that uses reality as its playground to such an extent that it can become indistinguishable from it. In addition, cyberpunk centred on themes of surveillance, alienation and exploitation in a corporate-dominated digitized society, and it created an aesthetic that became a blueprint for countless games.

For clarification, gamic novels need to be clearly distinguished from video game novelizations, that is, adaptations of existing video games into novels. While such adaptations are closely related to video games for obvious reasons, they differ most importantly in that they do not acknowledge the games as games. In fact, their main draw for the recipient is the full narrative immersion into the specific gameworld by means of the adaptation medium. Gamic novels, by contrast, are always aware and reflective of their subjects.

By looking at a few specific examples, I want to develop a more general and abstract sketch of some of the ways that video games are making their influence felt within contemporary literature. One could first of all argue that the move from passive reception of narrative (as reader, listener or watcher) to an active participation within the narrative implies a shift from the third-person perspective to the second-person perspective as well. Experiencing narrative and mentally projecting storyworlds mainly meant *looking at* someone or something. This was usually mediated through a specific perspective, which could be that of a detached narrator or of characters that are themselves part of the storyworld, but which is always understood to be distinct from that of the recipient. Participation blurs the boundaries between actors in the narrative and the recipient/player, and the most logical form to express this would be through the use of the second person. Indeed, CYOA books and early text adventures used it consistently, but it runs so strongly counter to the narrative form that we are accustomed to that it is rarely used outside of these examples. Even video games got rid of this device as soon as they could replace it with the more effortless visual perspective.

One of the few examples for the use of the second-person perspective in the context of a gamic novel is Charles Stross's *Halting State* (2007) and its successor *Rule 34* (2011). Both novels invite the reader to identify with a number of characters by being always addressed as 'you', whether it is an Edinburgh Detective Sergeant, an insurance fraud investigator for Dietrich-Brunner Associates or a recently laid-off programmer and expert on Massively Multiplayer Online Role-Playing Games.

I want to use Ernest Cline's *Ready Player One* (2011) as my key example to illustrate this particular media ecology of the gamic novel. *Ready Player One* is not the first gamic novel, but it is one of the most successful ones (becoming a *New York Times* bestseller and getting adapted into a Steven Spielberg movie in 2018), and it was immediately received as a high point in the narcissistic self-reflection of gaming culture, literalizing as it does the postmodern notion of 'gaming and play as a metaphor to describe the relationships between subjects and the cultural systems within which they are enmeshed' (Condis 2016, 2). In the novel, which is set in the not-too-distant future of 2045, a game-like virtual reality system called OASIS has become the place that almost all people spend most of their lives in, not only to play games, but also to work or go to school. The OASIS is certainly preferable to the dystopian real world that Cline describes, which is wrecked by an energy crisis, global warming and widespread societal collapse.

Of course, besides the futuristic elements, the most prominent feature of the novel is its nostalgia, which is directed at 1980s pop culture in all of its forms, but with early video gaming at its core. The fulfilment fantasy that is enacted by the novel is twofold: on the one hand, these trivial cultural artefacts (cf. the German term 'Trivialkultur') – which postmodern theory had claimed were an apt metaphor for reality – now *become* reality through the technical wizardry of advanced virtual reality. As part of the hunt for the novel's version of the Holy Grail, players fully and bodily inhabit simulated realities that are based on much less immersive earlier media. Whether it is a cult movie like *Wargames*, a part of the *Dungeons & Dragons* pen-and-paper role-playing game or an early video game like *Dungeons of Daggorath*, everything is rendered, and therefore experienced, as a complete, albeit simulated, reality; hence, it becomes (part of) reality. Thus, it is an imaginative fantasy, rendered in what is arguably the most low-tech medium (language used in a printed book), about how a speculatively advanced medial technology (virtual reality) can turn the imagined spaces of less advanced media technology (film, arcade video games) into reality. In other words, Cline asks his readers to imagine that they will no longer need to imagine.

The second way in which the novel is a fulfilment fantasy of nerd culture is that it develops a narrative situation in which everything that has been decried as trivial suddenly *really matters*. The driving force of the plot is the fact that the inventor (and therefore proprietor) of the OASIS, James Halliday, has devised a game in the form of a treasure hunt that will bring the winner into full possession of the OASIS. By raising the reward to such a ridiculous degree, the 'game' in the novel, with all of its minutest details, becomes the most serious endeavour on earth. Finding the right clues necessitates an encyclopaedic knowledge of the 1980s pop culture that Halliday grew up in and that he therefore elevates to an almost mythic significance, so that finally – at least in the world of the novel – the emotional relevance that pop-culture fans had always attached to their objects of adoration matches their real-world relevance.

Besides this, Ernest Cline's *Ready Player One* is also both story and game: hidden in the text is an Easter egg that takes its reader to an online video game competition, thus mirroring the story device of the treasure hunt. It is worth taking a closer look at the way that the first clue for Halliday's Easter egg is hidden in the novel, because it is another example of Cline's playful negotiation of media and their materiality:

> But then, buried among all those rambling journal entries and essays on pop culture, I discovered a hidden message. Scattered throughout the text of the Almanac were a series of marked letters. Each of these letters had a tiny, nearly invisible 'notch' cut into its outline. I'd first noticed these notches the year after Halliday died. I was reading my hard copy of the Almanac at the time, and so at first I thought the notches were nothing but tiny printing imperfections, perhaps due to the paper or the ancient printer I'd used to print out the Almanac. But when I checked the

> electronic version of the book available on Halliday's website, I found the same notches on the exact same letters. And if you zoomed in on one of those letters, the notches stood out as plain as day. Halliday had put them there. He'd marked these letters for a reason. There turned out to be one hundred and twelve of these notched letters scattered throughout the book. By writing them down in the order they appeared, I discovered that they spelled something. (Cline 2011, 65)

This could be described as a variation on the implication of literature's fictionality as it was sketched previously, now mapped upon differences in media technology: in printing, the concrete manifestation of the sign (a black shape on white paper) is, besides being a symbol (representing a letter), also an index of the real process of printing. An imperfection therefore bears an indexical relationship to the reality of this process, indicative of a corresponding imperfection in the printing machine – *and nothing else*. But in the digital medium, the concrete realization is only a simulation of the earlier form (a page in a pdf is made to *look like* a printed page), it is therefore a created reality in a similar way that narrative creates a reality, which is why an imperfection is not just there, but must have been put there, and consequently must have a meaning: 'Halliday had put them there. He'd marked these letters for a reason.' Again, it is the hand of the 'maker' (the original meaning of the word 'poet') that turns a mere representation into a game.

But the game does not stop there, because Cline mirrored the book's central conceit of the 'Easter egg hunt' onto itself, announcing a competition in which the winner could get a car (in fact, not just any car, but an exact replica of the DeLorean that had featured in the *Back to the Future* movies, flux capacitator and all), and for which the first clue was to be found in the book. And, indeed, Cline used the same 'trick' as described in the quote, with a series of 'imperfectly printed' letters in the book that spelled out a URL where contestants would find the 'first gate' of the hunt. This particular type of 'puzzling' is another characteristic of gamic novels in general that they have developed in their own way under the influence of video games.

As we saw, 'puzzle-solving' had always been a part of the literary experience, because figurative uses of language are in essence linguistic puzzles. The rise of detective fiction in the footsteps of Edgar Allan Poe's 'tales of ratiocination' expanded the principle to puzzle-solving within a narrative storyworld, an important precondition for all narrative puzzle-solving in video game genres like the adventure-games and many role-playing ones. What is new in the era of video games and the gamic fiction that is a reflection of them is the concrete manifestation of the puzzle (inside and outside the text) and the emphasis on (levels of) completion. The 'game of interpretation' had always been only very loosely delineated. Literature teachers might insist that an adequate understanding of a classic poem can be achieved only when allusions to ancient mythology or contemporary politics are detected and understood, but, at least for today's readers, this 'game' carries no intrinsically motivated prestige. The references hidden in gamic novels and other texts of 'geek culture', on the other hand, are not only more recognizable as an invitation to play, but there is also a specific cultural capital attached to 'winning'. A reviewer of Sarah Vaughn's 2021 gamic novel *Questland* asks: 'But does *Questland* go overboard with its geek-culture Easter eggs? That all depends on how leveled-up you are' (Heller 2021). And Condis writes about *Ready Player One* that '[i]t is possible to finish the novel, like a video game, with various levels of completion' (2016, 4). The ability to detect the references is part of what defines the player's identity. 'It is possible to view the geeky subcultural canon described in *Ready Player One* as a source of gaming capital, both for players within the diegetic world of the O.A.S.I.S. and for the novel's actual readers. In this case, the canon compiled by Cline (through Halliday) reflects the particular historical material conditions that shaped the origins of gamer culture' (2016, 8). It is clear that this 'gaming capital' cannot be gained by merely being a reader, but only by being a 'hunter' for hints and references. 'One cannot simply consume Cline's narrative. It must be played' (2016, 4).

A specific variant of puzzle-solving in the context of video games is the so-called 'Easter egg hunt'. Easter eggs in this sense originally described hidden features in video games, starting with a programmer for Atari in 1980, who secretly added his own name to the game, which became visible only to players who moved their avatars over a specific pixel in one part of the game. Subsequently, adding such hard-to-find 'secrets' to games became a standard feature, first, in video game design, and then, in transmedia storytelling. A few characteristics differentiate the Easter egg from other forms of 'literary puzzles': in contrast to a metaphor or allusion, the Easter egg is usually relatively unconnected to the original text's meaning, something closer to Johann Sebastian Bach's hiding his last name within the notes of his compositions than an arcane layer of meaning in a metaphysical conceit. On the other hand, its existence is, once found, undeniable, because it usually extends the hunt beyond the boundaries of the book. An additional meaning of a poem's metaphor can never be conclusively proven, partly because it does not have a concrete existence outside of the text. This is different with a series of clues that enable hunters to piece together the URL of a website – which does really exist. In consequence, there is also an expectation of completion, in a sense that it is possible to find all of the clues, an expectation that comes straight out of video games, where player progression towards 100 per cent is often monitored and published by the games themselves. This is, of course, quite a contrast to literature's gradual loss of 'definiteness' during the last 250 years.

Not less playful, but certainly less nostalgic than *Ready Player One* is Cory Doctorow's 2010 novel *For the Win*. Indeed, the book could well be understood as a continuation of the politically motivated agitprop literature of the 1930s rather than the narcissistic navel-gazing of the frequently apolitical postmodernist tradition. The settings are quite comparable, though Doctorow is much closer to our contemporary technological reality, but he also depicts a world in which games and virtual game environments have become dominant factors in social and economic life. Also comparable is the consequent merging of the activities of playing and working. But Cline wanted to have his cake and eat it, too – creating the fantasy that the essence of play suddenly acquires an almost religious significance and seriousness; Doctorow's point is the much bleaker observation that, because games are business, generating wealth, they also create a shadow labour force of people who work within them, in order to enable more 'fun' for the players. These are the so-called 'gold farmers' (who actually already exist), who continuously play in games that allow levelling up through repetitive activity in order to sell the levelled characters or currencies that are gained by such activities. *For the Win* follows a number of such 'playbourers' and soon focuses on their attempts to unionize and fight for better working conditions. In between action-filled and exciting narrative chapters, Doctorow intersperses instructive lessons in economy and workers' rights, further underscoring the ways in which our society is becoming game-like, for example, in the financial market. But at the same time that Doctorow is clearly criticizing the ways that capitalism uses games as a way to introduce new forms of exploitation in the guise of 'fun', he also emphasizes the ability of games to create new forms of (global) community as well as solidarity.

Through this, we can identify another way in which the gamic novel expands on existing concepts of the playful in literature. As we have seen, an increasing emphasis on playfulness also meant a more engaged participation by the recipient, who constantly had to 'up his/her game' to meet the demands of the text, by filling in gaps, choosing among ambiguous meanings or even choosing different paths to traverse through the text. What is new for recent 'gamic fiction' is the increasing emphasis on collaboration[4] in the context of participation. It is no coincidence that one common feature of the games that appear in such fictions is that they are online multiplayer games, where social interaction becomes a crucial aspect of the gameplay experience as well as the game mechanics.

Throughout its medial development from oral to written to printed discourse, literature had turned from a predominantly communal to a predominantly individual experience. Walter Benjamin has described this phenomenon in his essay 'The Storyteller' with a particular focus on the novel: 'A man listening to a story is in the company of the storyteller; even a man reading one shares this companionship. The reader of a novel, however, is isolated, more so than any other reader' (2006, 372). Silent reading and the immersiveness of realistic narrative created the image of the solipsistic reader, lost to the world around him/her, a male or female Quijote, a stereotype that became hypercharged when applied to players of video games, whose isolation was often seen as total. In reality, most games today have become partially or fully networked experiences that allow interaction and communication with other players, so that playing is more than ever becoming a social activity. This is reflected in the way that gamic novels emphasize the connectedness of not only players, but also readers. All the gameworlds described are also social networks, and characters usually need to collaborate to achieve their goals. The most extreme example is *For the Win*, which is literally all about organizing players/labourers into communal and collaborative groups that practise solidarity.

Through the communal emphasis of cooperative play another aspect comes into focus, that moves the discussion full circle back to the media ecologies of literature: copyright. Doctorow specifically is an author who has spoken and written extensively against the US Digital Millennium Copyright Act (DMCA) and as a representative of the Electronic Frontier Foundation against Digital Rights Management (DRM) software, 'he has criticized the shift in focus of copyright law – from a measure that protected the rights of such authors as Dickens to fair compensation to one that guards the exclusive control exercised over cultural products by moneyed corporations for ever longer periods of time' (Fletcher 2010, 81). The text of Cory Doctorow's *For the Win* is available to download for free in every file format imaginable. Doctorow has published the novel under the creative commons license CC BY-NC-SA 3.0, which stands for 'Attribution-NonCommercial-ShareAlike 3.0 Unported' and means that users are free to share – copy and redistribute the material in any medium or format, as well as to adapt – remix, transform and build upon the material – as long as they credit the original author and indicate the changes they have made. This invitation to creative appropriation is at the same time the most up-to-date development in the gamification of literature under the influence of digital media – and the oldest game in the book, the intertextual play of retelling, quoting, remediating that has been a core feature of literature ever since it emerged.

Notes

1 On reading as meaning-generation and its media ecologies, see Christoph Reinfandt in this volume.

2 See the discussion of *The Unfortunates* by Sabine Zubarik in this volume.

3 'The node can very generally be characterized as any point in a narrative that allows for more than one continuation and so enables a structural bi- or multifurcation' (Meifert-Menhard 2013, 45).

4 Cf. the notion of collaboration in Alexander Starre's discussion of Abrams and Dorst's *S.* in this volume.

References

Arsenault, Dominic. *Narration in the Video Game: An Apologia of Interactive Storytelling, and An Apology to Cut-Scene Lovers*. Saarbrücken: VDM Verlag 2008.

Benjamin, Walter. 'The Storyteller.' *The Novel: An Anthology of Criticism and Theory 1900–2000*. Ed. Dorothy J. Hale. Malden, MA: Blackwell, 2006. 361–78.

Carson, Don. 'Environmental Storytelling: Creating Immersive 3D Worlds Using Lessons Learned from the Theme Park Industry.' *Gamasutra* (2000). <gamasutra.com/view/feature/3186/environmental_storytelling_.php>. Accessed 23 August 2021.

Cline, Ernest. *Ready Player One*. New York: Crown Publishing Group, 2011.

Condis, Megan Amber. 'Playing the Game of Literature: Ready Player One, the Ludic Novel, and the Geeky "Canon" of White Masculinity.' *Journal of Modern Literature*, 39.2 (2016): 1–19.

Doctorow, Cory. *For the Win*. New York: Tor, 2010.

Domsch, Sebastian. *Amerikanisches Erzählen nach 2000: Eine Bestandsaufnahme*. München: edition text + kritik, 2008.

Domsch, Sebastian. *Storyplaying: Agency and Narrative in Video Games*. Berlin: De Gruyter, 2013.

Domsch, Sebastian. 'Hearing Storyworlds – How Videogames Use Sound to Convey Narrative.' *Audionarratology: Interfaces of Sound and Narrative*. Eds. Jarmila Mildorf and Till Kinzel. Berlin: De Gruyter, 2016 (Narratologia Series). 185–98.

Domsch, Sebastian. 'Dialogue in Video Games.' *Dialogue Across Media*. Eds. Jarmila Mildorf and Bronwen Thomas. Amsterdam: John Benjamins, 2017. 251–70.

Domsch, Sebastian. 'Space and Narrative in Computer Games.' *Ludotopia: Spaces, Places and Territories in Computer Games*. Eds. Espen Aarseth and Stephan Günzel. Bielefeld: transcript, 2019. 103–26.

Eagleton, Terry. *Literary Theory*. Minnesota: Blackwell, 2008.

Fletcher, Robert P. 'The Hacker and the Hawker: Networked Identity in the Science Fiction and Blogging of Cory Doctorow.' *Science Fiction Studies*, 37.1 (2010): 81–99.

Heller, Jason (2021). 'You Don't Have to Be a Complete Nerd to Love This Novel . . . But It Helps.' *NPR*, 23 June 2021. <https://www.npr.org/2021/06/23/1009195526/you-dont-have-to-be-a-complete-nerd-to-love-this-novel-but-it-helps>. Accessed 23 August 2021.

Jenkins, Henry. 'Game Design as Narrative Architecture.' *First Person: New Media as Story, Performance, and Game*. Eds. Noah Wardrip-Fruin and P. Harrigan. Cambridge, MA: MIT Press 2004. 118–30.

Kuehl, John. 'The Ludic Impulse in Recent American Fiction.' *The Journal of Narrative Technique* 16.3 (1986): 167–78.

Meifert-Menhard, Felicitas. *Playing the Text, Performing the Future: Future Narratives in Print and Digiture*. Berlin: De Gruyter, 2013.

Miles, Terry. *Rabbits*. New York: Del Rey Books, 2021.

Minnema, Lourens. 'Play and (Post)Modern Culture: An Essay on Changes in the Scientific Interest in the Phenomenon of Play.' *Cultural Dynamics* 10.1 (1998): 21–47.

Murray, Janet. *Hamlet on the Holodeck: The Future of Narrative in Cyberspace*. New York: Free Press 1997.

Stross, Charles. *Halting State*. London: Orbit, 2007.

Zubarik, Sabine. *Die Strategie(n) der Fußnote im gegenwärtigen Roman*. Bielefeld: Aisthesis 2014.

PART IV

Coda

11

Towards a media ecology of literature

The case of Romanticism

Ralf Haekel

Introduction

This volume set itself the task of applying a coherent media-theoretical approach to literature that would comprise a wide variety of already existing theories. The two main problems facing this approach may abstractly be defined as, first, the specific historicity of media theory, and, second, the flexibility of the media concept. The first problem refers to the fact that the most influential media-theoretical investigations start, historically speaking, at best with the invention of photography and the phonograph in the middle of the nineteenth century, and the majority of them focus on the new media of the digital age.[1] A media theory of literature, however, must necessarily apply a media concept that predates the so-called new media (see Gitelman 2006) and has to comprehend all forms of literary mediation, be they oral or written. Thus, the media concept must be as precise as it has to be flexible. This is also important regarding the second problem – the wide range of different media concepts and theories.

The definitions of the media concept range from the very material basis of the carrier of information – book, photograph, radio, television set, computer and so on – to a non-materialistic and conceptual theory of mediation focusing on practices and cultural techniques. The main argument of this book is that a theory of *media ecologies of literature* solves these two problems by historically looking at literature as part of a cultural media network that includes material and immaterial features, that is dynamic and yet relies on historically retrievable works and artefacts. In this coda, I will take a summarizing look at media ecology as a theory of literature, and I will focus on Romanticism as my example – a historical period that predates the invention of modern storage media. Charlotte Smith's relatively unknown Romantic poem 'Studies by the Sea' will serve as framework as well as case study for these general and largely theoretical considerations.[2]

Science and Charlotte Smith's 'Studies by the Sea'

The very title of Charlotte Smith's poem 'Studies by the Sea' suggests a proximity to the new scientific landscape emerging at the turn of the nineteenth century. The decades around 1800 witnessed the advent of new scientific disciplines such as biology, chemistry and geology. Smith is known not only for making numerous references to scientific discoveries in her masterpiece *Beachy Head* but also for having written and published scientific books – on history, botany, ornithology – with the primary goal of educating the youth. The poems she wrote late in her life are part of an erudite scientific media ecology – made obvious in her extensive use of endnotes in order to contextualize her allusions and topics. Hence, these poems not only refer to scientific publications: they are part of an entire system which aims at educating her readers and making them familiar with new forms of knowledge. At the same time, Smith's poetry is far more sophisticated than, for example, Erasmus Darwin's, who wrote poetry mainly to popularize his scientific findings.

This becomes obvious when looking at the meta-reflexive nature of her later works. 'Studies by the Sea' self-reflexively refers to its medial form as well as to the mediation of knowledge. In that sense, it is a reflection on the fact that the rise of the scientific system and of scientific knowledge had changed the perception of the world forever. The first two stanzas give evidence of this change:

> Ah! wherefore do the incurious say,
> That this stupendous ocean wide,
> No change presents from day to day,
> Save only the alternate tide;
> Or save when gales of summer glide
> Across the lightly crisped wave;

Or, when against the cliff's rough side,
As equinoctial tempests rave,
It wildly bursts; o'erwhelms the deluged strand,
Tears down its bounds, and desolates the land?

He who with more enquiring eyes
Doth this extensive scene survey,
Beholds innumerous changes rise,
As various winds its surface sway;
Now o'er its heaving bosom play
Small sparkling waves of silver gleam,
And as they lightly glide away
Illume with fluctuating beam
The deepening surge; green as the dewy corn
That undulates in April's breezy morn. (Smith 1807, 1–20)

The poem juxtaposes two different ways of looking at the world, an 'incurious' and an 'enquiring' way. Whereas the uninterested or indifferent gaze is incapable of recognizing anything in the sea but 'the alternate tide', the curious and inquisitive observation will discover 'innumerous changes'. This beginning is quite remarkable for a number of reasons. First of all, the sea that the speaker describes is not only the object of scrutiny, it also becomes itself a medium for the beholders. Yet, what the said beholders see or read in the ocean depends fundamentally on their capacity, that is, on their education, their knowledge and thus their access to the new media infrastructure that made the proliferation of science possible in the first place. Thus, two things need to come together to establish the nucleus of a media ecology of knowledge in literature: the expertise or learning of the readers and the material media that need to be part of a cultural network or infrastructure. At the turn of the nineteenth century, this media ecology of knowledge does not rely on new technological inventions but, rather, on the massive growth of print technology in the wake of the industrial revolution. This also triggered a transformation of the cultural techniques of knowledge acquisition. Scientific knowledge was – through public lectures, scientific transaction and encyclopaedias, but also monthly magazines – made available for the first time to lay readers who also participated in the remediation of said knowledge – through educational works or poetry. In effect, it can be said, with reference to Clifford Siskin and William Warner's important and influential book *This is Enlightenment*, that the advent of the scientific system of disciplines around and after 1800 is an 'event in the history of mediation' (2010, 1).

Charlotte Smith participated in this media ecology of Romantic science very actively: she published two volumes on the *History of England* (1806) and a *Natural History of Birds* (1807) that itself included poems and fables which were also published in her final volume *Beachy Head: With Other Poems* (1807). *Conversations Introducing Poetry: Chiefly on Subjects of Natural History. For the Use of Children and Young Persons*, published in two volumes in 1804, betrays the fact that science and education are an important part of her poetry and her poetic theory. Such an oeuvre can be approached only as a network of disciplines, genres and media, on the one hand, and of cultural techniques including writing and reading practices, education and knowledge acquisition, on the other. In other words, the media ecology in which such a short poem as 'Studies by the Sea' participates needs to be described in detail, but it must also be thoroughly theorized. To state my case, I will, for analytical reasons, focus first on the concept of knowledge and its relation to literature and subsequently I will turn to a more general investigation of the field of media theory and literature.

Knowledge and literature

Charlotte Smith's poems partake in a complex scientific media network or media ecology. Her poetry is intricately intertwined with the scientific discourse of the time, as she not only makes use of scientific theories and discourses, but also theoretically explores the nature of the relation of knowledge and mediation. Her poems display how knowledge is not only dependent on material media, but, rather, how this knowledge is indeed identical with external media, that is, books, journals, scientific periodicals and so on. Thus, her late poetry is a sophisticated rejection of subjective or immaterial conceptions of knowledge and thus also of the human mind in general.

In order to contextualize how the development of scientific knowledge shapes and influences literature and is thus part of the media ecology of literature in general, I will outline the main aspects of the theoretical discussion surrounding knowledge and literature. Knowledge in literature is closely linked to the academic discussion about the relationship between science and literature, which is as old as the division of the two discourses in the wake of the functional differentiation of society and the development of the modern scientific system in the early nineteenth century (see Pethes 2003, 188–91). The most prominent contribution to the debate is arguably C. P. Snow's lecture on the two cultures, which has become proverbial since 1959. In his systematic and comprehensive overview of the history of science and literature, the German scholar Nicolas Pethes summarizes the main trends of this debate from Thomas H. Huxley onwards. Up until the end of the twentieth century, the field was dominated by British contributions. This changed in the 1990s, when a sometimes fiercely fought-out debate about its legitimacy and systematic validity arose in Germany. This is relevant for the present context because it helps to highlight the preconditions that shaped the historical conceptions of consciousness and knowledge, in particular their rootedness in a mind-and-body dichotomy.

The German discussion was triggered by Joseph Vogl's writings of the 1990s and particularly his influential 1999 collection *Poetologien des Wissens um 1800* (*Poetics of Knowledge around 1800*). Vogl's works are influenced by Michel Foucault's discourse theory and based on earlier studies by Gaston Bachelard and Ludwik Fleck. In these studies, he aims at showing how scientific knowledge is shaped by pre-existing questions that are the outcome of historically determined discourse formations: 'The constitution of the fact does not lead from the object to the concept; rather it proceeds in the opposite direction: observation and experiment are only possible under the compulsion of previous trails' (Vogl 1999, 114).[3] In the present context I am not interested in the discussion on constructivism, that is, whether all scientific knowledge is fictional, made up and not factual – science *is* based on experiments and factual discoveries. What I am interested in, however, is the necessarily mediated quality of this knowledge. Scientific knowledge depends on discourse, language and, thus, on media. Knowledge, in a word, is always already mediated and cannot be separated or abstracted from its medial conditions.

The controversial debate which evolved from Vogl's work, conducted by Tilmann Köppe, Gideon Stiening, Roland Borgards and others, is noteworthy because it shows the extent to which the concept of knowledge is based on traditionally dualistic assumptions even today. In his attack against the poetics of knowledge, Köppe focuses not on the historical influence of science on literature but solely on the conception of knowledge by distinguishing two different theories: personal and impersonal knowledge, that is, the knowledge of people and the knowledge of books. The basic argument is rather simple. 'Personal knowledge,' Köppe argues, 'is, according to its logical structure, a *bipartite* predicate: it describes a relationship between a person and something this person knows. Somebody who knows something enters a specific relationship – that of knowledge – with a specific content or subject matter' (2007, 400).[4] Taking this rather undemanding description as the foundation for his further argument, he claims it to be nonsense that a text or a book can *know* something: 'Texts are not people; therefore, they cannot know anything' (2007, 402).[5] Now, one may dismiss his 'analytic' literary theory as a rather nit-picky witticism, but it helps to see the premises on which the concept of knowledge within the debate is based. Köppe's definition of knowledge presupposes a thoroughly dualistic conception of human nature, as it is grounded on the firm conviction that knowledge is something interior and subjective, something easily to be separated from the thing that is known. This knowledge can be stored or communicated in media, that is, in texts or books, but these media do not 'have' any knowledge themselves. This strict dichotomy has a long tradition in which the mind-and-body problem is possibly the most important strain. In arguing against this tradition, I contend that knowledge must be considered in a fundamentally different and non-dualistic manner, which may, in turn, illuminate the Romantic media ecology of literature.

There have been several attempts to transcend the strict mind-and-body dualism in recent years, most notably in the field of cognitive literary studies (Zunshine 2015), in the theory of embodied mind (Varela, Thompson and Rosch 1991) and in the studies on embodied cognition (Shapiro 2011). My own approach, however, focuses on mediation as a necessary condition of knowledge, and it is decidedly more historical. Recent developments in media studies, and particularly in actor-network theory, have focused on the historical dynamics of knowledge formation. From this perspective, the interplay of people, media and practices establishes the complex, dynamic and non-hierarchical social network that is the site of knowledge formation and proliferation. Accordingly, the human mind, that is, the concept of consciousness and its 'content' – knowledge – cannot be separated from these processes. The mind not only participates in this 'circulation of social energies' (Greenblatt 1988, 1), to borrow a well-established phrase; it is also established in this participation. Indeed, it can be understood and analysed only through its material manifestations – signs, speech, texts and so on. I would even venture a step further and claim that these material manifestations are what constitute the mind: this media ecology is necessary to define the concept of consciousness and knowledge in the first place.

Media theory and literature

Within recent years, media theory – especially in the German tradition – has gained importance in literary studies in general and in particular in the field of Romantic studies (see Burkett 2016). Before outlining the theory of media ecology, I will therefore briefly discuss the relevance of media-theoretical approaches with regard to the conception of knowledge.

There is little doubt that literature as a form of art is mediated and that it depends on carriers of mediation, be it manuscripts, printed books or other devices. The status of media studies within literary theory, however, is far from clear as it depends on the very definition of what constitutes a medium in the first place. Media-theoretical approaches to literature have changed fundamentally during the past decades. Friedrich Kittler's groundbreaking *Gramophone – Film – Typewriter* still focused mainly on the impact of technological inventions, arguing that new technology invented in the nineteenth century, which had no immediate connection to literary works themselves – like photography or sound recording devices – nonetheless changed the very nature of literature (see Kittler 1999, 3). The innovation of recording technologies, according to Kittler, displaced literature as the prime medium to record human emotions, thoughts and activities. Before this invention, literature had been the paradigmatic medium to portray human nature, while after the technological paradigm shift, this task was passed on to other media such as film. In order to make his argument, Kittler distinguishes traditional media like paper, handwritten letters, printed books and so on from technological media invented in the nineteenth century: photography, the phonograph, the telephone, film and, one might add, today's media technology – radio, television, computers, mobile phones and even the internet – Kittler already wrote about 'fibre networks' (Kittler 1999, 1) in 1986. The background to this distinction is the following: literature relies on language as an arbitrary sign system that bears no resemblance to its subject matter and thus has to rely on the power of the imagination. The new technology invented in the nineteenth century was able to record and store humans and human activity; mimesis, Kittler argues, was no longer the primary purpose of literature. Literature, in turn, became more self-reflexive and experimental. This is a powerful and convincing argument, yet it focuses solely on the technological means of artistic communication, which is the reason why Kittler is often dismissed as a techno-determinist, although this is, as mentioned in the introduction, far from justified.

This approach begs the question whether media theory can be applied to literary periods that predate the invention of new storage media and, indeed, Kittler himself already anticipates the answer because his own *Discourse Networks* sets in not with the paradigm shift in the middle of the nineteenth century but with a discussion of the cultural technique of silent reading and its impact on the concept of literature in the late-eighteenth century. In order to tackle this issue, I wish to correlate the historical period usually investigated by media theory with the history of the theoretical discipline itself. Media theory is a relatively new theoretical approach. As opposed to poetics or theories of literature, a theory of mediation was simply nonexistent prior to the invention of these new media technologies. Just like modern media technology was missing before the middle of the nineteenth century, there was also no theoretical or conceptual reflection on media and mediation. Does that mean that a media theory of earlier periods such as Romanticism is an anachronism? Recent investigations by the likes of Clifford Siskin (2010), Celeste Langan (2001), Andrew Burkett (2016), James Brooke-Smith (2013) and Christoph Reinfandt (2017) have argued to the contrary and shown that media theory is indeed of central importance to an understanding of earlier periods.

In his comprehensive survey of the 'Genesis of the Media Concept', John Guillory has argued that the concept was, indeed, missing because the 'proliferation of new technical media' set in only in the second half of the century: 'The very fact of remediation, however, suggests that premodern arts are also, in the fully modern sense, media but that for some reason they did not need to be so called, at least not until the later nineteenth century' (2010, 322). Guillory also argues that despite this lack of conceptualization a philosophical or theoretical need crystallized in a debate that moved towards filling the void: 'I argue that the concept of a medium of communication was absent but *wanted* for the several centuries prior to its appearance, a lacuna in the philosophical tradition that exerted a distinctive pressure, as if from the future, on early efforts to theorize communication' (2010, 321). In other words, although the technological media had not yet been invented, there existed a necessity to theorize communication, media and mediation, which he traces from the sixteenth century onwards. Thus, Guillory is able to show that the appearance of new media technologies in the middle of the nineteenth century does not change the discourse all of a sudden. Prior to their invention, there arose a demand for new ways to conceptualize what media do: communicate, store, process and proliferate information. This is particularly evident in the development of some of the key aspects of Romantic poetry, such as the origin and development of modern authorship and, in connection with this, central concepts such as the imagination and subjectivity.

A media-theoretically informed debate of Romanticism fundamentally relies on developments that at first seem to have little to do with the field of literature: the industrial revolution and the transformation of print. The literature of the eighteenth and early nineteenth centuries was fundamentally shaped by the changing book market; yet, the development of the capitalist print marketplace not only enabled authors to live off their trade but also changed the concept of literature as such (see Haekel 2017, 11–17). These changes left their mark on theoretical reflections on literature as well, particularly on the conception of subjectivity and selfhood in poetry as expressions of an inner self. These are, paradoxically as it may at first seem, an effect of media change rather than a countermovement. Christoph Reinfandt and others have argued that elements characteristic of Romantic poetry – sensibility, subjectivity, selfhood – which highlight the purported immediacy of poetic reception are, in effect, based on the development of print as a mass medium. The same is true for literary form. The popularity of blank verse and of ballads needs to be analyzed as a remediation of oral forms of literature into the written medium. The private communication with a speaker's mind in silent reading, which creates a sense of intimacy and immediacy, is dependent on the anonymity provided by mass publication. Reinfandt states:

> [M]odern literature's emergent sphere of the imagination more often than not displays a keen 'consciousness of mediation' and an awareness of the processes involved in transforming orality into print and of the new media environment in general. (2017, 130)

James Brooke-Smith highlights the same issue:

> [T]he ubiquity of print enables a new kind of subjectivity that looks beyond [. . .] the very technology on which it depends. Indeed, all of

> the studies that I have discussed in this essay characterize Romantic subjectivity in terms of its intimate yet occluded relationship to technologies of mediation. User-friendliness, audio-visual hallucinations, aesthetic autonomy, the lyric self – all integral elements of Romantic discourse – point away from the technologies of mediation that are their own conditions of possibility. (2013, 348)

Romantic poetry tries to create the impression of an immediate access to the speaker's innermost thoughts, thus rendering any material form of mediation invisible. As an effect, the material medium (language, text, book) becomes invisible, almost nonexistent in the minds of its readers.

The practice of remediation plays an essential role in this context. This whole process – the impression of intimacy, subjectivity and immediacy as an effect of mass capitalist print culture – becomes clearer if looked at in the light of this theory: the denial of mediation is, in fact, an effect of the remediation of oral forms into the medium of print. Although the theory of remediation was developed in order to describe art in the age of the internet, it can be easily applied to any other historical period. According to Jay David Bolter and Richard Grusin, the concept itself is characterized by a 'double logic', that is, a productive tension of immediacy and hypermediacy. As they put it: 'Our culture wants both to multiply its media and to erase all traces of mediation: ideally, it wants to erase its media in the very act of multiplying them' (Bolter and Grusin 1999, 5). On the one hand, media tend to render themselves transparent in order to simulate a direct – immediate – access to the mediated objects. In our age, there are several examples of this: virtual reality, the desktop metaphor on our personal computers and also realism in photographs or television: 'The transparent interface is one more manifestation of the need to deny the mediated character of digital technology altogether' (Bolter and Grusin 1999, 24). But, as Bolter and Grusin show, this is neither a new nor a surprising aspect of mediation. For instance, the technique of linear perspective in Renaissance painting or many of the eighteenth- and nineteenth-century realist novels also tend to deny their own mediality. The aim is to render a depiction most realistic and natural, foregrounding the illusion while denying the technique.

The double logic of remediation, however, can work only with immediacy's counterpart – hypermediacy: 'Where immediacy suggests a unified visual space, contemporary hypermediacy offers a heterogeneous space, in which representation is conceived of not as a window on to the world, but rather as "windowed" itself – with windows that open on to other representations or other media' (Bolter and Grusin 1999, 34). In other words, hypermediacy breaks the naturalist illusion and highlights the media technology. Again, this is not something particular to the digital age. In every age, hypermediacy acts as a counterpart to transparent immediacy, and in literature, the concept found its historical culmination in the period of classical modernism:

> In modernist art, the logic of hypermediacy could express itself both as a fracturing of the space of the picture and as a hyperconscious recognition or acknowledgment of the medium. Collage and photomontage in particular provide evidence of the modernist fascination with the reality of media. Just as collage challenges the immediacy of perspective painting, photomontage challenges the immediacy of the photograph. (Bolter and Grusin 1999, 38)

In the Romantic period, now, the tendency towards immediacy seems to be the dominant mode, but there are also examples that are highly self-reflexive and hypermedial in Bolter and Grusin's sense. Charlotte Smith is a prime example in this context as her extensive use of notes and references to the scientific discourses render the purported immediacy of Romantic consciousness *visible* and show it to be a medial construct. This also has epistemological overtones: contrary to the dominant idealist philosophy of the time, her concept of consciousness and knowledge is not interior but rather part of a cultural media ecology.

The origin of this specific kind of medial self-reflexivity, however, needs to be traced back to even earlier literary periods. In her study *Knowing Books*, Christina Lupton focuses on the concept of mediation which she carefully defines in contradistinction to both form and discourse, on the one hand, and materiality, on the other (see Lupton 2012, 5). Quoting Lisa Gitelman's insight that media are 'socially realized structures of communication' (Gitelman 2006, 7), Lupton concentrates not so much on the technological dimension as on the question of how self-conscious, that is, 'knowing' books have an impact on the consciousness of the readers by addressing 'the phenomenological question of what happens when mediation registers in discourse' (Lupton 2012, 10). Gitelman's insight is important in this context, as she shows how media work only in a social network 'where structures include both technological forms and their associated protocols, and where communication is a cultural practice, a ritualized collocation of different people on the same mental map, sharing or engaged with popular ontologies of representation' (Gitelman 2006, 7). By distancing herself from the tradition of technological determinism, Lupton likewise highlights the performative and processual dimension of mediation within a cultural network. With reference to Hegel's dialectic conception of mediation, Lupton pursues the question of

> how it is that self-conscious books contribute to the perceived autonomy of print mediation. The recognition of the reader, which shows up in the

> consciousness modelled by the book of its own mediation, and of the reader's categories of understanding, qualifies the book to perform as a partner in what is by rights a human process. (Lupton 2012, 16)

Lupton, of course, investigates eighteenth-century literature, but only a few decades later, during the early nineteenth century, immediacy and hypermediacy increasingly drifted apart.[6] Ultimately, this had consequences for the development of literary form. Both in the Romantic and the early Victorian realist novel or the Romantic meditative blank-verse poem, literature was ever more associated with the immediate expression of consciousness, that is, with the inward mind or the subjectivity of a speaker or narrator.

As argued earlier, this development was dependent on the changing book market. Celeste Langan likewise maintains that the impact of the medium of print ultimately led to the reinvention of poetry as a fundamentally modern form:

> the entire liberation, by 1805, of blank verse from its confinement to specific genres – tragedy, epic – and its implicit establishment as a norm marks the redefinition of English poetry by the medium of print. What occurs as a result of this 'blanking' of the auditory screen, however, is startling: a greater variety of audiovisual hallucinations. Read silently, the poetic figure seems that much more a sculptural or pictorial form; and, no longer subjected to the immediate sensory input of verbal melody, the silent reader gains access to the mediated (i.e., narratively evoked) musical scene of the poem. It is impossible to attribute this variety of audiovisual hallucinations to the poetic form as such; rather, they are intimately linked to the printed page. Although, quite obviously, varieties of rhymed and accentual verse continue to be written – even to proliferate – after 1800, the point is that blank verse comes to represent the achievement of a certain naturalized literacy. The particular magic of blank verse [. . .] consists in the way it occults its technology for producing 'soul'; it appears to reject artifice, and, uncannily like the 'general digitalization of information and channels' that according to Friedrich Kittler 'erases the difference between individual media', disavows any 'essential' difference from prose. 'Prose' then becomes itself less a generic term than a medium, and is virtually indistinguishable, in an imaginary horizon by which we are still framed, from print. (Langan 2001, 53)

This paradigm shift leads to a wholly new concept of literature according to which content is increasingly distinguished from medium and form: '"content" is not a substance, but rather the production through reading of an interior, of (literate) subjectivity as a virtual space modelled on the page' (Langan 2001, 58).

So far, I have argued that media and mediation need to be seen as part of a cultural network including human and non-human actors that is never static, a network that is necessarily always dynamic and processual. According to the logic of remediation, media either tend to render themselves invisible or, by means of a self-reflexive hypermediacy, are highly conscious of their own medial constitution. Within the period of Romanticism, it is particularly the remediation of several earlier, predominantly oral, media into print that creates the prototypical notion associated with Romantic poetry in the first place. What is more, the apparently dualistic state of consciousness in Romantic literature has its origin here, as consciousness is perceived as either wholly inward, which is ultimately the result of the silent 'invisible, inaudible medium of print' (Langan 2001, 54), or as self-reflexive and thus hypermedially visible as a physical, dynamic, and medial concept.

In the Romantic period, the immediacy of the poetic medium, particularly in the form of the blank-verse meditative poem by predominantly male authors such as William Wordsworth, may be the prevailing form, but it is by no means the only one. Charlotte Smith's 'Studies by the Sea', for instance, is a poem that is highly conscious of its own medial status. The reason why this poem highlights this hinges on the fact that it is not a remediation of an oral song but, rather, of earlier media of knowledge – scientific knowledge in particular. Smith's poem not only reflects the impact of scientific knowledge on the speaking subject; it also emphasizes that any consciousness is necessarily the result of mediation. Media theories less focused on technology but, rather, on the concept of mediation, such as the theory of cultural techniques, technography and, particularly, media ecology, enable us to understand how this kind of self-reflexive poetry generates a concept of consciousness that is always already mediated.

Transcending dualism: New approaches to media and mediation

The theorical field mapped out thus far is characterized by one problem: dualism and the difficulty of correlating two diametrically opposed factors, be that, on the one hand, mind and body or consciousness and nature/reality, or, on the other hand, technology and the human or material medium and content. Media-theoretically informed literary studies, however, has changed rapidly in recent years. The materialist focus on the impact of new media technology has made way for a more open approach characterized by a focus on how media need to be seen not as mere objects used for storing, processing and proliferating information, but, rather, as part of a dynamic interplay between technological inventions, *techné*, cultural techniques, dynamics and agency encompassing literacy, writing, education and knowledge acquisition. Yet, although the media-theoretical approach proposed in this coda is of a rather recent date, the problem of mediation is, I argue, already discussed in Romantic literature itself, particularly in self-reflexive poems like 'Studies by the Sea'. Current approaches to media theory – be that remediation, actor-network-theory or cultural techniques, which can be summarized under the umbrella concept of media ecology – offer a different or alternative view that may provide a way to transcend the described dualism.

A recent paper by James Purdon, published in 2018, approaches media theory with the aim of moving beyond its purported techno-centrism. Building on studies published in the fields of media archaeology (see Parikka 2012) and cultural techniques (Siegert 2015; Bayerlipp, Haekel and Schlegel 2018), he elaborates on the meaning and the scope of the more recent methodology of 'technography' (Pryor and Trotter 2016). Purdon refers to Martin Heidegger's philosophical and epistemological take on the term 'technology' with the expressed aim of stressing its dynamic and performative dimension. In order to highlight the opposition between the more recent and dominant understanding of technology as sets of mechanical equipment and the Greek dynamic definition of technology, he states that technology in Greek 'meant not a domain of objects but a genre of discourse' (Purdon 2018, 5). Purdon concludes that literature, through technology and technography, has always been linked to mediation:

> Literary works have never been simply purveyors of representational content, channels for messages or signals, or objects whose meanings can be made explicit either by traditional hermeneutics or by media analysis. This is not to suggest that works of literature always make a fetish of their own material media, but rather that literature is a name we have sometimes given to cases of writing which calibrate their formal processes with particular precision to the affordances and resistances of a specific environment of technological mediation. (Purdon 2018, 7)

More recent media theory, particularly the media theory of literature, has successfully overcome the strictly dualistic distinction between content and the material media through which this content is expressed in order to stress the dynamic dimension of mediation. Purdon's point is particularly important in this context, as it stresses the fact that literature as well as 'writing is technological, through and through' (Purdon 2018, 8). This reminder helps us to see that content – or knowledge – must in no way be separated from mediation. One may even venture a step further and claim that the notion of interiority is created by the technology of writing in the first place. This is a point already made in the 1960s by the Canadian scholar Eric Havelock in his study *Preface to Plato*. Here, Havelock claims that the concept of subjective selfhood is not a naturally existing entity but the immediate outcome of the invention of the technology of writing (Havelock 1963; see also Haekel 2014, 199). Writing as the 'separation of the knower from the known' (Havelock 1963, 197) enabled people to store knowledge which led to self-reflection and what Havelock terms 'the discovery of the soul'. Consequently, writing also enabled human beings to forget – which turned the written medium not only into an archive but also into a part of human consciousness. Writing as a technology and as a medium is therefore not opposed to subjective consciousness – it, rather, creates it in the first place.

The theory proposed in this volume that arguably best captures the non-essentialist and non-technocentrist approach to media and mediation is media ecology. The concept itself is as old as modern media theory and was first used by the Toronto school, in particular by Marshall McLuhan and Neil Postman. This traditional approach to media ecology has been criticized for its strictly hierarchical structure by a number of scholars after the turn of the millennium, most notably by Matthew Fuller. Postman's approach looked at a technological medium and its immediate environment – the people who use it and to which purpose and in what way it is put to use. In Fuller's terms: 'Here [i.e. in Neil Postman's sense], "media ecology" describes a kind of environmentalism: using a study of media to sustain a relatively stable notion of human culture' (Fuller 2005, 3). More recent approaches – again and in accordance with those media theories just discussed – are less static and hierarchical and more dynamic. It is little wonder that Matthew Fuller's game-changing book on media ecology begins with a reference not to Postman but to Kurt Schwitters. Schwitters's description of a Dadaist collage serves Fuller as illustration of his approach to media ecology, as Dada is the juxtaposition and confrontation of fragments, cut-outs and appropriated elements that, in a new arrangement, reject the notion of an organic work and highlight the dynamics and the transience of culture.

The theory of media ecology as mapped out by Fuller is therefore less influenced by the original concept of the Toronto school than by the post-structuralist writings of Gilles Deleuze and Felix Guattari. In particular, it is the latter's study *The Three Ecologies* that has made the most significant impact. The non-hierarchical and dynamic approach to mediation is also stressed by Michael Goddard and Jussi Parikka, who maintain:

> Media ecologies are quite often understood by Fuller through artistic/activist practices rather than pre-formed theories, which precisely work through the complex media layers in which on the one hand subjectivation and agency are articulated and, on the other hand, the materiality of informational objects gets distributed, dispersed and takes effect. (2011, 2)

In essence, the theory of media ecology encompasses the whole of culture, as Ursula Heise argues:

> Based on the assumption that media are not mere tools that humans use, but rather constitute environments within which they move and that shape the structure of their perceptions, their forms of discourse, and their social behavior patterns, media ecology typically focuses on how these structures change with the introduction of new communications technologies. (2002, 151)

Although Heise here mainly refers to digital technology, the introduction of new communication technologies, if applied to the Romantic period, also calls up the new media associated with the storage, processing, and proliferation of science and knowledge: scientific transactions, popular periodicals, encyclopaedias, museums, but also lectures, and poems like Erasmus Darwin's *The Botanic Garden*. Although neither of these medial forms were absolutely new at the time, the upsurge of the capitalist print market created an entirely different medial landscape (see St. Clair 2004), that in turn left its mark on literature. These repercussions are reflected upon in Smith's poem. In the following section, I will come back to 'Studies by the Sea' to briefly apply the aforementioned thoughts and reflections.

Poetry – science – media

The turn of the nineteenth century is often regarded as marking the dawn of modernity. Charlotte Smith's oeuvre is a case in point. While her early poetry, particularly the massively successful *Elegiac Sonnets*, was still heavily indebted to eighteenth-century lyrical modes and sentimentalism, her later poetic works as well as her scientific and educational publications bear witness to a paradigm shift towards a nineteenth-century view of the world shaped by science and by media competence. It is, therefore, important to read her as part of this changing dynamic media ecology. This also means that a media-ecological reading of a poem like 'Studies by the Sea' must begin with, but eventually move beyond, a historicist reading that merely contextualizes it, and it must consider the dynamics, cultural techniques and practices associated with the use of media in the said historical context. This also includes, in the sense of Latour's actor-network theory, the agency of the material media itself. The study of literature is nonetheless special because it is by definition a non-pragmatic and highly self-reflexive discourse and, as Jussi Parikka states, 'a media-ecological perspective relies on notions of self-referentiality and autopoiesis' (2005, n.p.).

'Studies by the Sea' was published twice – first, as part of the second volume of *Conversations Introducing Poetry* in 1804, then in the posthumous collection *Beachy Head: With Other Poems* in 1807. This publication history gives readers an insight into the reflection on the writing process as influenced by scientific studies, and because the first book is by definition an educational book for 'children and young persons', as passing certain cultural techniques associated with scientific knowledge on to her readership. A closer look at *Conversations* illuminates the project. In the preface to the first part, Smith writes:

> The poetry in these books was written without any intention of publishing it. I wished to find some short and simple pieces on subjects of natural history, for the use of a child of five years old, who on her arrival in England could speak no English, and whose notice was particularly attracted by flowers and insects. (1804, i)

Conversations takes the form of dialogues between Mrs Talbot and her children, Emily and George. The two children are introduced to topics of natural history, particularly botany and ornithology, which Mrs Talbot explains and then illustrates with short poems like 'To a Lady-bird' or 'The Snail'. Education, book knowledge and poetry thus establish a media ecology which becomes more sophisticated the more the children learn.

The dialogues have a plot as well, as the three of them go on a journey to the seaside. In the course of their travels, the scope of topics widens, as Mrs Talbot can now talk about economy, agriculture and other subjects as they pass along. That the poetry itself, however, is at times far too complex for non-native five-year-olds, is something Smith herself is fully aware of:

> It will very probably be observed, that the pieces towards the end of the Second Volume are too long for mere children to learn to repeat, and too difficult for them to understand. It is, however, impossible to write any thing for a particular age; some children comprehend more at eight years old, than others do at twelve; but to those who have any knowledge of Geography or Mythology, or who have a taste for Botany, the two last pieces will not be found difficult. (1804, iii)

'Studies by the Sea' is one of those two final poems mentioned here. The didactic intention nonetheless stays intact: poetry enables children to understand topics otherwise too difficult for them to comprehend. The cultural techniques of reading and remembering the verses are just as important as the media made use of – books, oral or written poetry.

Although *Conversations* is the fictitious remediation of an oral dialogue, the medium of the book is nonetheless central to the storage and proliferation of the knowledge discussed in it. This is made obvious on a number of levels.

First, in the preface Smith mentions her own lack of knowledge and her reliance on her library:

> Whoever has undertaken to instruct children, has probably been made sensible, in some way or other, of their own limited knowledge. In writing these pages of prose, simple as they are, I have in more than one instance been mortified to discover, that my own information was very defective, and that it was necessary to go continually to books. After all, I fear I have made some mistakes, particularly in regard to the nature of Zoophytes; but the accounts of this branch of natural history in the few books that I have, are so confused and incompleat, that I could not rectify the errors suspected. (1804, iv–v)

Although the concept of zoophytes – organisms situated between the animal and the plant kingdom – is no longer used or discussed in science, it was a subject matter of extensive scientific investigations in the eighteenth century. This shows that Smith strove to include contemporary specialized knowledge, and that she relied on her own books for that knowledge.

The manner of passing on this knowledge relies, of course, on the medium of print and thus on books, as well. The poems in this volume are not only embedded in the conversations between mother and children, but they are also heavily annotated. Just like in her other books, the notes take the form of endnotes, and there are no marks to point to their existence, so there is nothing on the page that indicates that they are there. It requires a skilled, that is, grown-up, reader to find them in order to look up the information hidden at the back of the book.

All this goes to show that a media-ecological investigation of literature depends on the consideration of all aspects involved in their historical moment: the material media – which a historical investigation necessarily relies on – the forms and genres in which the discourse becomes manifest and the remediations, that is, the inclusion of one medium in another which triggers the passing on and dissemination of discourse content and knowledge. This is particularly apparent once two different discourses intersect. In the case of Smith, scientific knowledge and poetry engage in a fruitful dialogue that enables us to see a small poem like 'Studies by the Sea' as part of a dynamic and constantly evolving culture. This media ecology involves the intersection of science and literature through remediation; it showcases the change of the state of knowledge, the advent of academic disciplines and the changing status of education; it finally enables us to see how cultural techniques develop and change, and that cultural practices such as reading, learning and knowledge acquisition evolve through a number of mediated discourses including literature. In a word, the historical analysis of literature as part of a dynamic media culture enables us to describe its place and function within a historical media ecology.

Notes

1 Of course, there are notable exceptions such as Harold Innis, Sybille Krämer or Bernhard Siegert.

2 This paper was written simultaneously with a book chapter on Charlotte Smith's (2022). The theoretical sections of both chapters overlap, but they are far longer and more elaborate in this chapter while the focus of the counterpart paper lies on the analysis of Smith's *Beachy Head* which, however, is not discussed here.

3 'Die Konstitution des Faktums führt nicht vom Gegenstand zum Begriff, sie verläuft vielmehr in umgekehrter Richtung; Beobachtung und Experiment sind nur unter dem Zwang vorausgehender Bahnungen möglich' (My translation, RH).

4 '[. . .] "personales Wissen" ist, seiner logischen Struktur nach, ein zweistelliges Prädikat: Es bezeichnet eine Beziehung zwischen einer Person und etwas, das die Person weiß. Wer etwas weiß, tritt, wie man auch sagen kann, in eine bestimmte Beziehung – eben die des Wissens – zu einem bestimmten Inhalt oder Gehalt' (My translation, RH).

5 'Texte sind keine Personen, sie können daher nichts wissen' (My translation, RH).

6 See also Mirna Zeman's chapter in this book in which she discusses the self-reflexive dimension of object narratives.

References

Bayerlipp, Susanne, Ralf Haekel and Johannes Schlegel. 'Cultural Techniques of Literature.' *Zeitschrift für Anglistik und Amerikanistik* 66.2 (2018): 139–47.

Bolter, J. David, and Richard A. Grusin. *Remediation: Understanding New Media.* Cambridge, MA: MIT Press, 1999.

Brooke-Smith, James. 'Remediating Romanticism.' *Literature Compass* 10.4 (2013): 343–52. <https://onlinelibrary.wiley.com/doi/epdf/10.1111/lic3.12052>. Accessed 4 March 2021.

Burkett, Andrew. *Romantic Mediations: Media Theory and British Romanticism.* Albany, NY: State University of New York Press, 2016.

Fuller, Matthew. *Media Ecologies: Materialist Energies in Art and Technoculture.* Cambridge, MA: MIT Press, 2005.

Gitelman, Lisa. *Always Already New: Media, History and the Data of Culture.* Cambridge, MA: MIT Press, 2006.

Goddard, Michael, and Jussi Parikka. 'Editorial: Unnatural Ecologies.' *The Fibreculture Journal* 17 (2011): 1–5.

Greenblatt, Stephen. *Shakespearean Negotiations: The Circulation of Social Energy in Renaissance England.* Berkeley: University of California Press, 1988.

Guillory, John. 'Genesis of the Media Concept.' *Critical Inquiry* 36.2 (2010): 321–62.

Haekel, Ralf. *The Soul in British Romanticism: Negotiating Human Nature in Philosophy, Science and Poetry*. Trier: WVT, 2014.

Haekel, Ralf, Ed. *Handbook of British Romanticism*. Berlin: De Gruyter, 2017.

Haekel, Ralf. 'The Media Ecology of Romantic Consciousness: Knowledge in Charlotte Smith's *Beachy Head*.' *Romanticism and Consciousness Revisited*. Eds. Joel Faflak and Richard Sha. Edinburgh University Press, 2022. 196–221.

Havelock, Eric A. *Preface to Plato*. Cambridge, MA: Belknap Press, Harvard University Press, 1963.

Heise, Ursula. 'Unnatural Ecologies: The Metaphor of the Environment in Media Theory.' *Configurations* 10.1 (2002): 149–68.

Kittler, Friedrich. *Gramophone, Film, Typewriter*. Trans. Geoffrey Winthrop-Young and Michael Wutz. Stanford, CA: Stanford University Press, 1999.

Köppe, Tilmann. 'Vom Wissen in Literatur.' *Zeitschrift für Germanistik* 17.2 (2007): 398–410.

Langan, Celeste. 'Understanding Media in 1805: Audiovisual Hallucination in the Lay of the Last Minstrel.' *Studies in Romanticism* 40.1 (2001): 49–70.

Lupton, Christina. *Knowing Books: The Consciousness of Mediation in Eighteenth-Century Britain*. Philadelphia, PA: University of Pennsylvania Press, 2012.

Parikka, Jussi. 'The Universal Viral Machine: Bits, Parasites and the Media Ecology of Network Culture.' *CTheory* 12.15 (2005). <https://journals.uvic.ca/index.php/ctheory/ article/view/14467/5309>. Accessed 4 March 2021.

Parikka, Jussi. *What Is Media Archaeology?* Cambridge: Polity Press, 2012.

Pethes, Nicolas. 'Literatur- und Wissenschaftsgeschichte. Ein Forschungsbericht.' *Internationales Archiv für Sozialgeschichte der deutschen Literatur* 28.1 (2003): 181–231.

Pryor, Sean, and David Trotter, Eds. *Writing, Medium, Machine: Modern Technographies*. London: Open Humanities Press, 2016.

Purdon, James. 'Literature – Technology – Media: Towards a New Technography.' *Literature Compass* 15.1 (2018). <https://onlinelibrary.wiley.com/doi/epdf/10.1111/lic3.12432>. Accessed 28 October 2021.

Reinfandt, Christoph. 'Popular and Media Culture.' *Handbook of British Romanticism*. Ed. Ralf Haekel. Berlin: De Gruyter, 2017. 116–34.

Shapiro, Lawrence A. *Embodied Cognition*. New York: Routledge, 2011.

Siegert, Bernhard. *Cultural Techniques: Grids, Filters, Doors, and Other Articulations of the Real*. New York: Fordham University Press, 2015.

Siskin, Clifford, and William Warner. *This Is Enlightenment*. Chicago, IL: University of Chicago Press, 2010.

Smith, Charlotte. *Conversations Introducing Poetry: Chiefly on Subjects of Natural History. For the Use of Children and Young Persons*. 2 vols. London: J. Johnson, 1804.

Smith, Charlotte. *The History of England, from the Earliest Records to the Peace of Amiens: In a Series of Letters to a Young Lady at School*. 3 vols. London: Richard Phillips, 1806.

Smith, Charlotte. *Beachy Head: With Other Poems*. London: J. Johnson, 1807.

St. Clair, William. *The Reading Nation in the Romantic Period*. Cambridge: Cambridge University Press, 2004.

Varela, Francisco J., Evan Thompson and Eleanor Rosch. *The Embodied Mind: Cognitive Science and Human Experience*. Cambridge, MA: MIT Press, 1991.

Vogl, Joseph. *Poetologien des Wissens um 1800*. Munich: Fink, 1999.

Zunshine, Lisa. *The Oxford Handbook of Cognitive Literary Studies*. New York: Oxford University Press, 2015.

INDEX